ABSENT-MINDED
BEGGARS

ABSENT-MINDED BEGGARS

BEGGARS

VOLUNTEERS IN THE BOER WAR

by

WILL BENNETT

LEO COOPER

First published in Great Britain in 1999 by
LEO COOPER
an imprint of
Pen & Sword Books Ltd
47 Church Street
Barnsley
South Yorkshire
S70 2AS

ISBN 0 85052 685 X

Typeset in 12/13pt Bembo by
Phoenix Typesetting, Ilkley, West Yorkshire

Printed in England by
Redwood Books Ltd, Trowbridge, Wilts.

This book is dedicated to my mother,
JOAN BENNETT,
who encouraged me to write it,
but who did not live to see it completed.

CONTENTS

INTRODUCTION

The volunteers who came forward in Britain and the colonies during the Boer War have been much neglected by military historians. Regimental histories, personal memoirs and books on the Volunteer Force such as Ian Beckett's *Riflemen Form* have all touched on aspects of the Imperial Yeomanry, City Imperial Volunteers and Volunteer Service Companies, but few attempts have been made to tell their story as a whole. Yet it was an important development in the history of the British Army. For the first time large numbers of volunteers, some from the auxiliary forces but many with no previous military experience at all, were allowed to serve alongside regular troops. The British Government's decision to accept volunteers was taken at a moment of high imperial drama. The series of reverses which the Boers inflicted on the British in December, 1899, in what became known as Black Week triggered one of the greatest crises in the history of the British Empire. The centenary of these events seems an appropriate time to tell the story of the volunteers.

Many of the volunteer units were wonderfully eccentric products of both the British class system and the nation's talent for improvisation. It is hard not to smile at the gentlemen rankers of the Duke of Cambridge's Own Imperial Yeomanry who paid their own way to South Africa only to find themselves prisoners of the Boers or at the conversational way in which CIV sergeants gave orders to their men. The CIV was a classic piece of early privatization, buying almost all its equipment, even artillery, on the open market with generous funds provided by the City of

London. The formidable upper class ladies who organized and despatched the well-equipped Imperial Yeomanry Hospital deserve to have their story told, while the chaos surrounding the raising of the second contingent of Imperial Yeomanry has rarely been looked at in any detail. Yet, amid the eccentricity and the humour, it should never be forgotten that the Boer War was a particularly brutal conflict. Boer homes were burned down, women and children sent to concentration camps where they died by the thousand in insanitary conditions and both sides on occasions shot prisoners. The conflict may have attracted gentlemen rankers but it was certainly not a gentlemen's war.

As far as the title of the book, *Absent-Minded Beggars*, is concerned I cheerfully plead guilty to having bent the rules. Strictly speaking Kipling's poem, which took the nation by storm in late 1899 and early 1900, referred to the reservists who were called from their civilian occupations and sent to South Africa. But *The Absent-Minded Beggar* quickly became the anthem of the volunteers who followed them. It was sung at almost every gathering held to mark the recruitment and despatch of the Imperial Yeomanry and other volunteer units. Indeed the lines "Cook's son – Duke's son – son of a belted Earl, Son of a Lambeth publican – it's all the same today" describe the Imperial Yeomanry very well. So there it is. I hope the purists won't object too much.

The decision on what to include and what to exclude from a book is not always easy. It was clear from the start that the Imperial Yeomanry, CIV, Volunteer Service Companies and medical volunteers ought to be included. I later came to the conclusion that a chapter on the non-South African colonial volunteers also ought to be incorporated. The Scottish Horse, although partly raised in South Africa, squeaked in because most of them were recruited in Scotland and Australia. I decided to exclude the South African colonial units because they are a complex subject deserving separate treatment and because most of them did not come from overseas to fight. I also rejected the militia, who were not volunteers, and the South African Constabulary, although I have mentioned them briefly, because they were regarded as a police force, albeit a paramilitary one. Most reluctantly of all, I decided to leave out the volunteers on the Boer side because I did not have easy access to the relevant material in the time available.

There are many to whom I am indebted. First of all I am grateful to my family, friends and my colleagues at the *Daily Telegraph*, few of whom have the slightest interest in the Boer War, for tolerating me discussing the progress of the book. Those who have provided me with material or permission to use material include John Sly, Ted Peacock, Mike Hibberd, Meurig Jones, Martin McIntyre, Professor Peter Beighton, the Museum of the Order of St John, and Lieutenant-Colonel Neil McIntosh of the Green Howards Museum. I am eternally grateful to the staff of the National Army Museum for their assistance and for the use of their archives while I was researching the book. I also acknowledge my debt to two of the great standard works on the period, *The Boer War* by Thomas Pakenham and *A History of the British Cavalry Volume Four* by the Marquess of Anglesey as well as to Amery's massive *Times History of the War in South Africa*. For the chapter on the overseas colonials I had less access to primary material and have leaned heavily on Brian Reid's excellent *Our Little Army in the Field* for the Canadians and R.L. Wallace's finely researched *The Australians at the Boer War*. It is only right that this should be acknowledged. I plead for the forgiveness of anyone who I have inadvertently omitted from this list.

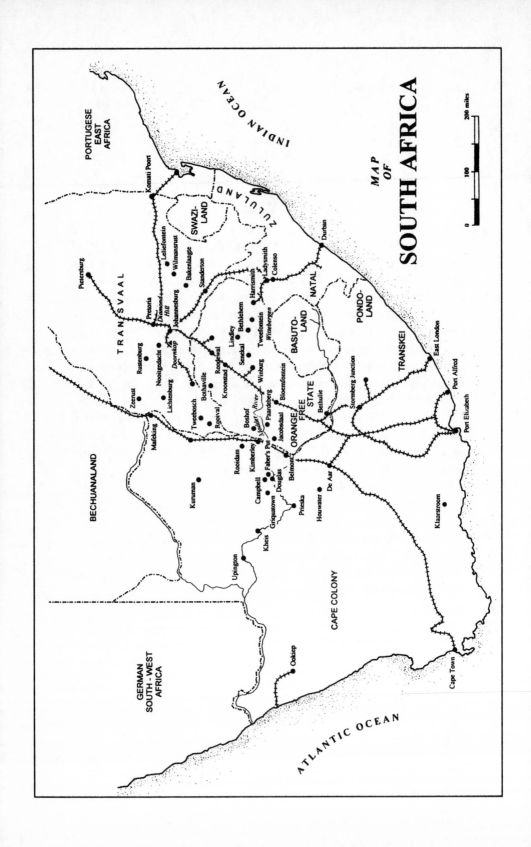

MAP
OF
SOUTH AFRICA

200 miles

100

0

INDIAN OCEAN

PORTUGESE
EAST
AFRICA

Komati Poort

SWAZI-
LAND

ZULULAND

Durban

Pietersburg

T R A N S V A A L

Leliefontein

Wilmansrust

Bakenlaage

Standerton

Diamond Hill

Pretoria

Johannesburg

Doornkop

Nooitgedacht

Rustenburg

Harrismith

Ladysmith

Colenso

NATAL

Bethlehem

Lindley

Tweefontein

Witteberge

BASUTO-
LAND

PONDO-
LAND

East London

Port Alfred

TRANSKEI

Port Elizabeth

Zeerust

Lichtenburg

Bothaville

Senekal

Winburg

Tweebosch

Roodeval

Kroonstad

Roodeval

Boshof

Bloemfontein

Stormberg Junction

Bethulie

Mafeking

Rooival

Modder River

Paardeberg

Jacobsdaal

ORANGE

FREE
STATE

Kuruman

Rooidam

Campbell

Kimberley

Faber's Put

Belmont

De Aar

Douglas

Prieska

Houwater

Klaarstroom

Griquatown

Kheis

Upington

BECHUANALAND

CAPE COLONY

GERMAN
SOUTH - WEST
AFRICA

Ookiep

Cape Town

ATLANTIC OCEAN

CHAPTER ONE

THE CRISIS

Dawn had not yet arrived and the street lamps of London were still burning under a clear night sky as the huge folding doors of the Honourable Artillery Company's drill hall in Bunhill Row were flung open shortly before 7am. As the men of the City of London Imperial Volunteers marched out behind the band of the London Rifle Brigade a roar of welcome from the huge waiting crowds greeted them. A large force of mounted police, their horses sometimes bucking nervously, struggled to force a way for the 500 men of the first contingent of the CIV as they began their march through the city which had raised them to Nine Elms railway station. There they would entrain for Southampton where they would board the troopships taking them to South Africa to fight in the Boer War.[1]*

London had not seen such an outburst of popular enthusiasm since the parade which celebrated Queen Victoria's Diamond Jubilee and with it Britain's Imperial high noon almost three years previously. The CIV's march to Nine Elms, south of the river, was supposed to take one hour and ten minutes. Instead it took three hours and twenty minutes for the men to force their way through the pushing, swaying crowds singing the patriotic songs popular in January 1900. Any pretence at an orderly march was soon abandoned and as they pushed onwards the CIV men smoked, chatted, sang snatches of songs and kissed the girls who

* See Source Notes p. 239

hung upon their arms. By the time they arrived at the railway station some of the men were exhausted and many pieces of equipment had gone missing, often snatched as souvenirs by the crowds.

Down the centuries the capital had often seen soldiers march off to war but the departure of the CIV was something new. In the past those leaving for the front had been professional soldiers or from the militia, men with no choice but to go. Now for the first time Britain was calling upon volunteers from its part-time soldiers to reinforce the regulars in significant numbers in a serious crisis which neither the Government nor the people had believed possible. As well as the CIV, which was drawn from the ranks of the part-time Volunteer Force, civilians with no military experience at all were being trained to go to South Africa. Professional soldiers shook their heads and said that no good would come of it and politicians watched warily. But the gravity of the situation and the strength of popular feeling left them with no choice. Fourteen years later on the outbreak of the First World War such recruitment would be repeated on a much larger scale with the raising of Kitchener's New Armies.

The Boer War had broken out in October, 1899, just over three months before the CIV left London. It was the culmination of almost a century of turbulent relations between the Afrikaners, then known as Boers, and the British. The Boers were the descendants of settlers who arrived after the Dutch East India Company founded a shipping station at the Cape of Good Hope in 1652. They were originally mostly Dutch Calvinists but included some German Protestants and French Huguenots and were dour, independent-minded and suspicious of European interference.

In 1806 the British took possession of Cape Colony because the Cape was a strategic naval base on the sea route to India and the East and soon the seeds of conflict were sown. When Britain ordered the emancipation of slaves throughout its colonies in 1834 about 5,000 Boers refused to give up their black slaves and set off north on the Great Trek. But British influence followed them and Natal, where some of the voortrekkers had settled, was annexed in 1843. Britain did recognize the Transvaal and the Orange Free State, the two Boer republics, in the 1850s, but in 1877 annexed the Transvaal in an attempt to federate South Africa. However four years later the Transvaal's independence was restored after the First Boer War which ended in humiliation for Britain with the defeat at Majuba in 1881.

The discovery of gold and diamonds in southern Africa destabilized the region, fuelling the ambitions of British imperialists and causing a wave of immigration into the Transvaal. Diamonds were found in Kimberley, just inside Cape Colony near the border with the Orange Free State. Cecil Rhodes made his fortune there from the diamond business and later became Prime Minister of the Cape and founded Rhodesia. In 1886 gold was discovered in the Transvaal making it the richest country in southern Africa and non-Boer immigrants, many of them British, arrived to take part in the gold rush. Known as Uitlanders by the Boers, they threatened to outnumber the latter in their own country but were denied the vote. In 1895 Rhodes and Dr Leander Starr Jameson hatched a plan for an Uitlander insurrection in the Transvaal backed up by an invasion from outside. This aimed to force the enfranchisement of the Uitlanders and so enable the election of a Transvaal government which would agree to Rhodes's plan for South African federation. It was a fiasco, with a feeble response to the call for an uprising and the defeat of Jameson's 500 men who had invaded from Mafeking. Rhodes had to resign as Prime Minister.

But the question of the Uitlanders' rights remained unresolved after the failure of the Jameson Raid, and the appointment of Sir Alfred Milner as High Commissioner for South Africa in 1897 ensured that British pressure on the issue would continue. Milner was a firm believer in imperial unity and viewed the 19th century in South Africa as a struggle for supremacy between Britain and the Boers. Convinced that the Transvaal would never introduce sufficient political reforms, Milner conspired to bring about the alternative solution. In short he planned to pick a fight. In the summer of 1899 Paul Kruger, President of the Transvaal, made concessions over voting rights but Milner had no intention of compromising and told the British Government that these were qualified by impossible conditions. The margin by which peace efforts failed was tantalizingly small, but the Government in London accepted Milner's advice that Kruger would give in to further pressure and agreed to send 10,000 men to reinforce the inadequate British forces in South Africa.

This and the news that more troops were mobilizing in England forced Kruger's hand and on 9 October, 1899, he issued an ultimatum to the British. He demanded that British troops should withdraw from the Transvaal border, that soldiers who had landed since 1 June should be removed from South Africa and that no British troops then at sea would be disembarked. Britain was given 48 hours to agree or war would result. The terms were unacceptable and the Boer War began on 11 October, 1899. Not for the last time the British public expected the war to be over by Christmas. Few people believed that the Boers would provide any serious resistance to the great army which was being sent against them. In fact the war was to last two and three-quarter years and cost over £200 million and 21,942 British and colonial lives.

Although the Boers failed to take advantage of the brief numerical superiority they enjoyed before their enemy was reinforced, within two months everything had gone horribly wrong for the British. Soon the Boers were besieging three towns, Mafeking, Kimberley and Ladysmith, and the British forces were hopelessly overstretched. General Sir Redvers Buller, commanding the British, abandoned the original plan to concentrate in Cape Colony and then advance into the Boer republics and instead divided his troops into four. Two forces were to protect Cape Colony, one was to relieve Kimberley and the other to lift the siege of Ladysmith. But in December three of the four commanders suffered serious setbacks in what was quickly dubbed 'Black Week'.

The worst week in the history of the British Empire began on 10 December when Lieutenant-General Sir William Gatacre was repulsed at Stormberg in the northern Cape Colony. Although instructed to take no risks until he had been reinforced, Gatacre made a night march with 3,000 men to attack a position captured by a Boer invasion force. Misled by his guides, he was ambushed and forced to retire, losing eighty-nine men killed or wounded and 633 prisoners.

The following day the force under Lieutenant-General Lord Methuen, who was planning to relieve Kimberley, was also thrown back at Magersfontein. Methuen's attack was beaten off with heavy loss, particularly among the Highland Brigade, which had attempted to turn the Boer flank by night but was instead pinned down in the open for most of the following day. Unable to make any impression on the Boers, the British withdrew to the Modder River having lost sixty-eight officers and 1,011 men killed and wounded.

Only four days later Buller himself was similarly humiliated at Colenso, south of Ladysmith. A frontal attack went badly wrong, the Irish Brigade on the left being led into a loop in the River Tugela, where they were a sitting target for the Boers on the heights above. On the right two batteries of artillery were led much closer to the Boer positions than Buller intended and became stranded. Two guns were eventually rescued with great heroism but the British had to withdraw having lost 143 killed, 755 wounded and 240 missing. Colenso was not a defeat but it was, as Buller termed it at the time, "a serious reverse".

Back in Britain the newspaper boys shouted the bad news from street corners and the papers themselves printed detailed casualty lists. Theatres and concert rooms were empty, the restaurant trade had a thin time and publishers complained that people only wanted to read war books. A nation used to easy colonial victories against opponents armed with spears and unsophisticated firearms had suddenly suffered more than 2,000 casualties in a week. Since the start of the war another 2,000 British troops had surrendered. It was a humiliation made worse by the wave of pro-Boer sentiment that swept across most of Europe. There was no sense of panic in Britain, little pressure for Government ministers to be sacked, but people were more worried than at any time since the Indian Mutiny, perhaps even since the wars against Napoleon. The Hon Sidney Peel, a barrister soon to volunteer for service in South Africa, later recalled that the gloom of Black Week was so all-pervading that "it was impossible to go on doing the ordinary things of life".

People were right to be concerned. Not only was Britain's dangerous isolation in Europe being exposed but so too was the slenderness of its military resources. On 1 October, 1899, the Regular Army was 235,602 strong, almost 14,000 below establishment. Of these 68,939 were serving in India and it was regarded as far too risky to withdraw large numbers of British troops from the jewel of the Empire. The use of Indian troops in South Africa had been ruled out for political reasons. This was intended to be a war waged by white troops against a white enemy, although both sides eventually used South African blacks. There were only 107,739 regulars in Britain on 1 October, including non-combatant units.[2] The best of these were soon on their way to South Africa but although, after the First Class Reserve had been called up, there were still nearly 100,000 regulars at home, it was estimated that 40 per cent of these were either too young or physically unfit for foreign service.[3] The Marquess of Lansdowne, Secretary of State for War, told the House of Lords that the men left at home were "in no sense a field army".

Britain's small army suddenly needed to be expanded rapidly. The Royal Commission chaired by Lord Elgin, which reported after the war, concluded: "At the outbreak of the war there were in the Regular Army and Reserve insufficient trained men of an age fit for foreign service to meet the emergency which arose, even when practically the whole Reserve had been used." The report added: "The defence of the Kingdom . . . was at this time dangerously weak."

Part of the response to the crisis was the traditional Victorian remedy of sending a hero to take charge. Field Marshal Lord Roberts, who had won the Victoria Cross during the Indian Mutiny and became the most revered soldier of his day with his march from Kabul to Kandahar in Afghanistan in 1880, was sent out to take command in South Africa. But the manpower problem remained and one of the answers was provided by the wave of emotion and patriotism which swept through Britain and the Empire in the wake of Black Week. Astonishment at the reverses in South Africa gave way to a sense of humiliation and anger at this snub to the imperial dream. People wanted to play a part in the war. For many this meant no more than roaring out the verses of Kipling's recently published poem *The Absent-Minded Beggar* in music halls. Others, including Queen Victoria herself, contributed to funds to buy gifts for the troops. Some, for whom such gestures were not enough, volunteered to fight. In the colonies, where people sympathized with both the mother country and with the Uitlanders, feelings also ran high. The shortage of troops and and the need to harness popular feeling meant that within a few days of Buller's setback at Colenso the Government decided to give those who wanted to volunteer the chance to go to war.

Britain's part-time soldiers had offered their services to the Government even before the Boer War began. On 19 July, 1899, as the South African crisis worsened, Lieutenant-Colonel Eustace Balfour, commanding the London Scottish, approached George Wyndham, Parliamentary Under-Secretary at the War Office, and suggested that a special service company should be raised from his regiment and attached to the Gordon Highlanders in the event of war. The following month Colonel Sir Howard Vincent, Conservative MP for Sheffield Central and commanding officer of the Queen's Westminster Volunteers, offered to raise a 1,000 strong volunteer battalion at his own expense. He was told that his offer had been sent to the War Office "through the wrong channel".

Both offers were renewed when war broke out in October and others came forward from the yeomanry regiments and the Volunteer Force.That month Colonel Alfred Lucas, a wealthy businessman commanding the Suffolk Yeomanry, suggested mobilizing a composite regiment of yeomanry for service in South Africa. In November Colonel Lord Lonsdale of the Westmorland and Cumberland Yeomanry offered to equip and transport 1,000 men to South Africa while among the others who came forward were the Middlesex Yeomanry and Colonel Lord Harris of the East Kent Yeomanry.

The great and the good of the auxiliary forces were straining at the leash but all were turned down. Vincent was told by the War Office that the Volunteer Act of 1895 provided no powers to send volunteers abroad. Sir Evelyn Wood, the Adjutant-General, said that volunteers would cost as much to transport as regulars and would not be as efficient. Vincent was turned down again in November and on the 26th of that month, only two weeks before the humiliations of Black Week began, Lucas was sent a curt letter by the War Office which concluded: "There is no intention at present of utilising the services of the yeomanry in South Africa." At the heart of the rejection of these offers lay two factors. Firstly professional soldiers despised the part-timers and the only previous occasion on which they had been used was when the specialist skills of a handful of Post Office and Railway Volunteers had been employed in the Egyptian campaigns in the 1880s. Secondly neither they nor the Government contemplated a situation in which the Regular Army would be seriously tested by the Boers. Like so many of their assumptions at the outbreak of the Boer War, they were quickly proved wrong.

Two offers of help were accepted. One was from the colonies, some of which proffered assistance as early as July 1899. It made political sense for Joseph Chamberlain, Secretary for the Colonies, to accept some help to cement Imperial unity at a time when Britain was deeply unpopular in continental Europe. For the colonies it was a chance to demonstrate their loyalty, an opportunity for them to show that they had come of age as nations, as well as useful campaign experience for members of their fledgling defence forces.

Even so, the War Office managed to demonstrate a mixture of muddle and apathy. It gave Chamberlain a controversial and misleading telegram to send to the colonies describing the soldiers required as 'infantry most, cavalry least serviceable'.[4] Instead of encouraging the sending of colonial mounted troops, the War Office wanted only token forces to attach to British units. Secondly, colonial enthusiasm was watered down by a British military hierarchy unable to accept that its professional army would need help. When the Australians offered 2,500 men, Britain told them to send less. Given that Australian mounted infantry were just the type of troops needed to fight the Boers, it was further evidence that the War Office had yet to understand its enemy. However despite this, the first contingents of 1,105 men from Canada, 1,271 from Australia and 203 from New Zealand[5] set sail for South Africa amid great scenes of popular enthusiasm in late October and early November. Many of them were volunteers from local regular or part-time units and they were the first of nearly 30,000 non-South African colonials who would serve in the Boer War.

Furthermore, it quickly became apparent that the Regular Army's medical services were hopelessly inadequate to deal with a conflict of this size. Casualties in the first few weeks of the war were greater than anticipated and diseases such as enteric fever, now called typhoid, soon began to take a dreadful toll. Voluntary medical organizations had anticipated that this might be necessary and almost a year before the war had combined to form the Central British Red Cross Committee to organize assistance to the Army's medical services. One of the organizations involved was the St John Ambulance Brigade which on 3 November was approached by the War Office to provide trained medical order-lies and on the 21st the first twenty-three men embarked for South Africa.[6] Eventually about 1,900 SJAB men served in hospitals during the Boer War. Civilian surgeons were recruited to ease the Army's shortage of doctors and funds set up to send private hospitals and hospital ships to South Africa.

Even before Black Week had reached its disastrous climax at Colenso, attitudes towards using non-regular troops were beginning to change at the War Office. On 13 December, two days after Magersfontein, Lansdowne held a meeting attended by Lord Wolseley, the Commander-in-Chief, and senior officers. Lansdowne asked for opinions on whether the yeomanry and volunteers should be offered a role in the war and Wolseley supported their use. That day Wolseley wrote to Lansdowne saying, "I would accept the services of eight or ten companies of mounted infantry from our yeomanry service. The same from the Volunteer Force." Setting out his proposals in a more detailed memorandum to Lansdowne the following day, Wolseley confessed, "We are now face to face with a serious national crisis and unless we meet it boldly and quickly grapple with it success-fully it may – in my humble opinion it will – lead to dangerous complications with foreign powers."[7]

Wolseley went on to outline a package of proposals for re-inforcing British forces in South Africa which included accepting all offers of additional contingents from the colonies, enlisting 1,000 yeomanry willing to serve as mounted infantry and 6,000 officers and men from the volunteers. He continued, "The employment of these detachments of our Auxiliary Forces is de-sirable. It will be very popular, it will raise the character of the forces concerned and it will free for active work against the enemy many regular battalions." The following day the Army Board met and put more flesh on the scheme. It suggested that for every English, Scottish and Welsh line battalion serving in South Africa two companies of volunteers should be raised, one to serve along-side the regulars and the second to be held in reserve. The Board estimated that this would provide 6,000 to 8,000 men for service against the Boers with a similar number in reserve. The yeomanry was to be asked to form ten 100-strong companies of mounted infantry. As far as colonial contingents were concerned, the Board thought "that offers should be considered on their merits and all those which are likely to prove beneficial should be accepted without restrictions as to numbers and that whenever possible we should try to get mounted infantry."[8]

Lansdowne himself was well aware of the political advantages of enlisting civilians and part-time soldiers. The rapid change of policy towards such recruitment had twin benefits for the Conservative Government which had drifted into the war and then badly mishandled it. Ministers could appear to be doing something decisive at a time of crisis while also providing a way for the public to let off steam. As Lansdowne put it when he wrote to the Marquess of Salisbury, the Prime Minister, on 15 December: "It seems to me to be impossible to refuse altogether and, apart from purely military considerations, I see some advantage in affording an outlet to public feeling, which is beginning to run very high."[9] The pressure to do something was indeed building fast. *The Times* published a letter from the writer Arthur Conan Doyle, creator of Sherlock Holmes, calling for civilian volunteers to be allowed to serve. "There are thousands of men riding after foxes or shooting pheasants who would gladly be useful to their country if it were made possible for them," he wrote.

Public feeling had already started to manifest itself by the formation of the City of London Imperial Volunteers. On the 15th Sir Alfred Newton, the Lord Mayor of London, offered to raise the CIV, as the unit became known. The formation of the CIV was a triumph of improvisation and was in many respects an early example of privatization. By comparison with the civil servants of the War Office, the merchants and bankers of the City of London and the leading lights of the Volunteer Force in the capital moved with lightning speed. The Court of Common Council voted £25,000 for the CIV and other large sums were donated by banks and livery companies. The first CIV draft left for South Africa less than a month after the regiment had originally been proposed.[10]

As official attitudes changed, events continued to race ahead of them. One of the catalysts was Buller himself who on the 16th, the day after Colenso, sent a cypher telegram to Lansdowne asking, "Would it be possible for you to raise eight thousand irregulars in England? They should be equipped as mounted infantry, be able to shoot as well as possible and ride decently. I would amalgamate them with colonials."[11]

A key player in the rapidly changing situation now emerged in the form of Wyndham, Lansdowne's Parliamentary Under-Secretary. Wyndham, Conservative MP for Dover, was the unofficial leader of Milner's supporters in the House of Commons and had reported to the High Commissioner behind Lansdowne's back as the South African crisis unfolded. He was a former chairman of the South African Association, the main jingoistic pressure group in Britain, and quietly manipulated both this body and the press to back Milner's uncompromising stance towards the Boers. Wyndham had a military background, having served in the Egyptian campaign as a Lieutenant in the Coldstream

Guards almost twenty years previously. He quickly saw the potential of using Buller's telegram to raise an entirely new type of force, to be called the Imperial Yeomanry. The day after the telegram arrived he told Lansdowne that British mobility must match that of the Boers. Then he suggested raising as "a matter of immediate urgency and permanent importance" 20,000 irregular mounted infantry from the Empire, at least 5,000 of whom would be recruited in Britain.

As well as helping relieve the military crisis in South Africa, the Imperial Yeomanry provided Wyndham, an officer in the Cheshire Yeomanry, with a vehicle for reforming the yeomanry at home. The part-time cavalry regiments, mostly formed in the 1790s to defend Britain against France, had become picturesque relics of little practical military use. They did not take their soldiering as seriously as the Volunteer Force and were committed to serve only in case of foreign invasion and then only within their own county. In 1899 the yeomanry numbered only 10,433, more than 1,400 below establishment.[12] But the raw material, particularly the gentry and farmers well used to riding and shooting, had immense potential. Indeed Wyndham advised Lansdowne to be guided by such people, some of whom were friends of his, in forming the Imperial Yeomanry. He explained in a letter to his father, "They are men of affairs, and as masters of foxhounds, they are in touch with the young riding farmers and horse-masters of this country."[13]

The concept of the Imperial Yeomanry caught the imagination of politicians, the press and the public. Only four days after Buller's telegram, Wyndham wrote to his mother, "The Imperial Yeomanry is my child. I invented it after lunch on Sunday and it is already a fine banting. To bring it to birth has been a business."[14] The birth was officially announced by a Royal Warrant dated 24 December. A committee of distinguished yeomanry officers was appointed to run an organization which was entirely separate from the War Office. As with the CIV, improvisation was to be the order of the day. The Royal Warrant specifically stated that the Imperial Yeomanry was to be recruited from a mixture of yeomanry, volunteers and civilians. It also announced the formation of the CIV and of the Volunteer Companies proposed by the Army Board.

Wolseley was not happy about having his scheme trumped by Wyndham. On 28 December he wrote an irascible memo complaining that he had not been consulted about the scheme and warned: "I was very anxious to supply the GOC in South Africa with 8,000 trained men accustomed to some sort of discipline but to go into the highways and byways and pick up any civilians who will volunteer to go to South Africa quite regardless of whether they have ever learnt even the rudiments of discipline and to form them into companies or battalions in the proportion of three of such men to one of the very imperfectly drilled and disciplined yeomanry men also volunteering is, according to my knowledge of war, a dangerous experiment."

But he had lost Lansdowne's support. The Secretary of State replied that it was not fair "to suggest that we are picking up in the highways and byways any civilians who will go to South Africa. We have laid down . . . certain qualifications which ought to ensure our getting really useful men who, with a little training and experience in the field, will be extremely valuable. The Boers are not, I suppose, very highly drilled or disciplined."[15]

CHAPTER TWO

GENTLEMEN IN KHAKI

Wyndham did not have to go into the highways and byways to recruit the Imperial Yeomanry. Even in his most optimistic moments he could not have dreamed that it would tap the popular mood with such stunning success. The recruiting centres were overwhelmed by applications, some men returning from abroad to enlist. Among gentlemen, unencumbered in many cases by either wives or the need to earn a living, there was a rush to join up. The foxhunting fraternity, men already comfortable in the saddle, showed particular enthusiasm for going to South Africa. In Ireland the 45th Company Imperial Yeomanry was recruited largely from the Ward Union, Meath and Kildare hunts and was commonly known as the Dublin Hunt Company.[1] They were the sons of county gentlemen or professional men in their own right, recruited in the Irish capital by Lord Longford. The 22nd Company was raised in mid-Cheshire by Captain Mosley Leigh, well known as a rider to hounds in the county. Some officers of the Royal Wiltshire Yeomanry were so keen to play a part that, being out with the hounds when the telegrams summoning them to a preliminary meeting arrived, they rode straight into Trowbridge in their hunting kits in order to attend.[2] In the words of the historian Thomas Pakenham: "In sporting circles there was a rush to abandon the fox and pursue the Boer."[3]

Thirty-four MPs and members of the House of Lords joined the Imperial Yeomanry. The Duke of Marlborough volunteered for the Oxfordshire contingent and the Duke of Norfolk for the 69th (Sussex) Company. Inevitably they and almost all the

14

members of the House of Commons received commissions, but at least one MP served in the ranks. As the involvement of volunteers turned the Boer War from being the last of the nineteenth century's colonial campaigns into the first of the twentieth century's national conflicts, a new breed of gentleman ranker was born. Nothing illustrated this more vividly than the formation of the so-called Special Corps, which came under the umbrella of the Imperial Yeomanry organization, but which had nothing to do with the existing yeomanry regiments, which were responsible for raising most of the force.

Pre-eminent among the Special Corps was the 47th Company Imperial Yeomanry, which soon acquired itself the less mundane title of the Duke of Cambridge's Own. The ageing Duke, Commander-in-Chief of the Army for thirty-nine years until 1895 and a bitter opponent of reform, accepted the presidency of its recruiting committee. Led by the Earl of Donoughmore, the committee set up offices in Duke Street in the heart of London's fashionable West End and recruited the sort of rank and file which the regular British Tommy was more accustomed to saluting. Most were the sons of the aristocracy or gentry, many were old Etonians, and every man agreed to pay the considerable sum of £130 for his own passage to South Africa, his horse and his equipment. If anyone was still in any doubt that they were gentlemen rather than players, the DCOs agreed to donate their pay to the Imperial War Fund for the Widows and Orphans of Soldiers. A popular joke at the time suggested that they were so socially superior that a special class of foe would have to be found for them as they could not possibly be expected to exchange bullets with the ordinary Boer.[4]

The Duke Street office was deluged with applications and on one day alone more than 100 men applied to join. The rank and file included William Allen, the Liberal MP for Newcastle-under-Lyme, two sons of the landowner Sir James Blyth and the Hon Norman Lubbock, son of Lord Avebury. Such was the demand to enlist in the company that one well-known African explorer, whose name was not made public, offered £2,000 and a Maxim gun if he could be assured of a commission. His offer was refused as he did not meet the guidelines established for the recruitment of officers. One volunteer who was rejected on medical grounds went off to get a second doctor's opinion, but was still turned down while another, who had been urged to join up by his wife, was so frightened of what she would say about his medical failure that he demanded a certificate of unfitness.[5]

Not far behind the DCOs on the social scale was Paget's Horse, the 51st, 52nd, 68th and 73rd Companies, which together comprised the 19th Battalion Imperial Yeomanry. They were public school-educated men recruited through advertisments in gentlemen's clubs. The battalion was raised by George Paget, the son of a British general and a compulsive amateur soldier with a penchant for getting himself involved in any conflict that afforded the chance of action. He never seems to have been a regular officer but served in the Russo-Turkish War of 1877–8 and the Greco-Turkish War of 1897, as well as the Zulu War in 1879. Although aged 46 when the Boer War broke out, he went out to South Africa as second-in-command of his regiment and proved himself to be a man of some courage, being wounded twice. A portly figure who felt at home in the dining rooms and smoking rooms of Pall Mall, Paget recruited 500 officers and men from a tiny, hopelessly inadequate room at the Imperial Yeomanry Committee's offices in Suffolk Street. However, it at least had the advantage of being only a short stroll from the clubs of which he was a member.

Paget's Horse wore a badge made up of the letters PH which provided a source of instant merriment for the wags on the streets of London, who suggested that it stood for 'Piccadilly Heroes' or more commonly for 'Perfectly Harmless'. Gentlemen troopers such as Cosmo Rose-Innes, a barrister, found that wearing their new uniforms in the capital produced a rich variety of reactions and some odd social contradictions. He later recalled: "The khaki drew to its wearer, however, many amusing experiences; the fervent 'God bless you' of old ladies in the bus, the friendly offers of navvies to ''ave half a pint' in the street, the respect of substantial citizens for one's opinion on the war. The ''ave half a pint' situation was the most embarrassing. We were clad as troopers but flattered ourselves we bore the impress of officers and hence a conflict of emotions, the desire to be rollicking good fellows qualified by surprise that our would-be host should not detect the gentleman under the plain khaki."[6]

Most of the Imperial Yeomanry was not of the same social background as these Special Corps, but nevertheless the recruits were of a far higher quality than the Regular Army obtained. Colonel the Earl of Scarborough of the Yorkshire Dragoons said that of 450 men he raised to go to South Africa 12.5 per cent were farmers, 9.25 per cent grooms, 9 per cent clerks, 8 per cent engineers, 4 per cent butchers and 2.5 per cent shoeing smiths. Some 4 per cent had no occupation, which may have been due to unemployment but more probably meant that they were gentlemen of private means.[7] The recruits also included "a few travellers, drapers and labourers". A draft of men for four companies from rural Welsh areas which made up the 9th Battalion consisted of 30 per cent clerks, 18 per cent shopkeepers and merchants, 14 per cent farmers, grooms and other rural occupations, 12 per cent skilled artisans and 6 per cent with no occupation. They included an artist, a musician, a modeller and a dentist, none of whom were likely to have ever joined the Regular Army. Of the 34 per cent with some form of previous military experience, almost all had served in the Volunteer Force, with only one man having been in the yeomanry and two being ex-regulars. Half described themselves as being "used to shooting game", which at least ensured some familiarity with firearms, even if shooting at Boers vanishing across the veldt required substantially greater skill than bringing down a pheasant in Denbighshire.[8] Of the first 100 recruits for the 22nd Company in Cheshire, fifteen were "gentlemen who had comfortable homes and had volunteered to go out as troopers," according to Captain Leigh, their company commander. It has been estimated that overall about half of the Imperial Yeomanry contingent of 1900 came from the middle class.[9]

Major-General John Brabazon, who commanded the Imperial Yeomanry in South Africa, described them as "Physically magnificent because they were the representatives of England, the yeomen of England, and intelligent men and there was a large number of gentlemen in the ranks. They were a vastly superior crowd of human beings to the men we have in the ranks naturally. They were the men I want to see in our ranks as soldiers, which other countries have."[10]

Not for the first or last time in a war, potential recruits lied about their age. The minimum age for joining the Imperial Yeomanry was twenty and the maximum was supposed to be thirty-five. Both limits were widely ignored and so great was the enthusiasm for getting to South Africa that if men were turned down by one recruiting centre they simply went to another. Any strings that could be pulled were grasped and tugged. Roy Rice applied to join one of the Middlesex companies but foolishly admitted that he was only nineteen. He wrote later: "The paper was torn up and I was told there was nothing doing. I was terribly upset but still determined to get to the war somehow. I had an uncle down in Wiltshire, so wrote to him and asked his help. He invited me down and said he thought he could get me into the Wiltshire Yeomanry. I went at once and he introduced me to Colonel Chaloner, officer commanding the regiment, who took us to lunch at Badminton, where we met the Duke of Beaufort, Sir Walter Long, the Marquess of Bath and his brother Lord Thynne. My uncle had been at school with the Duke and hunted with him for years." Connections proved stronger than regulations and Rice was allowed to join the 2nd (Wiltshire) Company as a private.[11]

Under-age recruiting was one of many problems which had to be dealt with by the Imperial Yeomanry Committee, the central organization of the new force. On occasions it came close to being overwhelmed by public enthusiasm for the war and the huge volume of correspondence which this unleashed. On one day alone the committee received more than 1,000 letters. One sixteen-year-old youth wrote offering to enlist because "as I am the eldest of five brothers I shall not be missed". Many anxious inquiries were received from parents who discovered that their sons had run away to join up. Mr H. Hicking of West Bridgford, Nottingham, wrote asking whether there was any news of his two sons, aged 19 and 18, who were believed to have enlisted in the Imperial Yeomanry in London. Inevitably there were also those who took advantage of the sense of national crisis. A Mr Thorpe was sought by police after obtaining food and lodgings by falsely claiming to be a member of the Sherwood Rangers Imperial Yeomanry contingent. In a letter to the Imperial Yeomanry headquarters, the constabulary described him as having a moustache and wearing light check cycling knickers.[12] A potentially more serious threat than this Victorian cad was an apparent attempt by Boer spies to enlist. *The Times* reported: "In more than one case there were very good reasons for believing that the applicant presented himself for enrolment in the interests of the enemy. But the vigilance of the authorities was sufficient to frustrate any such purpose." One cannot help thinking that there must have been more effective ways for the Boers to get intelligence about British military plans.

The Imperial Yeomanry Committee began life before Christmas, 1899, as an informal group of senior officers from the existing yeomanry regiments. The driving force was Colonel Alfred Lucas of the Suffolk Yeomanry, who had lobbied for the involvement of the auxiliary forces from the start of the war and who was to be a key figure in the organization of the Imperial Yeomanry throughout the conflict. He offered his services to the War Office who passed him on to Colonel Lord Chesham of the Royal Bucks Hussars, who later became Inspector-General of Imperial Yeomanry. Chesham asked him to take on the home organization of the force and Lucas agreed provided that he was given a free hand to choose his staff and draw up the rules. The new organization opened offices at 12 Suffolk Street, off Pall Mall, manned by a small staff. All was confusion, as what was still effectively an unofficial body made up the rules as it went along. The premises proved utterly inadequate and in January the headquarters moved a short distance to Cleveland House in St James's Square. Lucas had already pressed Lansdowne and Wyndham to "get the organization in proper order" and the committee was formally constituted by the War Office on 4 January. At its head was Lucas and also on the seven-strong committee, which met

19

daily, were the Earl of Lonsdale and Lord Harris, both yeomanry colonels who had previously offered to raise forces for South Africa, and Colonel Viscount Valentia of the Oxfordshire Yeomanry. Royal favour was bestowed when the Prince of Wales became Honorary Colonel of the force, and the committee set about its work which was effectively to act as a small-scale rival to the War Office. Lucas recalled: "Practically the whole of what I may call our professional staff was chosen from men of Indian experience – the Indian Staff Corps – and they brought to bear a very broad and open mind on all the questions that came before them. I think it was owing to their support that the work of the Yeomanry Committee was as successful as it has been."[13]

The task given to the committee was to raise twenty battalions of four companies apiece, each of the the latter consisting of 121 all ranks. The titles reflected the War Office's view that the Imperial Yeomanry was a mounted infantry force rather than cavalry. The infantry designations were widely resented and frequently ignored, the units often referring to themselves as squadrons and regiments. The rank and file liked to call themselves troopers, although technically they were privates.

The committee appointed battalion commanders and seconds-in-command, the emphasis being on previous military experience, and, with one exception, all the commanders of the battalions raised in 1900 were ex-regulars. Only four, including Chesham , a former cavalryman who commanded the 10th Battalion, were yeomanry officers. Junior appointments were made locally but all officers had to be approved by the committee and finding the right candidates was not always easy. The committee made a general rule that no officer would be accepted who did not have some kind of previous military experience. But the War Office banned Regular Army officers from joining the Imperial Yeomanry and many militia officers were being mobilized with their battalions to go overseas. This left the new force dependent on the yeomanry, the volunteers and ex-regulars as a source of officers. The officers were far better than those of the second contingent of Imperial Yeomanry recruited in 1901 but finding suitable captains and lieutenants as well as veterinary and medical officers became increasingly difficult. Recruiting efficient regimental staffs was also a major problem.[14]

The rank and file were recruited by the existing yeomanry units, except for the Special Corps and in Ireland, where there were no such regiments. The men enlisted for one year or for the duration of the war if longer and had to pass shooting and riding tests as well as a medical and be at least 5ft 3ins tall. Bachelors or widowers without children were preferred to married men and the force was to be paid the normal cavalry rate. Recruiting them was never difficult and far more could have been sent to South Africa if the War Office had been prepared to sanction it. Lucas said later that "offers from various gentlemen to raise forces amounting to over 5,000 men"[15] had been turned down for a variety of reasons by the committee and that a much larger force of Imperial Yeomanry could have been recruited. But within two months of the committee's foundation the War Office, still nervous about this new military phenomenon, started to apply the brakes on recruiting, setting a limit of 11,600. A few weeks later, emboldened by the modest success of the occupation of Bloemfontein, the capital of the Orange Free State, this was cut back to 10,500. Eventually 550 officers and 10,371 men embarked with the first contingent of the Imperial Yeomanry. The twenty battalions were made up of seventy-eight companies, the 8th and 16th Battalions being short of one company each.

Lansdowne had originally suggested that the ratio of civilians and volunteers to yeomanry should be three to one, which would have meant about 2,700 recruits from the yeomanry. Wyndham doubted that he would get more than 2,500 men from the latter force but in a more optimistic moment said that he wanted each company to consist of forty yeomen and seventy-five volunteers and civilians. He wrote to Lansdowne expressing the fear that "the yeomanry may organize itself into some twenty companies, take ship overseas and leave us to find the difference".[16] Wyndham need not have worried as all his projections about recruits from the yeomanry turned out to be optimistic. Of the rank and file of the Imperial Yeomanry only 1,898, less than one fifth, came from the existing yeomanry regiments.[17] As a source of men for overseas service, the ailing poorly-trained yeomanry failed its first-ever test. Not everybody was sorry. Peel, who joined the 40th (Oxfordshire) Company as a private, commented: "I do not think that this was at all a misfortune; certainly I never detected any particular aptitude for active service in old yeomen."[18]

Recruits for the Imperial Yeomanry did not only come forward out of patriotism, although those who did tended to downplay it. Peel recalled, "I only remember one man who declared that he had enlisted from reasons of patriotism and he was generally regarded as peculiar. If others were so influenced, they would by no means confess to it. Some came because they saw a chance of emigration at Government expense, some for love of sport and excitement, some because their domestic affairs were in a tangle from which enlistment offered a ready escape, some because they were tired of their present occupation, some because they wanted a job, some because they wanted a medal and some because others came." At the Imperial Yeomanry base camp at Maitland, near Cape Town, Sergeant Major Fownes of the 10th Hussars kept a confessions book to which many men contributed. Reasons given for joining the Imperial Yeomanry included: "to escape my creditors", "to escape the police", "because I was sick of England", "a broken heart", "vanity" and "sudden splash of patriotism upon visiting a music hall".[19]

Apart from arming the force, providing some funds and restraining recruitment, the War Office had little to do with the Imperial Yeomanry. Ironically many would-be recruits did not understand this and clogged its corridors offering their services. Indeed the two organizations became rivals in the desperate scramble to find equipment and horses for the reinforcements being sent to South Africa. The day after the formation of the force was announced, General Sir Henry Brackenbury, the Director-General of Ordnance made his view clear in a tetchy memo. "I cannot provide these 'Imperial Yeomanry' with anything except arms, ammunition and tents. They must provide everything else for themselves," he wrote. "We cannot get these things fast enough to supply the regular troops."[20]

The Imperial Yeomanry Committee and the county organizations took up the challenge. Even their machine guns and medical equipment were obtained privately.

The Government did provide some money, a capitation grant of £25 per man for clothing, equipment and saddlery, which was later increased by £10. If a man brought a suitable horse with him, a further £40 was permitted. The rest of the cost of the Imperial Yeomanry was met by private central and local funds and gifts of horses and equipment. The central fund run by the committee was given £66,000, of which £50,000 came from Wernher, Beit, the richest and most powerful of the Rand gold mining houses.[21] The company was closely allied with Milner's imperial ambitions, had already financed the raising of Uitlander regiments in South Africa and probably viewed the Imperial Yeomanry as a source of future loyal settlers. The Prince of Wales gave 100 guineas. The various county funds raised a total of £80,000, the amounts given varying widely from area to area, which proved a source of friction. The county organizations were allowed to equip their men entirely themselves if they were able to do so. The Irish companies, with no parent yeomanry regiments, were placed at a disadvantage by this system.[22]

Despite this hastily improvised procurement operation, the Imperial Yeomanry went to South Africa far better equipped than their regular comrades. Major Wyndham Knight, Chief Staff Officer of the Imperial Yeomanry, told the Royal Commission after the war, "There was no question of articles being too expensive if they were thought necessary. We could give them the very best of everything." The yeomen left for the war clad in khaki serge patrol jackets, hunting breeches made of Bedford cord or similar material, slouch hats or helmets, cavalry cloaks and good quality boots. Knight recalled: "The clothing supplied was of such superior quality that after the occupation of Pretoria, officers were offering men of the Imperial Yeomanry a good deal more than the original cost in order to obtain their jackets, hats and breeches."

Inevitably the competition between the War Office and the buyers from the Imperial Yeomanry forced prices up. This was particularly the case with horses, of which the Imperial

Yeomanry's central and local remount officers bought 13,512 costing £463,666[23] in the space of a few weeks. Every market in Britain, Australia, South Africa and even Austria was scoured and after the war some of the officers involved were accused of having corruptly lined their own pockets. Chesham later admitted that the competition "put the price up and was very unsatisfactory".[24] The House of Commons Public Accounts Committee was later scathing about the creation of this seller's market and accused the Imperial Yeomanry of buying sub-standard goods at inflated prices. However, the force's defenders pointed out that they only bought horses and equipment because the War Office could not cope and that much of the money spent came from private donors. Both sides in the argument however, agreed that this was a situation which should never be allowed to arise again.

The War Office, overwhelmed by the crisis in South Africa, managed to make a mess of the one part of the Imperial Yeomanry procurement operation over which it had retained control. The Lee Enfield rifles supplied to the force had been wrongly sighted, although at first the problem was blamed on the poor shooting of the recruits. Soon, however, it was realized that nobody could be guilty of such spectacularly bad marksmanship and the weapons were sent for adjustment. While this was done the men practised with the older Lee–Metford rifle but valuable time, which the recruits could ill afford to lose, was wasted.

Two units similar to the Imperial Yeomanry were recruited independently of the Cleveland House committee. Immediately after the British reverse at Magersfontein Lord Lovat approached the War Office and asked permission to raise Lovat's Scouts. He recruited 269 men from the Scottish Highlands, many of them ghillies and stalkers who were, as he put it, "thoroughly trained in the use of the telescope". On arrival in South Africa they were attached to the Highland Brigade as scouts. The second unit was also an aristocrat's private venture. Lord Loch raised Loch's Horse mainly from men with previous experience in southern Africa. At first he applied for his force to be part of the Imperial Yeomanry but quickly put the committee's noses out of joint by going directly to Lord Roberts for permission to recruit his men. He negotiated an agreement by which Loch's Horse was paid more than the Imperial Yeomanry, not put through any tests or inspections and not subject to discipline on board ship to South Africa. At that point the Imperial Yeomanry organization left him to his own devices.

The raising of the City Imperial Volunteers in London proved as popular as that of the Imperial Yeomanry. It was the only unit recruited from the Volunteer Force sent out as a complete regiment and was the product of an extraordinary, informal deal reached by Wolseley and Sir Alfred Newton, the Lord Mayor of London. On the day that Buller was repulsed at Colenso, Newton went to see the Commander-in-Chief, driving a mayoral coach and horses through all the usual War Office channels. The Lord Mayor took with him an outline scheme prepared by Colonel Charles Boxall of the Sussex Volunteer Artillery. Wolseley gave Newton verbal permission to raise the CIV and after that the project took on a momentum of its own. The first written permission for the CIV appears to have been a semi-official letter treating its formation as a *fait accompli*[25] and it was officially recognized in Army Orders only a week before the first men embarked for South Africa.

The CIV consisted of a battalion of infantry, two companies of mounted infantry and a four-gun artillery battery recruited from forty-seven Volunteer Force units in London. The infantry included a twenty-strong cyclists section provided by the Inns of Court Rifle Volunteers. The commanding officer and his staff came from the Regular Army and other officers were appointed by Wolseley from lists of candidates provided by the Honourable Artillery Company and the Metropolitan Volunteer Corps. The lists were approved by the Lord Mayor before they were passed on to Wolseley, an astonishing piece of civilian intervention in military affairs. The senior NCOs, the quartermaster sergeants, colour sergeants, orderly room clerk and pay sergeants were also regulars, but the remaining NCOs came from the volunteers. Recruits had to be aged twenty to thirty-five, at least 5ft 5ins tall, of good character, to have been passed as efficient volunteers for the past two years and be medically fit. The medical turned out to be less than rigorous and it was later estimated that up to ten per cent of the men would not have passed for the Regular Army.[26] They joined up for a year or for the duration of the war if longer and were paid one shilling per day, the same as regular infantrymen.

The CIV was raised in less than a month, which reflected the fact that some of the sharpest brains in the City of London were behind it. The Mansion House, the official residence of the Lord Mayor, took on a new role as the regiment's headquarters and Colonel Henry Mackinnon of the Grenadier Guards was appointed to command it. The Lord Mayor summoned all the commanding officers of the Volunteer Force in London, told them that there was a national emergency and asked them each for forty volunteers for the CIV, although eventually some units provided more and some less. Potential recruits flooded in and Mackinnon estimated that he received about 25 per cent more volunteers than he could actually accept. He said, "The men began to pour in long before we were ready for them, in fact we were not at all ready for them. The moment it got out in the newspapers, the Mansion House was inundated with people from all parts of the world who wanted to come into the service."[27] On New Year's Day 365 men were sworn in by the Lord Mayor at the Guildhall and three days later another 900 went through the same ceremony. The original plan had been to raise 1,000 men, but fundraising proved so successful that eventually sixty-four officers and 1,739 other ranks served in South Africa, including a later draft to the regiment.[28] The only real problem with recruiting was that unmarried men were preferred, which ruled out many volunteers. However, to Mackinnon's annoyance, some men rushed to wed their girl-friends after enlistment and before embarkation and he found, once out in South Africa, that at least five per cent of his soldiers had wives at home. Officers, mostly from the Volunteer Force, were through sheer necessity selected quickly and not always with the greatest of care. Sir Howard Vincent, the most deter-mined of all campaigners for the involvement of the auxiliary forces in the war, said scathingly, "It was rather like seeing footmen, only one made much less inquiry than one would have done when taking people into one's own service. It was impossible to do it, the pace was too severe."[29]

As with the Imperial Yeomanry, the quality of the recruits was something to which the Army was utterly unaccustomed. An analysis of 1,260 men of the CIV[30] found that they included nine barristers, sixteen solicitors, two bankers, a shipowner, two House of Commons Clerks, fourteen members of the Stock Exchange, four schoolmasters, three surgeons, a perfumery manager and a Queen's Messenger from the Foreign Office. By far the biggest contingent, almost 30 per cent of the total, were 367 clerks from banking, the civil service and elsewhere. Another twenty-five men were of independent means, these doubtless including the private to whom Mackinnon spoke on board the ship taking them to South Africa. Mackinnon recalled: "I asked a sentry what his profession was and he replied 'I have none sir but my amusement in life is archaeology and I was going this very week to Athens and the Levant.'"[31]

The City of London raised £70,000 for the CIV within ten days of Newton's meeting with Wolseley and by 12 January had passed the Lord Mayor's £100,000 target. The largest sum, £25,000, was donated by the Corporation of the City of London, with the Mercers', Grocers' and Goldsmiths' Companies giving £5,000 each. As ever with such projects, Wernher, Beit was involved, giving £5,000 to add to the money it donated to the Imperial Yeomanry. Wellcome & Co provided free medicines and shipping companies offered their vessels to take the new regiment to South Africa. With more money behind them than the Imperial Yeomanry had in its central fund for a much larger force, the staff at the Mansion House simply went out and bought the best of everything. Mackinnon told the Royal Commission: "There was no lack of money and no lack of the best business heads in London to do it for us and it was almost impossible that there should be much of a hitch."

Everything except rifles and ammunition was provided by the CIV from its own resources. The regiment even purchased its own artillery, four Vickers-Maxim 12½-pound quick-firing guns, and a supply of reserve ammunition for the entire campaign

27

because the Army had no guns of this type. With the battery came a team of workmen from the manufacturers who enlisted to help fire and repair the guns. They were the only CIV men from outside the Volunteer Force. As well as acquiring its own privatized artillery, the regiment went out into the market place for uniforms and equipment. The serge for its uniforms was of a better quality than that used by the Army and the boots, bought from a manufacturer in Nottingham, cost 15 shillings a pair, compared to 9 shillings for those worn by regular troops. The CIV's boots were so superior that when they got a new supply after six months in South Africa, the commanding officer of the neighbouring regular battalion begged Mackinnon to let him have the old ones for his men. However, not every aspect of the CIV's procurement proved so successful and the waterproof haversacks they bought quickly wore out. Getting waistbelts on the open market was also a problem, which was solved by borrowing more than 1,300 from the Queen's Westminster Volunteers.[32]

Vincent, Colonel of the Queen's Westminsters', praised the speed with which the CIV was raised but criticized the lack of help provided by the War Office and the frenetic atmosphere in which the regiment was recruited. He said: "What was done very rapidly, very hurriedly, extravagantly and, to some extent, badly, might have been done economically and leisurely." He thought that stripping the Queen's Westminsters of waist belts for the CIV "was an exceedingly defective way of equipping a regiment for the field".[33] Poor Vincent's sense of outrage was understandable. He had proposed a volunteer battalion similar to the CIV but recruited from the whole Volunteer Force two months before the war even began and had been rebuffed by the War Office. After all his lobbying on behalf of the auxiliary forces, he had been appointed to command the CIV's infantry battalion only to fail the medical because of a heart condition. He eventually got out to South Africa in an unofficial role, but there is more than a hint of bitterness in his attitude towards the raising of the CIV. His protestation to the Royal Commission that "I should not like it to be thought that I have any feeling whatever in the matter and

28

I tender these observations entirely as a matter of public duty" is not wholly convincing. However, despite the fact that recruiting and equipping the CIV was a triumph of imagination and enterprise, Vincent was right. This was no way to run a war.

The Volunteer Service Companies were the poor relations of the Imperial Yeomanry and the CIV, lacking their glamour and with far less patronage from either the business community or the landed gentry. This did not matter so much as it might have done because the companies were always firmly inside the official military system. They were the one surviving element of the scheme to use the auxiliary forces drawn up by the Army Board in December which was mostly overtaken by subsequent events.

The War Office decided that a "carefully selected" company of 116 all ranks could be raised from affiliated Volunteer Force battalions to serve alongside each regular battalion in or about to leave for South Africa. In fact many of the sixty-four companies which went to South Africa took more than the officially allocated number of men. The selection of the officers and the composition of the companies were controlled by Regimental District commanders in Britain and once out in South Africa the volunteers became an integral part of the regular battalions. The Irish regiments had no Volunteer Force units to call upon, but the 5th (Irish) Volunteer Battalion King's (Liverpool) Regiment provided a company for the Royal Irish Regiment and the 16th Middlesex (London Irish) one for the Royal Irish Rifles. In all about 9,000 men embarked with the companies in early 1900.[34] The War Office also decreed that "waiting companies" should be recruited to remain at home until they were required in South Africa but these proved unpopular, only 2,983 men enlisting, and some were never formed. More than 400 Royal Engineers Volunteers joined up and were attached to their Corps in South Africa and members of the Volunteer Medical Staff Corps and Bearer Companies were asked to enlist in the Royal Army Medical Corps for one year. Vincent estimated that about 6 per cent of the "really efficient" Volunteers in the country went to South Africa in 1900.[35] One unit formed from outside the

29

Volunteer Force was the Elswick artillery battery of quick-firing 12½-pounders, the men being recruited from the works of the guns' manufacturers at Elswick, Newcastle upon Tyne.

The qualifications for the Service Companies were similar to those for the CIV, the aim being to get the best men the Volunteer Force could offer, but equipping them was not an entirely free market enterprise like the one run from the Mansion House. The War Office provided a capitation grant of £12 per man to cover clothing and equipment and £12 per company was allowed to purchase camping material. However, many of the uniforms and much of the equipment appears to have come from Regimental Depots and the Volunteer Battalions. There were local appeals for extra funds to buy some of what was needed but these did not meet with the same success as those for the Imperial Yeomanry. In Cheshire £5,142 was raised for the two local Imperial Yeomanry companies, while just £459 was contributed for the Volunteer Service Company, £300 of which came from Chester City Council.[36] The Earl of Radnor gave £200 to the Wiltshire Regiment's company, and the Duke of Somerset and two local Volunteer colonels added £100 each. There were also some smaller donations, but the sums were only a fraction of the £7,000 raised for the county's Imperial Yeomanry. Despite this, partly because infantry were cheaper to kit out than mounted troops, the Volunteer Service Companies seem to have gone to war adequately equipped.

One of the problems with the War Office scheme was that it was extremely inflexible. In some urban areas with a large number of volunteer units, the Service Companies were hopelessly over-subscribed and on Merseyside seven battalions had to divide one company for the King's (Liverpool) Regiment between them. By early January sixteen officers and 650 men had volunteered and even the Liverpool Irish had almost twice as many men as they needed for their separate company. Godfrey Smith, who joined the Volunteer Service Company of the 2nd Scottish Rifles in Glasgow, later wrote that "every drill hall was inundated with names of willing aspirants for the Army". He added that "great trepidation was evinced by the would-be Tommies, those who passed being as much elated as the poor fellows who, being rejected on such trivial grounds as bad teeth etc were disappointed."[37] In Cheshire 167 men of the 2nd Volunteer Battalion, one of five battalions in the county, offered to go to the front, while in Buckinghamshire seventy-two stepped forward from a single detachment of the 1st Bucks Rifle Volunteers. By comparison a few companies, mostly from rural areas, went out under strength. During the the raising of the New Armies in the First World War similar differences in recruitment patterns were dealt with by transferring surplus men from some regiments to under-strength battalions in others.

Given the essentially parochial character of many volunteer battalions it was not surprising that local jealousies caused some difficulties. In counties where strong rivalries existed between different areas, men from one district resented serving under an officer from another. In one case feeling in a town which had presented a machine gun was inflamed by a plan to place it under the supervision of an officer from elsewhere in the county. The matter was raised in Parliament and a compromise reached.[38] There was also discontent among the volunteers that men who failed medicals for the Service Companies were subsequently accepted by the Imperial Yeomanry.

The social make-up of the companies which went to South Africa mainly reflected the dominance of the lower middle class and skilled working class in the Volunteer Force. Harold Bryant, who served with the Norfolk Regiment's Volunteer Service Company, said that his comrades "included most trades and professions," and added "there were artists, agricultural labourers, auctioneers, boiler-makers, bricklayers, bakers, bank clerks, chemists, carpenters, engineers, farmers, grocers, merchants, postmen, surveyors and many others."[39]

These citizen soldiers found themselves entering a strange new world very different from the easy familiarity of Volunteer Force camps. They worked hard with little time to themselves until late afternoon. Bryant remembered: "Reveille went at six o' clock and a few minutes later a cup of coffee was enjoyed. First parade was at seven o'clock during which various company drill was practised and some quarter of an hour's 'doubling' made breakfast at eight o'clock very welcome. This was followed by a parade at eleven o'clock for about two hours then dinner. In the afternoon, various parades for kit and off duty at four o'clock." It was a traditional Victorian soldier's training, strong on drill and an insistence on spotless equipment but with little direct relevance to the task which they faced in South Africa.

For the gentlemen rankers the difference between their old life and their new one was even more stark. Among them was Erskine Childers, a clerk at the House of Commons who had joined the CIV's artillery battery. Later he was to achieve fame as the author of the novel *The Riddle of the Sands* and immortality as an IRA hero executed by the Free State government during the Irish civil war. He recalled "the abrupt change one raw January morning from the ease and freedom of civilian life to the rigours and serfdom of a soldier's." The CIV gunners, drawn from the Honourable Artillery Company, underwent "a month of constant hard work, riding drill, gun drill, stable work and every sort of manual labour until the last details of the mobilization were complete".[40] Peel said that his first few weeks in the Imperial Yeomanry reminded him of his early days at Eton. "There was the same sudden plunge into utterly new surroundings, new companions, new discipline and a new mode of life."

The early parades of Paget's Horse at Chelsea Barracks were an extraordinary sight and the men tested to the limit the patience of their own officers and the Regular Army sergeants in whose charge they were placed. Outside the barracks there was a long line of hansom cabs which had brought the gentlemen troopers to be turned into soldiers, often with a complete disregard for the punctuality which the Army expected as a matter of course. Rose-Innes wrote: "I made my first appearance on parade three-quarters of an hour late and clad in a fur coat surmounted by a tall hat. I silently resented having to explain that a consultation at my chambers had detained me and thought it a piece of gross impertinence that the officer should meet my explanation with a curt 'Fall in, you must get your hair cut'." Their first attempts at drill were a complete shambles. According to Rose-Innes: "So simple a command as 'company – right turn' bred the most dreadful confusion. Some would right about, many would left turn and others perform such evolutions as the warning 'company' suggested as probable. In a few moments a well-ordered line became a disorganized mob."[41]

Regular Army officers commanding the new forces found that some of their non-commissioned officers struggled to shake off the more casual ways of the Volunteer Force. Mackinnon said that the volunteer sergeants in the CIV were "very deficient in the knowledge of how to instruct or even drill their men without instruction and some of the men are ignorant of the most elementary knowledge of drill." He added despairingly: "The conversational style in which some of them give commands to squads of men is not conducive to efficiency."[42]

Standards of marksmanship and, where necessary, horsemanship were laid down for all the units being recruited for the war. There were few problems with accuracy among the CIV and the Volunteer Service Companies, who were recruited from the best shots of the Volunteer Force, which had always had many of the characteristics of a civilian shooting club. But some had little idea of how to look after their weapons over a prolonged period and no concept of the Regular Army's traditional need for disciplined firepower directed at the enemy. Mackinnon wrote: "There is a lamentable ignorance of fire discipline and I am constantly finding crack Bisley shots who spoil their section's shooting and, what is more remarkable, these men seem to be the most nervous of all the rank and file. I don't mind these good shots having unmilitary positions, I don't object to their wearing glasses nor to their blacking their sights, but I cannot stand their ignorance of the use of the magazine or of the elementary rules for the management and handling of the rifle." His frustration was later eased by the ability of an unusually intelligent rank and file to learn quickly and by the fact that many of these highly strung, thoroughbred shots would prove useful in a war which was very different from those to which the Victorian Army was accustomed.

The shooting of much of the Imperial Yeomanry was very

poor. According to the Army Orders which laid down their conditions of enlistment and service they had to be "marksmen according to the yeomanry standard". This meant that they had to pass the ordinary yeomanry first class shooting test by scoring fifty points out of eighty-four, firing seven rounds standing and seven kneeling 200 yards from the target and seven lying down at 500 yards. To be able to shoot well was crucial to the effectiveness of the Imperial Yeomanry but the tests were inadequate, a blind eye was turned to many failures and the men given little opportunity to practice. Only fifty rounds per man was issued for use before they embarked. Peel was contemptuous. "Such a test, and even this was not rigidly enforced, hardly proves more than that the man can shoot in the required direction," he wrote. "Not more than five or six of my company had ever shot at anything else than a target or at uncertain ranges; most had never fired a rifle before in their lives. But for some reason or other we were given no practice at all and most of us never discharged the rifles we carried in the field until we fired them at the enemy." The situation was not improved by a shortage of suitable rifle ranges around the country and the 12th (South Nottinghamshire) Company had to embark without having finished its musketry course because the local range was flooded.

Not all the Imperial Yeomanry were such chronically bad marksmen. The Sharpshooters, as befitted their name, were recruited from men who passed a much tougher shooting test. They comprised the 18th Battalion Imperial Yeomanry, the 67th, 71st and 75th Companies being recruited in London and the 70th Company raised in Edinburgh. The corps was the brainchild of Henry Seton-Karr, Conservative MP for St Helens, and was raised by a committee led by the Earl of Dunraven. Unlike some of the other Special Corps, it was not a unit for gentlemen, many of its recruits coming from what a newspaper of the time called "the artisan class". All the men were expected to be excellent shots and those with overseas experience in the colonies or elsewhere were preferred. The recruits who came forward, more than 500 in the first few weeks, included prize shots from contests at Bisley and in Scotland, big game hunters, men who had fought in the

Matabele War in Rhodesia and former members of the Canadian police and colonial irregular units.[43]

The yeomen were better horsemen than they were marksmen but even so many of them struggled to master their mounts. Roy Rice had only been on a horse a few times before, but teamed up with Tom and Herbert Brown at the barracks in Trowbridge where the Wiltshire contingent was training. The Browns, Rice said, were "Wiltshire farmers, fine horsemen and good horse-masters" who "gave me all the tips and managed to get me a decent horse". It was the start of a partnership between the suburban teenager and the brothers from a village near War-minster which was to endure until Tom Brown's death in action. Not everybody was as lucky as Rice. Peel and his comrades in the Oxfordshire company had "a little, only a very little, training," and in some units the difficulty of obtaining horses meant that riding practice was almost non-existent. This was aggravated by appalling winter weather making open-air riding sessions difficult, a problem which one recruiting centre overcame by hiring a circus tent. The standard of horsemanship among the CIV's mounted infantrymen was dreadful and they mostly had to learn to ride while on active service because they were sent up-country soon after they arrived in Cape Town.[44]

In theory all such deficiencies in riding and shooting were supposed to be weeded out before the men were sent to South Africa. Lieutenant-General Sir Leslie Rundle, Deputy Adjutant-General at the War Office, wrote to all the officers commanding military districts in Britain issuing clear instructions for the vetting of the Imperial Yeomanry. "You will at once take steps to have each company thoroughly tested in musketry, riding and general efficiency," he wrote, adding that all the officers and men had to meet the qualifications laid down in Army Orders. "As soon as the inspection is completed you will be good enough to telegraph at once to this department whether you are satisfied that the company fulfils the qualifications laid down and whether in your opinion it is fit for service in South Africa."[45] The telegrams poured into the War Office, all assuring Rundle that the Imperial Yeomanry companies were ready to go to war.

It would have been a brave inspecting officer who would have offended local pride and the powerful men who financed and sometimes commanded the battalions and companies by rejecting them. The competition between counties to get their companies out to South Africa as quickly as possible was intense and was a source of both strength and weakness to the Imperial Yeomanry. The positive side was that they were raised and despatched quickly and the nation felt a sense of involvement in the war. At the same time their deficiencies were largely ignored and they went out inadequately trained to fight a resourceful enemy.

Most of the British public had no doubts that the volunteers were heroes fighting for a just cause. Before they left, the men were fêted at dinners and municipal ceremonies throughout the country and given gifts ranging from pipes, purses and compasses to commemorative cards and scrolls. The Earl of Harrington, Colonel of the Cheshire Yeomanry, donated a sovereign to be given to each man of the county's Imperial Yeomanry companies as pocket money. The Norfolk Volunteer Service Company was presented with khaki-covered bibles, while in Glasgow the local Imperial Yeomanry and the Service Companies bound for the Scottish Rifles and the Highland Light Infantry were given the freedom of the city. The men of the CIV were accorded the same honour by the City of London and each contingent of the regiment went to St Paul's Cathedral for a service before it embarked. They marched to the cathedral led by the pipers of the London Scottish and the drums and fifes of the Artists Rifles. The Church of England preached that it was a just war. The Bishop of London, the Right Reverend Mandell Creighton, told one contingent of the CIV: "A period of national trial is a test of national qualities. We thank God that in such an hour as this England is at one."[46] The men of the Green Howards Volunteer Service Company listened to an uncompromising sermon from the Venerable William Danks, Archdeacon of the North Yorkshire town of Richmond. "This is a righteous war," the Archdeacon thundered. "Do not doubt it, nor let any talk of what might, could, would or should have been, cloud your clear conscience. You are fighting for the equal rights of men in South Africa."[47]

First to leave was the CIV, the initial 500-strong contingent marching through London amid great popular enthusiasm on 13 January and embarking on the vessels *Briton* and *Garth Castle* at Southampton that afternoon. Another 800 men of the regiment left for the war a week later and the remainder of the infantry on 29 January. The CIV artillery battery missed out on such a rapturous farewell, leaving St John's Wood Barracks in north London at 2am on 3 February with three inches of snow on the ground. "In utter silence the long lines of horses and cloaked riders filed out through the dimly-lit gateway and into the empty streets," recalled Childers. "Hardships had begun in earnest, for we had thirteen miles to ride in the falling snow and our hands and feet were frozen." Only a handful of people were on the streets to cheer the gunners on their way and a solitary policeman rushed up and shook Childers' hand. Except for a draft sent out in July, 1900, the raising and despatch of what had been dubbed 'The Lord Mayor's Own' was complete.

The Volunteer Service Companies, even if they lacked the charisma of the CIV and the Imperial Yeomanry, were left in no doubt as to the public mood as they marched off to war. Bryant recalled the scene as the Norfolks left Norwich station on 11 February. "The station was crowded with relations and friends and many a good health was drunk and 'he's a jolly good fellow' sung. A whistle from the engine was a signal for the massed bands to strike up 'Rule Britannia' and amid great enthusiasm the Volunteer Company steamed out with 'Auld Lang Syne'." Smith had a similar experience as the Scottish Rifles marched through Hamilton, near Glasgow. "Our march to the station was a memorable one," he wrote. "Great cheering crowds lined the streets, breaking, after a few yards, the formation of the marching company, the more enthusiastic spirits insisting on carrying their friends shoulder high." The company going out to join the Green Howards marched to Richmond station in a torchlight parade accompanied by the corporation band. The *Green Howards Gazette* recorded that "there was a seething crowd on the platform through which the men had almost to fight their way and the train steamed away amid vociferous cheering".

The embarkation of the Imperial Yeomanry was conducted at quite remarkable speed but was never the smooth operation which some of its founders had planned. The workload at head-quarters was unrelenting and the overstretched staff found themselves dealing with myriad problems, including the demands of aristocratic officers used to having their every whim catered for. Lord Dudley was one of several officers who wanted to take his own charger out to South Africa and the committee had to waste precious time getting permission from the authorities to put the horse on board ship at Liverpool.[48]

By 15 January the committee knew that 3,000 men would be ready to sail within the week and another 5,000 by early February.[49] In theory the companies should have been assembled into battalions which would then sail for South Africa, but the reality was much less tidy. As companies became ready they were sent out as soon as a ship was available to take them, although the War Office gave preference to regular troops. Companies which had friends in high places ruthlessly used these contacts to get early embarkation while others with less influence kicked their heels in Britain. Some battalions were broken up as their constituent parts boarded different ships at different times. The first of the men, the 6th (Staffordshire) and 8th (Derbyshire) Companies, left Britain on 27 January, but the rest of the 4th Battalion did not follow until later. The 3rd Battalion, two companies from Yorkshire and two from Nottinghamshire, were next to go, departing as one unit on the 28th. But the 13th Battalion, the Duke of Cambridge's Own and three Irish companies, left in three ships spread over nearly a month. The last seven companies, four of them from the Rough Riders, another of the Special Corps, sailed on 14 April. The entire embarkation had taken seventy-seven days.

The scenes accompanying their departure were as enthusiastic as those experienced by the CIV and the Volunteer Service Companies and sometimes bordered on the hysterical. At Chester between 20,000 and 30,000 people packed into the railway station as the 21st and 22nd Companies left. The huge crowd had initially gathered outside but the pressure on the massive doors of the station was so great that it was feared that they might collapse. They were opened slightly to avoid such a disaster and the crowd poured through onto the platform and scenes of utter chaos followed. A number of people were injured in the crush and the soldiers had the greatest difficulty in forcing their way through to the train.

As the Duke of Cambridge's Own marched through the centre of London on 18 February a hint of spring sunshine was in the air. The news from South Africa matched the weather for a week previously Roberts had begun his march towards the Boer republics. Unknown to most of those watching the gentlemen make their way to Nine Elms station, the British artillery had begun pounding a trapped Boer army at Paardeberg the day before in a battle which was to produce a much-needed victory. A section of the Metropolitan Mounted Police Reserve and the band of the Grenadier Guards led the DCOs through the streets, the musicians playing 'The Absent Minded Beggar' as they entered the station. The journey to Southampton to see them board the *Dunvegan Castle* was a day out for the committee which had raised the company, the parents of the men and others from London society. The train which steamed into the port carried the Duke of Aberdeen, the Earl of Donoughmore, Lord Arthur Hill and the Duke of Cambridge himself. Severe weather earlier in the week had stopped the old Duke from inspecting the men and now he had come to say goodbye and to praise them for volunteering to risk their lives without pay. The company gave him three cheers before boarding their ship. By now the earlier sunshine had vanished and it was raining as the *Dunvegan Castle* sailed down Southampton Water taking the men to an uncertain future.[50]

Among all the volunteers setting out for the war the greatest fear was that it might be over before they got to South Africa. Percy Ross, who joined the 69th (Sussex) Company, said that the men of the Imperial Yeomanry were constantly greeted with remarks in the streets such as, "Ha, going out to South Africa, why it'll all be over before you get there" or "Well, it'll be a pleasant little trip there and back for I don't suppose they'll land you."[51] More than a year later as they grumbled about not being sent home, the volunteers looked back at such concerns with grim amusement.

CHAPTER THREE

HARSH REALITY

At Maitland Camp the Imperial Yeomanry breathed dust, ate dust and drank dust. The flies were everywhere. The force's base camp at McKenzie's Farm, Maitland, five miles from Cape Town, provided the yeomen with their first experience of life in South Africa. The base was set up on an undulating sandy expanse which was soon dotted with hundreds of bell tents as the companies disembarked from the ships which had brought them to South Africa. As with most of the Imperial Yeomanry's organization at this early stage of the war, it was completely separate from arrangements made for the rest of the British Army. The Imperial Yeomanry Committee's original plans for the base were ambitious. It was to be manned by fifteen officers and 608 other ranks, most of whom would be in the remount section, providing horses for the yeomen.[1] In reality the staff at Maitland never reached anything near this number and when it was at its busiest in April and May, 1900, totalled only 320.[2] This left the camp struggling to cope with the workload caused by most of the Imperial Yeomanry companies arriving within the space of a few weeks. At a parade at Maitland on 14 April, 5,000 men, almost half the total force, provided an imposing spectacle as they marched past the base commandant, Lieutenant-Colonel Henry Graham, formerly of the 16th Lancers.

Behind this outwardly impressive show of strength, the problems at Maitland were multiplying and produced an acrimonious exchange of letters and telegrams between the Imperial Yeomanry Committee and Graham, who had retired from the Regular Army two years previously. The latter, although he faced daunting problems, appears to have possessed few diplomatic skills and thoroughly irritated the committee both by complaining about virtually every aspect of camp life and by going to Roberts behind its back. Graham protested bitterly that he had too few officers and men to run Maitland, and, among other complaints, was unhappy about the shortage of native labour, the men's lack of shooting practice, poor saddlery sent out with some companies, and the force's waggons, which he said were "absolute rubbish". He received a series of increasingly weary replies from Lucas on behalf of the committee, which in any case was in the final weeks of its existence. It was dissolved on 25 May because the War Office considered its work to be over, and thereafter only a small office remained in London to deal with residual matters.

The War Office was becoming increasingly assertive in its dealings with the Imperial Yeomanry and refused to sanction the original establishment of officers and men planned for Maitland. Lucas told Graham that efforts were being made to get the War Office to change its mind and that he had already been sent sixteen officers for the base "which is in excess of your requirements". Shortly after the committee was abolished, Lucas, who remained as Deputy Adjutant General of the Imperial Yeomanry, finally lost patience. He wrote to Graham: "You state that you have positive knowledge that no regard whatever was paid by the Imperial Yeomanry Committee to your requests or suggestions in regard to the personnel required and that, as far as you are aware, it had no official rank under which it was entitled to address you. This view, I beg to observe, is not in accord with that taken by the Secretary of State for War."[2]

While this feud went on, conditions at Maitland were getting worse. The weather was extremely hot, the water supply became difficult to manage and reports of insanitary conditions were received by the committee.[2] The number of cases of sickness rose, the officers seeming to be particularly vulnerable, and many of these were treated at the nearby hospital set up by the Imperial Yeomanry Hospital Committee. Some of the yeomen began to grumble. Lieutenant Charles Awdry of the 1st (Wiltshire)

Company wrote to his mother from hospital: "You know sitting idle here makes one think that it was a great pity to have come out at all simply to do nothing." He complained that even before he went to hospital he had grown tired of seemingly pointless routines such as parading for an hour to do only fifteen minutes drill.[3] The yeomen were starting to learn the harsh realities of life in the Army, which had always had a fondness for meaningless tasks. When Peel and his comrades in the Oxfordshire company later reached Kimberley they were ordered by their sergeant-major to repitch tents they had set up two feet out of line. Peel recalled: "I remarked to him as he passed my tent, 'Sergeant Major, don't you know that this kind of thing is the ruin of the Army.' With a sudden burst of angry candour he replied, 'Do you think I have been in the Army all my life without finding that out? But you must do it all the same'."[4]

Some Imperial Yeomanry companies kicked their heels at Maitland for weeks amid these dusty and insanitary conditions. This was partly because the railway line from Cape Town to the north-east was struggling to move the men, horses and supplies needed by Roberts for his march into the Boer republics. Frustrated by this bottleneck, Brabazon, just appointed as commander of the Imperial Yeomanry, fired off an angry telegram to Roberts complaining that his battalions were not being sent up-country. "Have applied frequently for units but have always been refused on the score of other troops having precedence over Imperial Yeomanry and the insufficiency of rolling stock," he wrote.[5] But the Commander-in-Chief had more pressing matters on his mind. In any case he was unlikely to take much notice of Brabazon, who he had recently sacked as commander of the 2nd Cavalry Brigade because he was too old and too fond of comfort. The appointment of someone so out of favour to lead the Imperial Yeomanry and the fact that the force was so often at the back of the queue for trains speaks volumes about the Regular Army's doubts about its new recruits. Brabazon was soon to find that his post as commander was a sham.

Another reason that so many of the Imperial Yeomanry remained at Maitland was that the war had temporarily moved into a quieter phase. After the surrender of Cronje and his Boer army at Paardeberg in February, the pressure for urgent reinforcements was off and the sense of crisis which pervaded Britain after Black Week had eased. This proved to be a blessing in disguise for the yeomen who, despite the unpleasantness of Maitland, were given badly needed time for training and acclimatization before having to face the Boers. In particular the horses which they had brought from Britain were given a chance to get used to their new surroundings. Chesham was convinced that this period was crucial to the yeomen. "They had a certain amount of time to get together," he told the Royal Commission. "It was just after Paardeberg when the Boer forces were more or less scattered and had not got together again."[6]

A handful of the volunteers who had arrived from Britain were present at Paardeberg. The CIV's two companies of mounted infantry arrived in Cape Town at the beginning of February and were sent north after only ten days. Their lack of riding experience was painfully obvious as they mounted the Basuto ponies which the Mansion House organization had bought in South Africa. Lieutenant Edward Manisty of the CIV MI wrote to his mother: "Some of the men appear never to have seen a horse before but they are shaking down and I think will prove a good lot."[7]

The mounted infantry was involved in its first action on 15 February at Jacobsdaal, south-east of Kimberley, the day that the latter was relieved after a siege lasting 124 days. Jacobsdaal was on the British line of communications and had been reported clear of Boers the previous day. But by the 15th 200 Boers under Commandant Martins had occupied it, much to the surprise of the CIV's mounted men. As both sides opened fire, the CIV MI was ordered to advance by its commanding officer, Lieutenant-Colonel Hugh Cholmondeley. He trotted forward with his men and told them to dismount as bullets came past from both friend and foe. Manisty was baffled by the order but later discovered that Cholmondeley had been told to draw the enemy's fire, so revealing their position. He told his mother that when Cholmondeley then ordered them to retire, "I ran to my horse but it would not stand, so I dodged behind a dead horse and lay down. I then found the horse I was behind was a dark one so wriggled back on my stomach about ten yards away from it and lay still."[7] Luckily most of the men did not hear the order to pull back as two of Manisty's section who did mount their horses were immediately hit. The young lieutenant later admitted that he was "in a blue funk" during his first taste of action. As the British infantry advanced to clear the village, the CIV MI joined them and the Boers mounted their horses and retreated. Three of the CIV were wounded in this minor action, but Britain's volunteers had been blooded and the Lord Mayor of London sent Cholmondeley a congratulatory telegram.

Roberts' advance into the Orange Free State, which had begun on 11 February, was grinding remorselessly forwards. Not only had Kimberley been relieved but by the 17th General Piet Cronje and 4,000 Boers had been surrounded at Paardeberg to the east. After a British infantry assault had been bloodily repulsed, the Boers were pounded by artillery and Roberts ordered all available guns to be brought up. The CIV MI was told to escort the guns of the Naval Brigade to Paardeberg, arriving on the 20th, and was then split up for various tasks and singled out for special favour by Roberts, who paid regular visits to its horse lines. Whatever his doubts about the volunteers in general, Roberts had great affection for the CIV and in March became the regiment's Honorary Colonel. The MI was not involved in fighting at Paardeberg but six men became gallopers for generals and one was sent into Cronje's camp with a message. After the Boer surrender on the 27th, when Roberts and Cronje met in one of the most memorable scenes of the war, it was the CIV MI who escorted the defeated general, his wife, grandson and staff into captivity. "I suppose it is a bit of an honour," wrote Manisty, "but I am afraid we shall lose some fighting."[7]

The CIV infantry arrived in Cape Town in February and was put on sentry duty at Government House, where Milner complimented the men on their smartness. On 20 February they set off on a three-day train journey north to Orange River Station, near the border with the Orange Free State. When they arrived their marching was a shambles and they were unfit. "They had no idea of march discipline, they fell out of the ranks and fell in just whenever they liked," said Mackinnon. "I thought the regiment would fall to pieces."[8] Within days, two companies of the regiment and its cyclists were sent off to help suppress a Boer rebellion in the vast, empty region of the north-west Cape Colony. Three British forces marched into the area, the cyclists being attached to the column commanded by Brigadier General Henry Settle while the infantrymen were with Colonel John Adye. One company was with Adye when he clashed with nearly 400 Boers near Houwater, north of Britstown, on 6 March. The rebels forced Adye to fall back during an eight-hour fight and the CIV failed its first fitness test in the punishing conditions of South Africa. As well as seven wounded, six other CIV men were missing or taken prisoner after the Boers repeatedly outflanked the small force, whose speed of retreat was dictated by the exhausted infantry. Adye blamed the losses on "the difficult nature of the ground, the heat of the day and the want of condition of the City Imperial Volunteers".[9] It was hardly surprising that men who until recently had been civilians, mostly with sedentary jobs, should struggle to cope. The company returned to the regiment under no illusions about the tough task which lay ahead of it.

Two weeks after Bloemfontein fell to the British on 13 March Mackinnon went to the Orange Free State capital to see Roberts, who told him that the CIV infantry would soon join his army. "He evidently takes great interest in the CIV," wrote Mackinnon[10], and the Commander-in-Chief proved as good as his word. A month later the infantry arrived in Bloemfontein to join the 21st Brigade, part of a new force commanded by the dashing Lieutenant-General Ian Hamilton, Roberts's greatest favourite. The two months' training before they joined the army marching on Pretoria, capital of the Transvaal, had been vital. Roberts said later that he had deliberately "nursed" the CIV infantry[11] while Mackinnon described the men as "pretty hard and pretty fit" by the time they left Bloemfontein on 29 April.[12] They needed to be as Roberts's 43,000 strong army marched north-eastwards through fiercely hot days and tried to sleep through

46

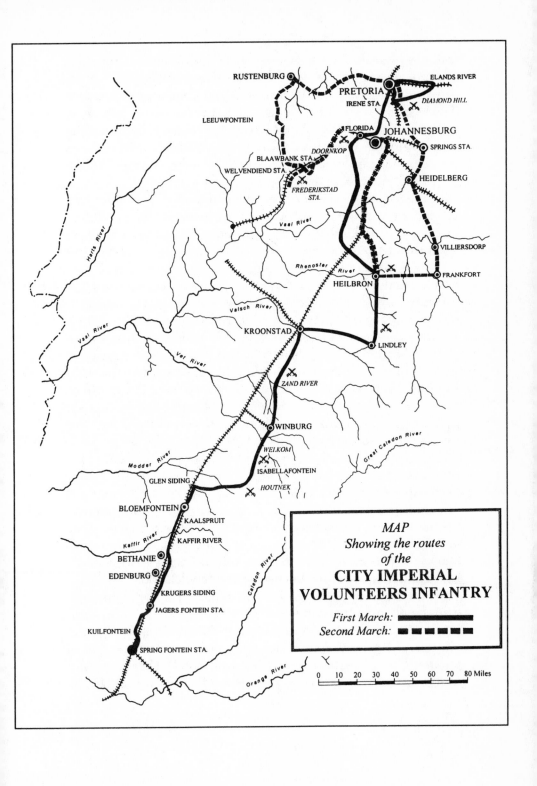

RUSTENBURG

ELANDS RIVER

PRETORIA
IRENE STA.   DIAMOND HILL.

LEEUWFONTEIN

FLORIDA   JOHANNESBURG

DOORNKOP   SPRINGS STA.
BLAAWBANK STA.
WELVENDIEND STA.   HEIDELBERG
                  FREDERIKSTAD
                        STA.

                                          VILLIERSDORP

          Vaal River

          Rhenoster   River   FRANKFORT
                             HEILBRON

          Valsch River

KROONSTAD   LINDLEY

                  ZAND RIVER

          Vet River

                  WINBURG

Modder River   WELKOM
                      ISABELLAFONTEIN
GLEN SIDING   HOUTNEK

BLOEMFONTEIN
          KAALSPRUIT
    Kaffir River   KAFFIR RIVER
BETHANIE
EDENBURG
          KRUGERS SIDING
          JAGERS FONTEIN STA.
KUILFONTEIN
          SPRING FONTEIN STA.

Harts River

Vaal River

Great Caledon River

Caledon River

Orange River

MAP
Showing the routes
of the
CITY IMPERIAL
VOLUNTEERS INFANTRY

First March: ━━━━━
Second March: ▬ ▬ ▬ ▬ ▬

0   10   20   30   40   50   60   70   80 Miles

freezing nights. The columns stretched for mile after mile, crawling at oxen pace, the wagons creaking, whips cracking, the drivers shouting and the infantry plodding along mostly in silence. The Boers hardly needed scouts, the dust clouds could be seen for miles. Roberts's main column stayed within reach of the railway line while Ian Hamilton's force, consisting of two infantry brigades, one cavalry brigade and some mounted infantry, was ten to twenty miles to the east.

On 1 May the CIV infantry came under fire at Kaalfontein, advancing without casualties, and by now were even fitter, marching 18 miles that day. The Boers retreated time and time again throughout Roberts's advance. At Welkom on 4 May the CIV was ordered to clear a hill, advancing as naval guns bombarded it. John Barclay Lloyd, who served with the battalion's cyclists, recalled: "when the enemy saw us coming up one side, they went down the other and we captured that kopje without a single shot being fired on either side with the exception of a scattered volley directed at our little stack of bicycles".[13] The column swept on through Winburg and caught the Boers by surprise at Zand River, where the CIV waded waist-deep through the water under artillery fire, and the enemy fled from their positions on the north bank when the British charged with the bayonet.

They marched through Kroonstad, Lindley and Heilbron, even those who had once thought of the war as an Imperial crusade thinking less and less about such grand concepts and more and more about their stomachs. The rations were down to seven hard biscuits for two days, one lump of raw meat daily, which they had to cook themselves, and a quarter of a pot of jam once a week. Despite cooking a lump of dough "with infinitely nasty results", Lloyd said that even this concoction seemed delicious. He wrote: "It is the small things that seem to us now of more importance than the big ones through which we have passed. The provisions for the day, the fowl we caught at Isabellafontein and stewed in our tins, the packet of cornflour we bought at a farm and tin of sardines that came, as it were, from heaven." They were not supposed to buy chickens and certainly not to steal them, because the CIV was told to be , as Lloyd termed it, "more regular than the regulars" when it came to obeying Army regulations. They watched in hungry frustration as other British units blatantly ignored the rules and the colonial irregulars looted their way across the Orange Free State with aplomb. But exhaustion, hunger and boredom was mixed with a sense of pride and the CIV was starting to feel like part of the Army. After two skirmishes and more than 100 miles marching, Lloyd wrote: "I think that we are amateurs no longer."[13]

On 26 May the CIV crossed into the Transvaal and three days later arrived at Doornkop, south-west of Johannesburg. Doornkop was an emotive place for the British, not regarded with quite the same burning sense of humiliation as Majuba, but still somewhere where a score should be settled. It was on this rocky ridge that Dr Jameson's raid had finally been crushed by the Boers in 1895. It was also only a few miles from the gold mines of the Rand that had played such a key role in the slide into war in South Africa. It was a fitting place for the CIV to face its greatest test. A full account of the battle will be found in Chapter Five, but the volunteers proved not only that they were no longer complete amateurs but that they could teach some professionals a thing or two. They stormed the hill, advancing in rushes, using cover intelligently and suffering only light casualties. Two days later Johannesburg fell and on 5 June Roberts marched into Pretoria.

The capture of Pretoria was supposed to be the defining moment of the war, the crushing psychological blow that would force the Boers to their knees. On the morning of the 5th when the CIV climbed a hill outside the capital Mackinnon recalled that "the city burst upon our view and I must say it was an impressive moment".[10] They marched into Pretoria having come 523 miles in fifty-one days, forty of which were spent on the march, a daily average of 13 miles. That afternoon the CIV took part in the victory parade into the city and Roberts acknowledged the regiment with what seemed to be a fatherly smile. "I do not believe that any man who took part in that triumphal ceremony can ever or will ever recall a moment of greater elation," wrote Lloyd.[13]

The emotions felt by Lloyd were shared by Sergeant Charles

Mackenzie of the Green Howards who by chance became the first British volunteer to march into Kruger's capital that day. Mackenzie, from Redcar, just outside Middlesborough, had landed in Cape Town almost three months previously. The Green Howards were not the first of the sixty-four Volunteer Service Companies to disembark, that honour being shared by the Royal Warwickshires, Norfolks, Suffolks, Royal Welch Fusiliers, East Lancashires and Hampshires, who all landed on 5 March. But while some of the companies languished near Cape Town or joined their regiments on quiet fronts, the Green Howards were soon on their way to join Roberts's advance from Bloemfontein. The volunteers marched across the endless veldt of the southern Orange Free State, covering 25 miles on one day that Mackenzie said "none of us will ever forget". Unused to the sun, footsore and agonizingly thirsty, they trudged on. Mackenzie wrote in his diary: "I am beginning to think the cause of almost all the suffering in this country is the want of water."[14] An old soldier in a detachment of regulars with the newcomers told him: "Fighting the enemy is not nearly so bad as marching to meet him."

The Green Howards were in the 11th Division, commanded by Major-General Reggie Pole-Carew, which was part of Roberts's central column. They quickly found themselves in action during the advance from Bloemfontein to Pretoria and Mackenzie claimed that lying prone for two and a half hours under shellfire was not as terrifying as he had thought it might be. He recorded: "Contrary to my expectations, I had no feeling of fear exactly, a quickened beating of the heart, some excitement, wondering where the next shell would fall and what people at home at that particular moment were doing." Unlike the CIV, the Green Howards saw no fighting outside Johannesburg but had a memorable march into the city. A well-dressed lady stood among the cheering crowds and as the Green Howards passed cried: "Three cheers for Tommy Atkins. God bless you, every one of you." Mackenzie felt a lump in his throat.

The Boers made a brief stand outside Pretoria at Six Mile Spruit on 4 June and Mackenzie's section alone fired nearly 1,000 rounds at a kopje 1,500 yards away. "We found we occupied a position absolutely in the open without any cover," he wrote. "Bullets began to bang past pretty lively." Apparently imbued with the often fatal *sang froid* favoured by some regular officers of the time, he strolled up and down his section before lying down. He admitted: "It was very uncomfortable for a few minutes, for the same man kept taking pot shots at me, disappointed, I suppose at not managing it the first time."

The volunteers serving with the 2nd Battalion Norfolk Regiment came under fire for the first time at Six Mile Spruit and Bryant found that the reality of battle bore no relation to the illustrations in the British press which "showed the regiment dashing up with flashing bayonets led by their officers with drawn swords". But the officers no longer carried swords and the company "just climbed up" the kopje they were ordered to take after a furious exchange of fire. There was no dashing.[15]

The next day Pretoria surrendered and the Green Howards volunteers from Redcar, convinced that the war was over, sang the hymn 'At the end of our journey, we shall wear a crown'. The Guards led the parade into the capital and behind them were the Green Howards with Mackenzie, the first of the Volunteer Service Company to pass Roberts. Their uniforms were in rags and their boots thin at the toes but it scarcely seemed to matter as the crowds waved handkerchiefs and cheered. The Transvaal flag came down and the silk Union Flag, specially woven by Lady Roberts for such triumphal occasions, fluttered over the city.

For most of the volunteers there were no such moments to savour. The company sent out to join the 2nd Battalion Hampshire Regiment was among the first to land but did not link up with the regulars for more than three and a half months. They were given the monotonous job of guarding a railway line about 70 miles from Cape Town and even when they moved further up-country found themselves doing chores on the lines of communication. On the Natal front, where Buller was still trying to push through the Boer defences into the south-east flank of the two republics, Smith and his fellow volunteers with the 2nd Scottish Rifles were also having a dull time of it. The nights were so cold that when they woke their blankets were covered with frost and their water bottles frozen and there was little action to take their minds off the fact that they were perpetually hungry.[16]

As Mackenzie's decision to stroll up and down in full view of the Boers at Six Mile Spruit had shown, the volunteers did not lack courage and on the Natal front two men of the Dorset Regiment Volunteer Service Company won the Distinguished Conduct Medal. Colour Sergeant B.S. Verdon and Private A.E. Williams won their medals for gallantry under fire at Alleman's Nek on 11 June, a battle which outflanked the Boers at Laing's Nek and finally cleared Natal of its invaders. Despite heavy fire from the front and both flanks, the 2nd Dorsets took a kopje at the mouth of Alleman's Nek and then seized the heights to the north of the pass at bayonet point. The action cost the battalion ten killed and fifty-four wounded.

The volunteers were much more intelligent than Regular Army recruits and Winston Churchill, then a war correspondent, described five companies which arrived in Natal as "fine-looking fellows with bright, intelligent eyes which they turned inquiringly on every object in turn".[17] The York and Lancaster Regiment found its volunteers useful for tasks needing intelligence and initiative and the commanding officer ordered the company to watch the crucial passes at Majuba and Laing's Nek.[18] But their NCOs remained a weakness. Sergeant Gavin of the London Scottish, which sent men to serve with the Gordon Highlanders, recalled an orderly sergeant who, when told by some of his men that they were too tired to go on picquet duty, would meekly go and ask somone else.[19] Regular soldiers, although mostly friendly towards the volunteers, watched such incidents with astonishment.

After taking Pretoria Roberts marched east to confront 6,000 Transvaalers under Botha in one of the last major set-piece battles of the war at Diamond Hill. The Boers were scattered for thirty miles along a range of hills, making it difficult for Roberts to employ his usual outflanking tactics. The CIV infantry was on the British right as the attack began on 11 June and the men, un-usually, found themselves fighting near the regiment's MI, who were being used as scouts. The infantry advanced across a river and up the slopes beyond under artillery and rifle fire, seven men being wounded. They carried the ridge from which the firing had come but as usual the Boers had gone by the time they got to the top and there was another ridge beyond. Leaving enough men to hold the crest, the CIV returned to the river to sleep.

On the 12th they pushed forward again, twenty men of 'A' Company advancing on to Diamond Hill itself "watched", as Mackinnon put it, "with breathless interest by the whole division".[10] They took it without opposition, but as the CIV advanced again it came under heavy fire from a kopje 1,500 yards to the north. The men lay down as they found themselves in the middle of an artillery duel. Lloyd remembered the shells coming "closer and closer until we felt that the next series would be clean among us".[13] The Boer rifle fire grew fiercer and each man found a rock to huddle behind, while some of the regiment stayed in the gully through which they had ascended the hill. Casualties began to mount and Lieutenant Brian Alt, whose father commanded the 22nd Middlesex Volunteers, was shot through the head. Alt, who had been wounded in the arm earlier in the day, was the only CIV officer to be killed in action in the war. The stretcher bearers were busy as the fire continued for much of the afternoon, killing one man and wounding seventeen others, two of whom later died. Then, after a final fusillade, the firing on both sides stopped and the CIV moved back to bivouac at a farm. The next morning when the British edged forward they found the Boers had abandoned their positions completely. The indecisive battle had cost the CIV its heaviest casualties of the war. Both sides claimed victory and Roberts had secured his eastern front for a total loss of twenty-eight killed and 145 wounded. But the battle had given the Boers renewed hope and confidence, qualities which were to sustain them in the guerrilla war to come.

Gradually the Imperial Yeomanry had begun to make the long journey north from Maitland Camp to the war zone. As with their departure from Britain, the influence of their officers played a key part in deciding which units got priority on trains. Two of the first companies to leave were the 21st (Cheshire), commanded by Lord Arthur Grosvenor, and the Oxfordshire Company, which included the Duke of Marlborough, who within weeks found himself a comfortable berth at Roberts's headquarters. Aristocratic string-pulling also proved effective further up the line. When the 69th (Sussex) Company left the rest of the 14th Battalion behind in Bloemfontein and temporarily joined Roberts's bodyguard, Ross was certain that it was "thanks to the fact of his Grace the Duke of Norfolk being attached to our squadron".[20]

The yeomen were hopelessly over-equipped as they left Maitland. Rose-Innes and his comrades in Paget's Horse must have presented an extraordinary sight. "Nothing could have been more supremely ridiculous than our marching order in those days," he recalled. "Imagine a heavy saddle with high, arched pommels and cantle. In front two huge holster bags stuffed to bursting and over these strapped a rolled cavalry cloak. Behind a rear pack, that is a tight roll about three feet long and containing blankets, an assortment of clothes and waterproof sheet. Already one might suppose the horse sufficiently burdened but we must not forget the trooper with belt, bayonet, bandolier, water bottle, field glasses, revolver and haversack and carrying his rifle supported in a 'bucket' attached to the saddle. Huge balls of hay in nets strung over the horse's withers complete the picture of a light horseman destined to pursue the flying Boer over the trackless veldt. After a few months experience we carried most of the impedimenta in waggons."[21]

In theory the distribution of the Imperial Yeomanry was perfectly simple. Four battalions, the 3rd, 5th, 10th and 15th, commanded by Chesham, were ordered to join Lord Methuen at Kimberley. In March he was told to clear the Boshof area, cross the River Vaal and push towards Mafeking, which was still besieged. Another six battalions, the 1st, 4th, 6th, 9th, 11th, and 13th, led by Brabazon, were to join Lieutenant-General Sir Leslie Rundle's 8th Division in the Orange Free State. Rundle's task was to advance behind Roberts's columns on the right flank between Thaba 'Nchu and the Basutoland border sweeping up any opposition and preventing any Boer breakthrough southwards. Lord Erroll was put in command of four battalions, the 7th, 12th, 14th and 19th, in the Orange Free State, while the 2nd

Battalion was sent to join Sir Charles Warren in Griqualand, who was still engaged in crushing the Boer rebellion in the north-west Cape. The 8th, 16th and 20th Battalions were to remain on the lines of communication in Cape Colony, while the 17th and 18th sailed to Beira in Portuguese East Africa to join Lieutenant-General Sir Frederick Carrington's Rhodesian Field Force.[22] The latter was to complete the British ring around the Boer republics by travelling across Rhodesia and invading the northern Transvaal.

In reality such arrangements soon began to fall apart because of the desperate need for mounted troops and the increasingly fluid character of the war. Some battalions never came together as units at all and many of the rest were gradually split up and used wherever they were needed. The Royal Commission into the war summed up: "The whole force was used as a mass of mounted troops, of a plastic character, who might be distributed by squadrons in any way that appeared to be convenient." When the commission asked Brabazon in what sense he had commanded the Imperial Yeomanry, he replied: "Absolutely in no sense, except as being gazetted to command them. I was to have had six regiments of yeomanry, which were never given to me, which I never saw, because in the exigencies of the service they were wanted here and there and every plan that was made was upset the day after." Instead he found himself attached to Roberts's staff as an Imperial Yeomanry representative. He admitted with considerable honesty and some bitterness: "I was never consulted and on the one or two occasions on which I did give a very force-able opinion was put on one side and overruled." One of Brabazon's protests was over officers going home on leave for personal or political reasons before the war was over, but Roberts was never going to back someone he regarded as a has-been against anyone with influence. "I refused them leave," recalled Brabazon, "but then they went to Lord Roberts and if they had any family interest they got their leave." In December, 1900 Brabazon left what had become a completely meaningless command and returned to Britain.

The fragmentation of the Imperial Yeomanry happened so

quickly that soon there was hardly a column or a garrison in South Africa without its quota of the new force. But its early fighting was principally in three areas, all on the fringes of the conflict away from the main theatre of operations, which was indicative of Roberts's doubts about the usefulness of the Imperial Yeomanry. It was first in action with Methuen, who by the time of Roberts's arrival at Bloemfontein, was reconstructing the 1st Division at Kimberley. Methuen had two main tasks, the first to protect Roberts's far left flank during the general advance and the second to divert the Boers' attention from the plan to relieve Mafeking. It had been originally intended that Methuen should carry out the relief, which had become a political imperative, but, because of the shortage of mounted troops in Kimberley, the task was given to a flying column commanded by Colonel Bryan Mahon. In early March Methuen occupied Boshof, north-east of Kimberley, aiming to put pressure on both the Boers guarding the River Vaal at Fourteen Streams and those in the Kroonstad area. On 5 April the Imperial Yeomanry was in action for the first time near Boshof, surrounding and capturing a Boer force mostly consisting of foreign volunteers commanded by the Frenchman Count de Villebois-Mareuil, who was killed (a detailed account of this action is in Chapter Five). It was a successful start for the Imperial Yeomanry, providing its champions with evidence to use against the force's critics. But it was not typical of the fighting which the Imperial Yeomanry was to experience, because the foreign volunteers allowed themselves to be surrounded, whereas a Boer commando would have slipped away as the British drew close.

Methuen pushed ten miles forward to Zwartkopjefontein but Roberts ordered him to retreat to Boshof because Boer reinforcements had left him exposed. During the retirement, Methuen's column was harassed by General Andries Cronje, giving the Imperial Yeomanry a much more realistic taste of what lay ahead. The 3rd Battalion under Lord Scarborough covered the right flank and rear as nearly 2,000 Boers swirled around the slow-moving wagons. A determined rush by the enemy to try to destroy the rear of the convoy was driven off and it reached safety after five hours. Most of the yeomanry casualties were suffered by the 9th (Yorkshire Hussars) Company from Doncaster which lost two killed, four wounded and eleven men taken prisoner. The 12th (South Nottinghamshire Hussars) Company had one man wounded and three missing. Methuen told Roberts that the yeomanry casualties were higher than they might have been because their English horses sometimes panicked under fire. But he added: "The steadiness and good conduct of the troops left nothing to be desired."[23]

As Mahon set off on his successful mission to get to Mafeking in early May, Methuen and Major-General Sir Archibald Hunter, whose 10th Division had been ordered over to Roberts's left flank, began to move north-eastwards. Methuen had lent Hunter three companies of Imperial Yeomanry, the 11th (Yorkshire Dragoons) and the 14th and 15th , both from Northumberland, which helped drive the Boers from their position at Rooidam, eleven miles south-west of Warrenton. The Boers were occupying a series of kopjes and low connecting ridges extending for about four miles, a position which the Imperial Yeomanry reconnoitred on 4 May. The following day the yeomanry and some artillery were sent to turn the enemy's right flank and the Northumberland men swept round and pushed back the Boer outposts. As the artillery opened fire, the Yorkshire Dragoons under Major Lewis Starkey galloped forward and seized a kraal and from there advanced to a farmhouse enfilading the main Boer position. As the British infantry attacked in the centre, the Boers retreated, pursued for three miles by the Imperial Yeomanry. British casualties were light and the Northumberland Yeomanry lost one killed and three wounded and the Yorkshire Dragoons three men taken prisoner during the action and the reconnaissance the previous day. The fight at Rooidam not only forced the Boers back but also cleared the way for Mahon, who was able to hurry on unopposed for some time. Mafeking was relieved on 17 May, leading to scenes of hysterical celebration in Britain, and that day Methuen, advancing north-eastwards, occupied Hoopstad. From there, the yeomanry he had lent to Hunter having returned to him, he marched to Bothaville, accepting the surrender of many Boers on the way. Roberts then ordered his division to Kroonstad to guard the rear of the central columns and protect the main railway.

The Boer rebellion in the north-west Cape, which the CIV had been involved in attempting to suppress in March, was still not wholly under control. After Adye's reverse near Houwater, General Lord Kitchener, Roberts's Chief of Staff, had taken personal charge. The British reorganized and marched back into the area but the rebellion south of the Orange River collapsed within weeks without a fight. The Transvaal commandos who had incited it retreated homewards as Roberts's main advance continued and the local rebels laid down their arms. Kitchener left for more important duties but some of the Imperial Yeomanry he had brought with him stayed on. The 21st (Cheshire) Company trekked endlessly across the region. "It seems scarcely more than a picnic we are out on," wrote Lieutenant Robert Barbour. "Nobody shows any signs of fighting."[24] The Cheshire yeomen eventually garrisoned the dreary desert town of Upington, enduring dreadful sandstorms and longing for home.

But north of the Orange River the rebellion was still very much alive among the tough Boer farmers of the region and two British forces set out to deal with them. One, commanded by Adye, left Prieska on 22 May to clear the rebels from the far bank of the river north of the town. A week earlier a larger force, under Lieutenant-General Sir Charles Warren, marched out of Belmont, south of the Modder River. Warren's task, as the new governor of the region, was to capture Douglas, Campbell and Griquatown, pacify Griqualand West and then march north to Kuruman and Bechuanaland.

Adye's force, which had been joined by the 5th (Warwickshire) and 32nd (Lancashire) Companies Imperial Yeomanry, fought a fierce action to clear 400 Boers from the river at Kheis, between Prieska and Upington, on 28 May. The rebel laager was directly opposite the crossing point at Kheis and therefore Adye decided to leave part of his force there to keep the Boers busy while the rest went across another drift six miles up the river. The artillery, escorted by the Warwickshire Yeomanry, opened fire on the

Boers at Kheis while the Lancashire Yeomanry and the remainder of the force brushed aside light resistance at Tesebe and forced a passage. Adye then moved quickly down the right bank towards the laager, which the Boers had evacuated because of the shell-fire. They retreated into some low bushy hills to the north where they made a stand. The Lancashire Yeomanry under Captain L.H. Jones was sent to outflank them, Adye holding back the main attack until they were in position. The Boers resisted fiercely as they were attacked from two sides and Sergeant A.D. Ward, land-lord of the Waterloo Inn in Wigan, was hit by three bullets as the yeomanry went forward. Private F.J. Roberts, a glassworker from St Helens, dismounted and pulled Ward into the cover of a bush. He was attending to him when another bullet hit the sergeant in the back, passed out through his chest and struck Roberts just above the knee.[25] He later had to have his leg amputated and in all the Lancashires lost three killed, including Ward, and seven wounded, Captain Jones being among the latter. Finally the Boers broke and fled, but the yeomanry was prevented from cutting off their retreat by the British artillery which carried on firing for too long. The laager contained 100 Boer women and children, guns, 30,000 rounds of ammunition and a large number of cattle and other livestock.

Meanwhile the Warwickshire Yeomanry had been involved in an unnecessary mishap at the drift at Kheis. The officer in command there, seeing that Adye had captured the laager and was fighting the other side of it, asked Major James Orr-Ewing, commanding the yeomanry, to see if the drift could be crossed. Lieutenant J.S. Forbes and Corporal A. Baxter volunteered to try but came under fire from a small group of Boers hiding on a thickly wooded island in mid-stream. Their horses were killed and, as they struggled back, the corporal was mortally wounded. Orr-Ewing, the son of a baronet and a former regular cavalryman, and Private E.P. Ashley ran to help Baxter but the officer was killed and Ashley wounded. Further rescuers were also hit and the Warwickshires's final loss was three killed and six wounded at the hands of a well-concealed enemy. Six Boers later surrendered and several others escaped. The engagement at Kheis restored

Adye's reputation after his reverse at Houwater and pacified the Orange River area until early 1901. It also taught the Imperial Yeomanry how costly even a small action could be.[26]

To the east Warren occupied Douglas with little opposition and on 26 May reached a farm called Faber's Put, 12 miles north towards Campbell. He waited there to collect sufficient transport and supplies for his advance and pondered how best to attack the Cape rebels. They solved his problem by attacking first, believing that they would have an easy victory over his force of mainly inexperienced volunteers. Warren had with him half a battalion of South African infantry from the Duke of Edinburgh's Own Volunteer Rifles, four guns of the Royal Canadian Field Artillery, the 23rd (Lancashire) and 24th (Westmorland and Cumberland) Companies Imperial Yeomanry under Colonel Crawley, a few men of Paget's Horse and about thirty Warren's Scouts, raised from Boers fighting for the British. Warren's defensive measures left a lot to be desired. His camp was surrounded by thick scrub and bounded by low ridges to the east and south. The force was spread out along a shallow valley between the ridges, with Warren's headquarters in a farmhouse and the Imperial Yeomanry and Canadian artillery occupying some native kraals. The DEOVR had picquets to the north and east and the yeomanry a post on the hill to the south and a sentry in a garden near the kraals, but there were gaps between them and no connecting patrols.

It was not difficult for the attacking force of 600 Boers to creep through the scrub close to the camp. Their plan was to launch one assault from the hill to the east, then a second by picked marksmen through the garden, followed by a third from the southern ridge. But at 5.30am on 30 May, just before the attack was due to start, a yeomanry sentry saw figures looming towards him and fired a shot. All hell let loose immediately as the Boers attacked from all three directions. For the Imperial Yeomanry it was a sudden and brutal introduction to the realities of warfare. Rose-Innes was among the Paget's Horse contingent which had escorted a convoy in the night before. "For a moment all was excitement and confusion, the greater part were instantly awake and sought such cover as could be found," he recalled. " 'Keep down man,' shouted the sergeant to one of ours as a bullet whistled through the boy's helmet. Poor lad, for one instant he raised his head again and his skull was blown to atoms."[27] Warren's men, confused as to where their attackers were coming from, rolled out of their blankets and hastily organized themselves. The DEOVR drove back the assault from the eastern ridge. While Paget's Horse remained by the yeomanry's Colt Guns, giving supporting fire from the northern end of the garden, Crawley led the 23rd and 24th Companies against the southern ridge, where their picquet was still holding out. They suffered many casualties in the open ground as they came under fire from the hill and were enfiladed from the garden. A party under Lieutenant Arthur Huntington covered the flank by shooting point blank into the garden until the DEOVR drove the Boers out of it. When the rest of the yeomanry reached the top of the southern ridge with fixed bayonets, the Boers as usual headed for their horses and the action was over after an hour. The yeomen were unable to pursue the Boers because most of their horses had stampeded during the engagement. Although the Colonel commanding the DEOVR had been killed, most of the casualties came from the yeomanry. The 23rd and 24th each lost six killed and a total between them of eighteen wounded and Paget's Horse four killed and four wounded, of whom two later died. The Boers suffered thirty-eight killed and fifty wounded. The volunteers from Britain, Canada and South Africa had all fought well and Warren was very lucky that he had not suffered a major disaster. Instead the engagement so disheartened the Boers that the rebellion in the northern Cape collapsed totally.[28]

But Methuen's campaign and the revolt in the northern Cape were minor affairs compared to the trouble that was brewing for the British east of the railway line which bisected the Orange Free State. This was a region inhabited by some of the most redoubtable of the Boers. It had a barren, brooding quality but was in fact good farming land, the granary of South Africa. More crucially its hills, mountains and valleys provided unlimited opportunities for the Boers to attack and then escape and here a

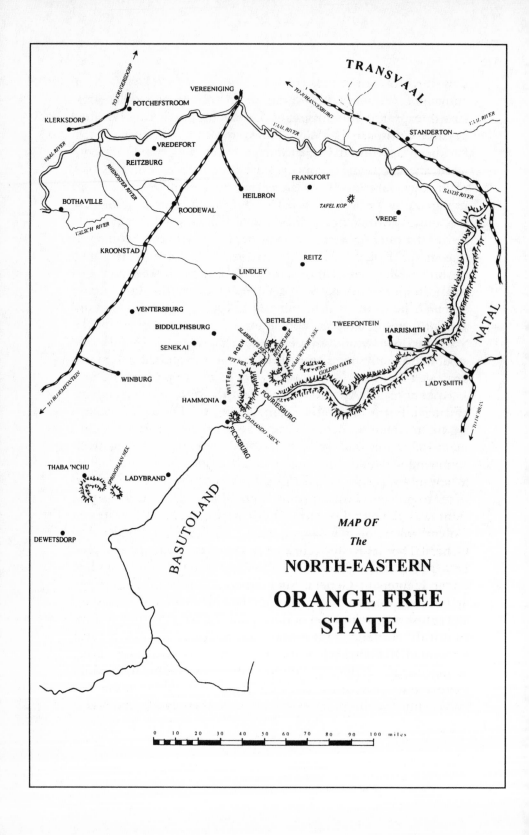

TRANSVAAL

TO KRUGERSDORP

TO JOHANNESBURG

VEREENIGING

KLERKSDORP

POTCHEFSTROOM

VAAL RIVER

STANDERTON

VAAL RIVER

VREDEFORT

VAAL RIVER

SANDS RIVER

REITZBURG

RHENOSTER RIVER

FRANKFORT

NATAL

BOTHAVILLE

HEILBRON

TAFEL KOP

VREDE

ROODEWAL

VALSCH RIVER

KROONSTAD

REITZ

LINDLEY

VENTERSBURG

BETHLEHEM

TWEEFONTEIN

HARRISMITH

BIDDULPHSBURG

SLABBERTS NEK

RETIEFS NEK

NAAUWPOORT NEK

SENEKAI

WITTEBERGEN

GOLDEN GATE

LADYSMITH

WINBURG

WIT NEK

TO BLOEMFONTEIN

HAMMONIA

FOURIESBURG

COMMANDO NEK

TLELA NEK

FICKSBURG

THABA 'NCHU

SPRINGHAAN NEK

LADYBRAND

DEWETSDORP

BASUTOLAND

MAP OF

The

NORTH-EASTERN

ORANGE FREE STATE

0   10   20   30   40   50   60   70   80   90   100 miles

new form of warfare developed. It was approved by a Boer council of war held at Kroonstad on 17 May, four days after the British captured Bloemfontein, and its architect was the formidable Christiaan De Wet. This tough and resourceful leader had been appointed Commandant-General of the Free State forces after his predecessor had been accidentally shot dead by one of his own sentries. De Wet realized the utter hopelessness of trying to stop Roberts's steamroller by conventional methods and was already formulating plans for a guerrilla war. He wanted the best of the Boer fighters to operate as raiding columns behind the line of the British advance, travelling light, hitting hard and vanishing before retaliation could be organized. Already there had been some successes using these methods and the Boer leaders accepted his plan in principle. Although the last of the conventional battles were still to come and even in the Orange Free State the Boers would still sometimes bar the passage of a British column by occupying a kopje, the war began to move into a new phase.

Roberts had always regarded his right flank as a potential source of danger. Firstly the north-eastern Orange Free State was the one region in which the writ of President Marthinus Steyn's government still ran in mid-1900. Secondly he was worried that Boer commandos would slip through and cause trouble to his rear as he advanced. Before he left Bloemfontein he organized his forces to try to prevent this happening. Behind Hamilton's force on his right was the 9th Division under Major-General Sir Henry Colvile; following that came Rundle's 8th Division, Lieutenant-General Thomas Kelly-Kenny's 6th Division, Major-General Sir Edward Brabant's Colonial Division and finally the 3rd Division under Lieutenant-General Sir Herbert Chermside. Altogether 40,000 men were to sweep through the eastern Orange Free State and at first the pacification of the region seemed to be progressing smoothly. Indeed by 17 May, as the Boer leaders met at Kroonstad, Roberts felt sufficiently confident to change these arrangements, sending Chermside from Dewetsdorp to Bloemfontein and some of Colvile's force to Ventersburg, nearer the railway line. Such optimism was about to be proved unfounded.

Substantial numbers of the Imperial Yeomanry were deployed with the various forces in the eastern Free State in keeping with Roberts's policy of using most of them on the fringes of his command. Even before the Boer council of war they had experienced a taste of what was to come when the 8th (Derbyshire) Company together with a company of the Scots Guards fought off an attack on a convoy they were escorting ten miles west of Thaba 'Nchu on 29 April. The Derbyshires performed well, perhaps helped by fighting alongside regular troops, but it was all too easy for the yeomanry to get itself into trouble against such a wily foe. At Senekal, a ramshackle Boer town consisting mostly of one-storey wooden buildings, a party of the 34th (Middlesex) Company was taught a sharp lesson on 25 May.

The 8th Division was marching through the area with little sign of opposition when Rundle sent about sixty of the Middlesex Yeomanry under Major Henry Dalbiac ahead of the column. Dalbiac was a famous athlete, a daring steeplechase rider and an experienced former regular solder who had served in the Afghan and Egyptian campaigns. But he was fatally impetuous and, while he cannot be faulted for courage, this was not matched by any great intelligence. Frustrated because the company had seen little action, he galloped his men nearly all the way to Senekal, failing to keep in touch with the main column. No Boer forces were in the town, so posts were placed on the outskirts and the rest of the yeomanry dispersed. Some went to find something to eat and drink in the town's hotel while others were ordered to confiscate arms from citizens who had decided to accept Roberts's surrender terms. At about 1pm shots were heard from a plateau east of the town where two of the posts had been placed. Dalbiac rushed out of the hotel, rounded up all the men he could find, numbering about thirty, and without a moment's thought galloped flat out towards the hill. They came under a withering crossfire from Boers to the north and south and Dalbiac was killed immediately, shot through the neck. Three of his party were also killed and four others wounded. Thirteen unwounded men surrendered, but the rest, led with great coolness by Sergeant-Major George Roller, managed to escape, Roller rescuing one of the wounded under fire. He was recommended for the Victoria Cross but awarded the Distinguished Conduct Medal and later commissioned as an officer. Dalbiac's charge had been a completely unnecessary piece of bravado as the yeomen who had remained in the town, including a party from other units which had arrived separately, held on until Rundle's artillery came up and drove off the encircling Boers. Senekal was then occupied by the column and the Boers vanished, having lost only one man, who was accidentally shot by his own side.[29]

Much worse was to follow within a few days. On 18 May the 13th Battalion Imperial Yeomanry was ordered by Roberts's headquarters to join Colvile's 9th Division at Ventersburg. The 13th was the most glittering and well bred of all the Imperial Yeomanry formations. One of its four companies was the 45th, the Dublin Hunt Company, whose young men rode to hounds with such style. Another was the 47th, the Duke of Cambridge's Own, the cream of London society who had all paid their own way to South Africa. Alongside them were the 46th and 54th Companies from Belfast, Ulster Unionists who added a powerful whiff of Irish politics to a unit which already fascinated the British public. The events which led to the capture of the entire battalion at Lindley in the Orange Free State on 31 May were the most controversial in the short history of the Imperial Yeomanry and created a huge furore in Britain. A full account of the Lindley episode will be found in Chapter Five. For the moment it is sufficient to say that the battalion found itself surrounded at Lindley and, rather than try to break out with his inexperienced troops, its commanding officer, Lieutenant-Colonel Basil Spragge, sent for help. None was forthcoming and after a siege lasting four days they surrendered after a corporal panicked and raised a white flag. The man's immediate commander foolishly felt bound to respect this flag and ordered his men to surrender, rendering the position untenable. For the Boers it was a major propaganda coup, for the British a sharp reminder that they had yet to master the art of warfare in this unforgiving land. The Imperial Yeomanry in particular was taught that enthusiasm and good breeding were no substitutes for experience.

The north-eastern Orange Free State became a running sore for Roberts, the commandos seeming able to attack at will. In early June the trouble reached the railway, the vital but vulnerable artery along which British supplies and reinforcements had to come. Little was safe, not even the baggage of the increasingly irrelevant Imperial Yeomanry headquarters. On 5 June this was being escorted north by three headquarters orderlies and thirty-two men of the Imperial Yeomanry Scouts, a South African unit recruited to be the eyes and ears of the yeomanry. This small column, led by Captain Wyndham Knight, the Imperial Yeomanry's Chief Staff Officer, was camped north of Kroonstad when it received an appeal for help from the commander of Roodewal station, who feared an attack. The men saddled up and reached the station next morning but the attack never materialized. They continued four miles north to the railway bridge over the Rhenoster River, where they were joined later in the day by the raw militia of the 4th Battalion Derbyshire Regiment. Knight and the Scouts occupied a range of kopjes a mile north of the bridge where they were attacked and almost surrounded by Boers under Froneman at 3 am on the 7th. They managed to get back to the camp near the bridge where all was chaos. Captain William Anderson of the Scouts later reported: "I descended to the camp and found the utmost disorder, men running in all directions for cover, some with guns and some without. No orders whatever were given. I took my men to a position where I thought they would be most useful."[30] The Boers brought up artillery and six hours after the first shots had been fired some of the militia began to hoist white flags. Their officers managed to prevent them for a time but by 10.30am they surrendered. The Imperial Yeomanry contingent was also captured, along with the luckless Brabazon's baggage. Froneman destroyed the bridge and swept on to join De Wet at Roodewal where they captured a huge quantity of supplies and clothing destined for Roberts's army in Pretoria.

The fight at Roodewal involved a group of British volunteers who had not expected to find themselves in the firing line. At the start of the war three officers and eighty-nine men of the 24th

Middlesex Volunteers, which was recruited from London post offices, had gone to South Africa to serve in the Army Post Office Corps. Strictly speaking they were reservists rather than volunteers because they had specially enlisted in the Army Reserve to make themselves available for foreign service. At Roodewal Lieutenant Preece and nineteen of his men put down the parcels they were sorting, picked up rifles and fought in the defence of the station. Two were killed and three wounded, all the survivors, including Preece, being taken prisoner.

By the middle of June Roberts decided that it was time to crush the commandos in the Orange Free State and the Imperial Yeomanry found itself more fragmented than ever. The core of Roberts's problem lay in the area east of four towns, Heilbron, Lindley, Senekal and Ficksburg. His plan was to garrison the main towns and the vulnerable points on the railway and to organize four flying columns which were to be constantly on the move through the eastern districts. Three of the four columns included units of Imperial Yeomanry, while the garrisons of Lindley, Frankfort and Senekal also had yeomanry in their ranks.

Roberts's decision marked the beginning of a seemingly endless existence of trekking for the volunteers who had come from Britain with so many romantic notions of warfare. They trudged or rode for day after day, either chasing an enemy who would only fight on his own terms or escorting convoys from one bored, depressed garrison to another. The 8th Division, far from the railway and short of supplies, became so gaunt from starvation that its men were nicknamed 'Rundle's Greyhounds'. "The daily trekking, often starting before daybreak and existing upon this half-cooked, ill nourishing diet and bad water had reduced many erstwhile robust soldiers to lean, half-starved individuals, fit candidates for sickness and disease," wrote Thomas Wetton, of the 1st Sussex Volunteer Infantry Brigade Bearer Company. The medical volunteers, like the yeomanry, found themselves scattered among the columns and garrisons. "Often we began the day's trek while the stars were still twinkling in the cold night air," Wetton recalled. "On the veldt the hours just preceding dawn are the coldest of the night and the fierce frost made the ground like iron. Bundled out of our warm blankets at unearthly hours with shivering frames and chattering teeth into the cold blackness of the night, the whole camp was soon in a state of commotion."[31] The flying columns scarcely flew and the convoys crawled along. Childers, escorting a convoy with the CIV artillery, found that "the standard of speed is the trek-ox, lurching pensively along under his yoke, very exacting about his mealtimes and with no high notions about supreme efforts when he has to get his wagon out of a bad drift."[32]

Even when there was the possibility of action, the new-style war in the Orange Free State could be a desperately frustrating business. On 23 June three companies of the 4th Battalion Imperial Yeomanry were sent to help a force of colonial troops engaging the Boers at Hibernia. After an appalling all-night march along bad roads and across treacherous river crossings they arrived just before daybreak to find the fight over and the Boers gone. But on the same day the 41st (Hampshire) Company at least had the satisfaction of driving off Boers who had crept to within 400 yards of a convoy which they were escorting near Senekal. They then pursued some of the enemy whom they captured in a farmhouse before burning down the building as the rest of the Boers watched from the heights nearby. Some of the yeomanry did not perform well in these trying conditions. On 26 June men of the 35th (Middlesex) Company disgraced themselves by fleeing from a Boer attack north of Senekal, in which they lost one man killed and one wounded, and not drawing rein until they reached Ventersburg. Eighteen of them were taken prisoner or were missing after this incident. For all the yeomen the conflict became, as Private Joseph Rogers of the 1st (Wiltshire) Company later told his family "a chasing about war".[33]

At the beginning of July the British began to march on Bethlehem, which was held by the Boers. One of the two columns was commanded by Major-General Arthur Paget and included the 53rd (East Kent), 57th (Buckinghamshire), 58th (Berkshire) and 62nd (Middlesex) Companies Imperial Yeomanry, as well as a company of Imperial Yeomanry Scouts.

Paget sent his 800 mounted men, consisting of the yeomanry and some Australian and South African troops, on a wide sweeping movement to his left as he advanced. The 38th Battery Royal Field Artillery and two guns of the CIV battery were attached to this force, which was commanded by an Imperial Yeomanry officer, Colonel Arthur Brookfield, who was the Conservative MP for Rye.

The action which followed at Bakenkop, near Bethlehem, on 3 July almost ended in disaster. The Boers barred Brookfield's progress with three guns on a ridge. Keeping most of the yeomanry to the rear, he posted his guns in three sections of two on a kopje with the CIV on the left. However, each pair was invisible to the others. Major Henry Oldfield, commanding the 38th Battery, ordered the Imperial Yeomanry escorting his guns to retreat behind him to the right. The officer commanding the party of yeomanry repeatedly told Oldfield that in his new position he could see neither the guns nor the enemy and therefore was useless as an escort. He was ignored and an artillery duel began.

After several hours Oldfield began to run short of ammunition and ceased fire, while the CIV gunners, who used different shells, continued to shoot intermittently. The Boers, believing that they had knocked out the battery, then crept forward and attacked the 38th's guns. Because they were unescorted three were captured, only one getting away to join the CIV, and Oldfield was mortally wounded. On the left the CIV gunners were in great difficulty, but, their guns now trail to trail, kept firing. The whole of Brookfield's force faced disaster, but the Boers delayed their advance while they took time to secure their prisoners and the captured guns. This gave one of the CIV's officers, Captain Charles Budworth, who had been with Oldfield when he was hit, time to gallop back. He asked the South Australian Bushmen, who were retreating amid the general confusion, to save the guns and the day. They turned and, led by Budworth, stormed the hill, recapturing the guns and driving off the Boers. Shortly afterwards some of the Imperial Yeomanry arrived on the ridge and opened fire at the retreating enemy. The 38th Battery had suffered heavy casualties and one of the rescued artillery pieces was served for the rest of the day by drivers from the CIV. Brookfield's force then continued on its way to rejoin Paget's column,[34] but had it not been for Budworth's quick thinking and bravery the British advance on Bethlehem, which was captured after a half-hearted Boer defence, would have been endangered.

As the British columns advanced across the eastern Orange Free State, almost 9,000 Boers withdrew into their last great redoubt in the Brandwater Basin. This was a fertile series of valleys inside a 75-mile-long horseshoe formed by the Wittebergen and the Roodebergen, the White and Red Mountains. These mighty peaks, viewed with awe by the tired British troops as they trudged towards them, were next to the Basutoland border, which formed the base of the horseshoe and which neither side were allowed to cross. The decision of the Boers to retreat into the basin was a strange one which showed that their transition to fighting a guerrilla war was not yet complete for it was as much a trap as it was a fortress.

The British forces gathered around them, the speed of their preparations hampered by shortages of supplies and adequate maps. Even as they assembled, De Wet and President Steyn with 2,600 men slipped through Slabbert's Nek, one of six wagon roads through the mountains, and escaped. It was a major setback for the British, but also sealed the fate of the remaining Boers who, deprived of their two most charismatic leaders, began to squabble among themselves. It was not until after De Wet had gone that Major-General Sir Archibald Hunter, commanding the encircling forces, finalized his plans. Most of the Imperial Yeomanry involved were along the western side. Rundle had four companies totalling twenty-six officers and 410 men, part of the 1st, 2nd and 11th Battalions, at Hammonia, near the southernmost entrance at Commando Nek. Another force of yeomanry was further north at Rooikranz and Bezuidenhout and 200 men from the Yorkshire and Wiltshire companies were at Witnek, the next main pass in the west. The 6th (Staffordshire) Company was with Major-General Ralph Clements's force which joined Paget to attack

Slabbert's Nek in the north of the horseshoe. Paget had with him 300 Imperial Yeomanry and two guns of the CIV battery. Nearly 200 men of Lovat's Scouts, who had done good work reconnoitring the mountains, were with Hunter himself outside Retief's Nek, the next northern pass.

On the 22nd Hunter ordered that simultaneous attacks should be made next day on Retief's Nek, Slabbert's Nek, Witnek and Commando Nek. At the first of these the Boers were well dug in in naturally strong defences and Hunter sent off Lovat's Scouts, Rimington's Guides and the Black Watch to seize a long narrow-backed kopje half way towards the main Boer position. By nightfall the British attack had been halted by heavy Boer fire. During the night three of Lovat's Scouts discovered that a hill shaped like Gibraltar situated between a ridge captured by the Black Watch on the left and the Nek itself had been left unoccupied. The Boers often temporarily evacuated positions during the hours of darkness. Early on the 24th the Scouts guided the Volunteer Company of the Highland Light Infantry up to seize the hill. But they were pinned down on the summit by fire from Boers on the hills beyond and it was not until the afternoon, when the Seaforth Highlanders captured the most easterly part of the ridge and got behind the Boers, that the enemy retreated.

Paget and Clements joined forces two miles north of Slabbert's Nek, where the Boers were also entrenched, on the morning of the 23rd. The mounted troops were sent to capture a spur on the British right and there the Staffordshire Imperial Yeomanry had a piece of luck. A small group led by Captain William Bromley-Davenport advanced towards some rifle pits dug by the Boers near an African kraal at the summit. The pits were empty, again evacuated during the night, and when the yeomanry realized this they dashed forward and jumped in. They were just in time, beating the Boers by a short head. Bromley-Davenport, evidently no great admirer of the Boers, said later: "The position is enormously strong and against any troops in the world except Boers we should have had hardly any chance of taking it." A couple of hours later they were joined by two companies of the Royal Irish Rifles and were ordered to advance with fixed bayonets. "Why not?" said the man lying next to Bromley-Davenport, getting up and walking calmly forward.[35] The position was carried and the following morning, after the Royal Irish Rifles and the Wiltshire Regiment had seized a crucial height, the Boers fled.

In the west the Boers were driven back through Witnek while the British forces at Rooikrantz kept the enemy in front of them busy enough to prevent them sending reinforcements elsewhere. Rundle made a similar demonstration against the entrance to Commando Nek which he occupied on the 25th without opposition. He sent scouts on to Fouriesburg, the main town in the basin which had become a temporary capital for the Free State government. They reported that the Boers had evacuated it and Rundle immediately sent forward the Imperial Yeomanry and other mounted troops to occupy the town. From Fouriesburg the British advanced east to Slaapkranz where the road to the two most easterly passes divided. There the yeomanry was used to try to turn the right flank of the Boers, who were becoming increasingly demoralized. By midnight on the 28th the position was taken.

Negotiations for the surrender of the Boers began and on the afternoon of the 29th they agreed to lay down their arms. Not all were prepared to give in, another 1,500 escaping through the Golden Gate pass to the east which the British had been too slow to block. But 4,314 men, three artillery guns and nearly two million rounds of ammunition were captured in the greatest success since Paardeberg. Manisty of the CIV mounted infantry, who with thirty-six of his men had escorted an ammunition column during the operations, helped disarm the burghers. He wrote to his mother: "Going round a bend we found a commando which we had not noticed in the dusk about half a mile away from the others, about 150 men. I formed them up and marched them down to where the others were disarming. I little thought when I came out that I should actually command and ride at the head of an armed commando."[36] The prisoners were marched to Fouriesburg, each batch of 200 being escorted by twenty Imperial Yeomanry from Rundle's Division. Hunter

72

was complimentary about them, telling Roberts: "The yeomanry is daily gaining experience in actual warfare, which is all they ask for and all they require to make them rank with the best. This they now do."[37]

But, whatever the scale of the victory, most of the Boers who surrendered were those with little fight left in them. De Wet and Steyn, those twin pillars of resistance, were away and a great chase across the veldt ensued. As he fled from the Brandwater Basin De Wet fought a skilled rearguard action to brush off an attempt by a British force, including Imperial Yeomanry and CIV gunners, to stop him getting away. At the end of July he took refuge near Reitzburg, seven miles south of the Vaal River. With heavy hearts he and his Free Staters prepared to leave their homeland and cross into the Transvaal to link up with commandos there. On 6 August he made a dash for it with Kitchener at his heels. The British were desperate to stop him getting to the Transvaal and Methuen's force, including 600 men of the 3rd, 5th and 10th Battalions Imperial Yeomanry, was sent to block the drifts on the northern side of the Vaal. But Kitchener, acting on false information, sent Methuen to the wrong river crossing and by the evening of the 8th De Wet's whole force was in the Transvaal. Methuen pursued him across the plain, leaving behind his infantry and transport, the task of trying to catch him falling on the Imperial Yeomanry.

A series of fierce rearguard actions ensued. At Rietfontein on the 9th the Yorkshire Dragoons and South Nottinghamshire Hussars heard that De Wet was just three miles ahead. Galloping after him they raced the enemy for a kopje which commanded the rear of De Wet's convoy. The Boers won by a short head but twenty yeomen carried the kopje at bayonet point and this brave handful then seized the next hill where Lieutenant Alfred Knowles of the South Nottinghamshires was killed by a sniper. Three other yeomen were killed and five wounded and by now they were in danger of being overwhelmed. Lieutenant-Colonel George Younghusband, commanding officer of the 3rd Battalion, decided to cross to the other side of his main position in full view of the Boers to organize reinforcements.

73

Nonchalantly lighting his pipe he appeared to stumble before reaching his destination. The hard-pressed yeomen were relieved and the Boers retreated but it was not until afterwards that Younghusband revealed that he had been shot through the thigh. In another action near Cyferbult on 12 August the 10th Battalion captured a gun and sixteen ammunition wagons and released sixty British prisoners. Sometimes Methuen made his men march through the night and once they rode eighty-one miles in fifty-nine hours, fighting an action in the middle of that. It was a magnificent effort by the yeomanry but all to no avail. Ian Hamilton failed to block Olifant's Nek, one of the passes into the Magaliesberg mountains west of Pretoria, despite being ordered to do so by Roberts. De Wet slipped through the unguarded pass and disappeared into the safety of the mountains. Soon the western Transvaal, where the Boers were led by General Koos De la Rey, was causing the British as many headaches as the Orange Free State.

Efforts to snare Commandant Olivier, one of the leaders who had escaped from the Brandwater Basin via the Golden Gate, proved equally unsuccessful. A force including Lovat's Scouts and men from the 6th and 15th Battalions Imperial Yeomanry engaged him at Spitzkop in the Orange Free State on 13 August, but Olivier vanished.

The Imperial Yeomanry now spent much of its time patrolling, searching for arms and ammunition and seizing livestock from Boer farms. There was only sporadic resistance but it was always potentially dangerous work. On 20 August a patrol of the 2nd (Wiltshire) Company, including the brothers Tom and Herbert Brown, rode up to a farm near Senekal. With them was Roy Rice whom the two farmers had helped through riding tests in England. Suddenly a volley of shots came from the house, killing Tom Brown and two others. The patrol had had no idea that there were armed Boers there. The survivors retreated and two days later Herbert wrote a heartbroken letter to their parents in the Wiltshire village of Upton Scudamore. "The life and nerve seem to have completely left me and I feel more like an old man," he admitted. "You cannot dream how I miss him. For nearly five months, we have slept, messed, rode and fired side by side, never thinking of going anywhere without the other." The harsh reality of war had struck home. Those carefree days when the brothers had enlisted together in England seemed to belong to another world.[38]

CHAPTER FOUR

DISILLUSION AND DEPARTURE

On the evening of 25 September, 1900, Roberts sent for Mackinnon of the CIV and told him that the regiment could go home. That day the British had reached Komati Poort on the border between the Transvaal and Portuguese East Africa. For the Boers it was literally the end of the line, the point at which the vital railway link crossed the frontier on its way to the coast. For Roberts, still thinking in conventional military terms, it represented the effective end of the war. The remnants of the Boer forces in the eastern Transvaal either scattered or surrendered. There were still some loose ends to be tied up, particularly those tiresome commandos in the Orange Free State and the western Transvaal, but he felt confident that he could send some of his army home. Mackinnon recalled: "Although he said it was not very convenient to spare them just now, still they had done so well that he was determined to let them go as he knew how important their engagements were at home."[1] The decision to dispense with the CIV's services was not an implied criticism of their performance. Roberts, as Honorary Colonel of the CIV, had a genuine affection for the regiment and had constantly praised its work. Sending it back to London was a typical piece of Roberts's favouritism.

After Diamond Hill the regiment had begun to waste away, 120 men volunteering for government jobs in South Africa, up to 400 being absent sick at any one time and a few being invalided home. Like the rest of the volunteers, the CIV infantry had experienced the dreary chores of convoy escort duty and then acted as the garrison of first Heilbron and later Frederickstadt. In the latter town in the Transvaal two men of the regiment were killed and four wounded in a Boer attack at the end of July. Even the CIV's good quality uniforms had been reduced to rags and with their numbers down to less than 600 out of the 1,045 who had landed in February they were ready to go home. Many of them, as Roberts had said, did have pressing business responsibilities. When Mackinnon told his men of Roberts's decision "there was much cheering". The regiment's gunners felt the same way and when Childers heard the news two days later he described it as "a red letter day".[2] Even the ever enthusiastic Manisty of the CIV mounted infantry confessed to his mother that he would "not be sorry to get into civilization again, although I enjoy this life immensely."[3]

The reaction in other units was one of astonishment and bitterness. Ross of the Sussex Imperial Yeomanry wrote, "The British Army feels aggrieved at the praise bestowed on the CIV regiment and its early return to England. To hear a discussion on our poor unoffending and former comrades is to have a sad exhibition of envy, hatred, malice and all uncharitableness." Some wag, possibly Ross himself, composed an extremely witty parody of Kipling's *Absent-Minded Beggar* which ran as follows:

When you've said 'the war is over' and 'the end is now in sight,'
And you've welcomed home your valiant CIVs,
There are other absent beggars in the everlasting fight,
And not the least of these your Yeoman please.
He's a casual sort of Johnnie and his casualties are great,
And on the veldt and kopjes you will find him,
For he's still on active service, eating things without a plate,
And thinking of the things he's left behind him.[4]

The Army's mood was not improved by the ecstatic welcome which the CIV received when it arrived back in London at the end of October. Four trains took the regiment from Southampton to Paddington and the men then marched through the streets of London to a thanksgiving service at St Paul's and a formal welcome at the Guildhall. For the CIV it was an intensely moving experience. Childers remembered "a dream of miles of upturned faces, of dancing colours, of roaring voices, of a sudden dim hush in the great cathedral, of more miles of faces under gaslight, of a voice in a packed hall saying 'London is proud of her . . .' ." The *Illustrated London News* published a special welcome edition, the Corporation of the City of London held a banquet at Finsbury barracks and everywhere the men were feted as heroes. But back in South Africa, Wetton, still serving as a medical volunteer and marooned in Bethlehem in the midst of the hostile Orange Free State, commented sourly: "Men remaining at the front felt that London's enthusiastic welcome to her citizen soldiers at this time was rather premature."[5]

Wetton's bitterness was understandable. As the CIV was dining in London the garrison of less than 1,000 men in Bethlehem, which included the 62nd (Middlesex) Company Imperial Yeomanry and some of the medical volunteers, was virtually under siege. The British had a string of outposts on kopjes outside the town and the Boers a similar ring about 3,000 yards further out. The only communication with the outside world was by heliograph from a hill near the town and signalling parties and anyone else who ventured outside the perimeter were likely to be attacked.

Where they were not under siege, yeomen were used as advance and rear guards and flanking patrols on convoys, each column needing a fringe of horsemen two to three miles out. It was exhausting, hungry work and the men often only had the vaguest idea of where they were. Peel recalled "an incessant round of early reveilles, long marches, night guard and picket and all the other ordinary routine, apparently without any aim or purpose whatsoever. When we did come up with the enemy, the attack never seemed to be pressed home."[6] The weight carried by the yeomanry's horses was still far too great, averaging nearly 300 pounds, and the animals suffered badly because many of their riders were poor horsemasters.

The shortages of supplies, particularly for Rundle's 8th Division in the Orange Free State, soon honed the yeomen's talents for foraging. Other troops nicknamed them the "farmyard scouts" and "bread and jam soldiers"[5] because of their skill at finding something to eat in even the most unpromising abandoned Boer home. Any early scruples and regulations against looting had long since been abandoned. Where supplies were plentiful, the yeomanry could live well off the land. Ross described a typical Rough Rider of the 72nd Company returning to camp. "Across his saddle, *à la* open scissors, would be two large pieces of wood, usually fence posts; oranges dropping from his nosebag; on one side of his saddle a fowl and a duck on the other; a small porker from his haversack."[4]

But such scenes of plenty were the exception rather than the rule and disillusion began to spread like a cancer through those who had volunteered with such enthusiasm less than a year previously. The Imperial Yeomanry first found itself burning food supplies at Boer farms to deny them to the commandos and later setting the buildings themselves ablaze. The policy of farm burning was adopted by Roberts in the summer of 1900 to make an example of Boer families suspected of helping the guerrillas and deter others from doing so. Forcing out women, children and the elderly onto the veldt before setting their homes ablaze was hardly the kind of warfare which the men had envisaged when they offered their services. As Captain Sir John Gilmour of the 20th (Fife and Forfar Light Horse) Company put it: "It is not a glorious job lifting women and getting potted by the husband."[7] Some accepted farm burning as a necessarily harsh measure in an increasingly bitter war. "The women and children were loud in their lamentations as the red flames blazed and the dense smoke rolled away on the fresh breeze," wrote Ross. "They cursed us and wept idle tears but they had their own dear friends, husbands and sons to thank after all, as nearly all the sniping in this lovely valley is being done by the farmers who live in it."[4] Other yeomen found even destroying food supplies a repulsive business and Lieutenant Barbour of the 21st (Cheshire) Company tried to soften the blow. "Some of the scenes are heartrending as the bags of corn go out to the fire or river," he wrote home. "It may be against exact orders but I never leave a house bare but always leave sufficient to keep the family going for some time provided they give none away to marauding Boers."[8] The problem with such generosity was that the commandos were as likely as the British to help themselves to anything that was denied them. Chivalry was in short supply on both sides and within months whole valleys had been laid waste by the British, once fertile farms left blackened and lifeless. The policy failed, stiffening the resolve of the hardy *volk* of the veldt and causing outrage in Britain. In theory it was abandoned in November, 1900, but in reality farms continued to be destroyed, wood stripped off for camp fires and tin roofs removed to build British blockhouses.

Endless convoys, weary garrison duties, screams of hatred from Boer women and children and the dogged resistance of the commandos all combined to send morale plummeting. Rose-Innes decided that he had had enough of life with Paget's Horse after a convoy which he was escorting took a week to travel 35 miles. Using his barrister's persuasive skills he "explained to the doctor frankly that unless I could get away from what looked like a prospect of horrible inactivity and attend to my work and private affairs, the consequences to my health would be very serious indeed."[9] The doctor sent him to hospital and soon afterwards he was discharged. Peel and his Oxfordshire comrades in the 40th Company soldiered on, but he confessed: "When it seemed that we might go on doing this interminably, a curiously strong wave of homesickness began to sweep over our country-bred ranks. There was a great deal of grumbling."[6] Lieutenant Sir Thomas Fowler of the 1st (Wiltshire) Company complained in a letter home: "We have now been at Leeuw River a month. I have very little to do here; sometimes I am sent out on patrol. It is not a very satisfactory existence and if fighting is over, we would rather have the option of either taking our discharge or enlisting in the local police."[10]

The strength of the Imperial Yeomanry declined as quickly as its morale. The root of the problem was that no system of drafts had been allowed by the War Office despite pressure from Lucas, the force's Deputy Adjutant General. He wrote a series of letters to the War Office advocating the sending of regular drafts to replace casualties but was told "it has been decided to utilise the existing recruiting agencies for this purpose."[11] In fact no recruits were sent to the companies from any source and the force began to waste away. The decision not to organize drafts for the Imperial Yeomanry's 1900 contingent was later criticized by the Royal Commission which investigated the conduct of the war.[12]

The drop in numbers was not just the result of the relatively light battle casualties and the much greater losses from disease. The well educated ranks of the Imperial Yeomanry were also a prime source of new Army officers and a recruiting target for government departments and the police in South Africa, who were better paid and delighted to take them on. About a third of the 22nd (Cheshire) Company joined the police along with fifty men from the 69th (Sussex) Company. Ross said that, quite apart from the higher pay, "many who were not desirous of joining the police have finally done so thanks to the innumerable fatigues, pickets on the surrounding kopjes and the crowning discomforts of the rainy nights."[4] The post office and railways were similarly keen to get men from the Imperial Yeomanry. The CIV had suffered from the same problem when it was in South Africa and of its nineteen cyclists only five were still with the regiment by the time it went home. As they had been recruited from the lawyers and clerks of the Inns of Court Volunteers they were particularly employable. Lloyd, who had chronicled their progress across South Africa, had become Crown Prosecutor in the Orange Free State, now renamed the Orange River Colony. One of his comrades had become secretary to the Military Governor of Bloemfontein, another was Assistant Crown Prosecutor in Johannesburg and four had received commissions in the Regular Army. "In short the CIV has proved itself a famous cover to draw for useful persons to assist in the civil and military administration of the newly conquered country," wrote Lloyd.[13]

The result of this attrition was that by the summer of 1900 the Sussex company was reduced to twenty-one men out of the original 120 and as early as July was temporarily absorbed into a composite unit formed with the remnants of those from Dorset,

Devon and Somerset. The 1st (Wiltshire) Company fared better but was still down to seventy men by November and only just over one third of the two Cheshire companies returned home with their original units in the summer of 1901. By that time the average strength of an Imperial Yeomanry company was thirty-five men.[14]

Not all the fighting in the autumn of 1900 was hit-and-run guerrilla warfare. At Ladybrand, tucked up against the Orange Free State's border with Basutoland, a siege in September illustrated once again the Boers' inability to attack well-organized defences. The commander of the small garrison in Ladybrand was Major Frederick White of the Royal Marine Light Infantry, a veteran of the Egyptian campaigns in the 1880s. He had with him eighty men of the 1st Battalion Worcestershire Regiment, forty-three from the 1st (Wiltshire) Company Imperial Yeomanry and thirty local volunteers. On 1 September White heard that an enemy force was approaching and the next morning its leader, Commandant Fourie, sent in a message demanding the town's surrender. White told Fourie that if he wanted Ladybrand "he had better come and take it" and retired to some previously prepared entrenchments on a hill to the west of the town.[15] The small British force had hardly reached its defences when the first of 382 shells fired during the siege hit its positions. The surrounded garrison behaved with great gallantry amid shell-fire and continous rifle fire from 3,000 Boers with nine artillery pieces and two machine guns. Corporal Bert Phipps of the yeomanry wrote home: "They found out our positions with their big guns and then we had it hot I can tell you. The first shell that was directed against our side of the hill took the right-hand corner of our trench away but no one was hit."[16] The British had dug themselves in so well that they lost only seven wounded, while their attackers suffered twenty-four killed and thirty-five wounded, many of them during an attempt to rush the trenches on the first day. On the evening of the third day of the siege the Boers fired a parting volley and retreated, and the following morning a relief force, which included 300 men of the 29th (Denbighshire), 30th (Pembrokeshire) and 31st (Montgomeryshire)

Companies Imperial Yeomanry, arrived. Phipps leapt out of his trench and shook hands with the Montgomeryshire men, who were the first to reach the garrison.

White was awarded the Distinguished Service Order and his men hailed as heroes, yet the margin between triumph and disaster was narrower than was admitted at the time. On the evening of the first day White saw a white flag flying in the centre of the position. "I called out and said if it was not at once put down I would fire at the man holding it and it was then lowered," he reported. When he asked Captain George Graves of the Wiltshire Imperial Yeomanry if he knew who was responsible Graves blamed one of his men, Sergeant Drayson. But Graves later admitted that he had ordered Drayson to raise the flag and the captain was arrested. Doctors discovered that he was suffering from "severe nervous debility" and he was put on the sick list instead of being court martialled.[17] The matter was hushed up and Graves was sent home and allowed to resign quietly. The defence of Ladybrand received considerable press coverage at a time when the British public needed some good news. Roberts did not want the inconvenient fact that one officer had cracked up to spoil the story of a genuinely heroic defence by the rest of the garrison. But had it not been for White's decisive action the white flag might have proved as fatal as it had at Lindley and Ladybrand could have fallen, providing yet another humiliation for the British.

On 20 October Lieutenant Alexis Doxat became the only man of the Imperial Yeomanry to win the Victoria Cross. Whilst serving as an intelligence officer with a British column, he was reconnoitring a position held by about 100 Boers near Zeerust, in the far west of the Transvaal. Suddenly a group of the enemy opened fire from a range of 300 yards and as the British retreated one of them lost his horse. Seeing his predicament, Doxat, a 33-year-old stockbroker who had come out to South Africa with the 11th (Yorkshire Dragoons) Company, galloped back under heavy fire and rescued him. But despite such individual acts of heroism, there was little opportunity for glamour in the guerrilla conflict. Lieutenant-Colonel Younghusband remembered this phase of the war as being "on the whole a weary, dreary nightmare and not worth writing about".[18]

De Wet, who was beginning to acquire an almost supernatural reputation among the British trying to capture him, was at the heart of the trouble. At the beginning of November the second great De Wet hunt began and came within a whisker of success. The Boer general was near Bothaville, on the Orange Free State side of the Vaal River, when the British stumbled across him on 6 November. De Wet, who had Steyn, the Orange Free State President, with him, was planning an incursion into Cape Colony but this time it was he who was caught napping. He was being hunted by forces commanded by Major-General Charles Knox, which included the 17th (Ayrshire) and 18th (Queen's Own Royal Glasgow) Companies Imperial Yeomanry.

At 4am on the 6th an advance party of the 5th Mounted Infantry captured a Boer picquet asleep before they could give the alarm. As the day broke, the MI advanced to the top of a low ridge and found themselves looking down on De Wet's laager. It was a moment the British had dreamed of for months, but they had to seize their chance while they had the advantage. Led by Major Kenneth Lean they opened a furious fire from the ridge. There was panic in the Boer camp but amid the chaos De Wet and Steyn hurled themselves onto their horses and galloped away with most of their men. About 130 Boers who could not get to their mounts retreated to a walled garden and fought a stubborn, bloody action. More British troops arrived , including forty-two men from the 17th and 18th Companies Imperial Yeomanry, led by Captain Coates and Lieutenant Boulton, who protected the right of U Battery Royal Horse Artillery and were soon heavily engaged. But the 170 British troops now at the scene were threatened by a counter-attack organized by De Wet who had rallied some of the fleeing Boers. The pressure eased as British reinforcements arrived throughout the four hour battle and the noose was finally closed around the Boers in the garden. Resistance only collapsed when the 5th MI and eighty West Australians were ordered, within earshot of the Boers, to go in with the bayonet and the surviving burghers immediately surrendered. The British had lost

84

thirteen killed and thirty-three wounded, the casualties including the gallant Lieutenant-Colonel Philip Le Gallais, commanding the mounted infantry and yeomanry, who was mortally wounded. The yeomanry escaped lightly, just two being wounded. The Boers had seventeen killed, seventeen wounded and ninety-seven were taken prisoner unwounded. All De Wet's artillery and wagons were captured but the fox himself had escaped and surprisingly there was no attempt at pursuit.

It was not long before the Boers had their revenge, this time not in the Orange Free State but in the valleys of the western Transvaal which had become De la Rey's hunting ground. On 13 December the Boers surprised a force of 1,500 men led by Clements, including 200 from the 20th (Fife and Forfar Light Horse), 26th (Dorset) and 27th (Devon) Companies of the Imperial Yeomanry, at Nooitgedacht in the Magaliesberg. After his pickets on the mountains above were forced to surrender by a sudden Boer onslaught, Clements managed to prevent a humiliation from turning into a complete disaster by retreating to a defensive position known as Yeomanry Hill. The action will be described more fully in Chapter Five but the Boers' inability to press home their advantage eventually allowed Clements to retreat with the remnants of his force. However the action cost the British 638 killed, wounded and captured, including more than fifty among the Imperial Yeomanry.

The advantage flickered backwards and forwards between the two sides, often dependent on good intelligence, fast reactions and mobility, all of which usually counted in the Boers' favour. But at Springhaan Nek, near Thaba 'Nchu in the Orange Free State, Colonel G.W. Forbes of the Montgomeryshire Yeomanry displayed the kind of initiative which was normally the prerogative of his enemies. On 14 December he learned from a native scout that a commando led by Commandant Haasbroek was contentedly cooking its evening meal about four or five miles away. He immediately set off at the gallop with 130 men of the 16th Lancers and 185 Welshmen from the 9th Battalion Imperial Yeomanry. As the yeomanry seized a kopje overlooking the Boer camp, the Lancers charged into the middle of it. According to one account the regular cavalrymen fired from the saddle as they galloped into the camp, while another says that they used clubbed rifles.[19] Whatever the truth, it was an early example of British cavalry charging with the rifle. Eight Boers were killed, thirty-three wounded and seventeen captured while the Lancers had just one man wounded and the yeomanry no casualties at all.

Two days later 2,000 Boers led by Commandant Pieter Kritzinger and Judge Barry Hertzog invaded Cape Colony. It was a bold move, although typically not characterized by any effective overall strategy, and it sent shivers up the spines of the British. Cape Colony may have been marked red on every schoolboy's map of the Empire but most of its white population were Boers and in its vast rural areas there were few loyalists. The British had always feared that rebellion could spread quickly among those who were only nominally Queen Victoria's sub-jects. The Boers calculated that for political reasons there could be no destruction of farms or reprisals against civilians in British territory.

On 17 December at Hamelfontein the invaders ran into a stubborn little garrison of twenty men of the 32nd (Lancashire) Company Imperial Yeomanry and nine from the 3rd Battalion Grenadier Guards, all under the command of Lieutenant William Fletcher of the yeomanry, a renowned Oxford University oarsman. A few of the yeomen in an outpost near the main farm spotted the Boers first. "Blaze away lads," shouted Private Swan, who was in charge. He was hit in the side almost immediately, but tried to sing to encourage his comrades as he lay dying. The three other men in the outpost realized that their position was hopeless and surrendered but in the farmhouse Fletcher was preparing an epic defence. Some rough barricades had been constructed and behind these the twenty-six remaining British fought off their attackers for eleven hours.[20] One of the yeomen was killed and seven of the garrison wounded before Kritzinger decided that there must be easier pickings in Cape Colony and moved on. Fletcher was awarded the Distinguished Service Order for his leadership and bravery. Kritzinger continued to roam the region for months causing the British major problems, but the feared mass uprising of Boers in Cape Colony failed to materialize.

By now Roberts was on his way home. He left Cape Town on 10 December, handing over command in South Africa to Kitchener and returning to a hero's welcome, £100,000 from a grateful nation and the post of Commander-in-Chief in London. Despite some mistakes, his public image was still that of the man who had marched to Pretoria and his status as the most popular Victorian military hero was undiminished. Before Roberts left South Africa he told an audience in Durban that the war was "practically over". It was a hopelessly over-optimistic judgement and many of the Imperial Yeomanry had already reached a very different conclusion. "I don't believe this war will be over for a very long time, that is if they want to go on with it," Lieutenant William Power of the 8th (Derbyshire) Company told his family in a letter.[21]

The Boers pounced on the slightest mistake by the British and were sometimes able to assemble large enough forces to over-whelm isolated garrisons. A small convoy which left Krugersdorp for Modderfontein, near Johannesburg, on 29 January, 1901 was guarded by eighty men of the South Wales Borderers, twenty of Marshall's Horse and twenty-five men of the 59th (Oxfordshire) Company Imperial Yeomanry. Foolishly the escort, commanded by Captain Magniac of the Oxfordshire Yeomanry, did not tell the Modderfontein garrison that it was on its way and was soon in difficulty. After struggling to its destination with the help of a party sent from the town, it then found itself under siege. Smuts attacked Modderfontein with 2,000 men and the yeomanry desperately built their own shelters and trenches under fire. After an assault lasting forty-three hours the British garrison and convoy escort, totalling just over 200, were finally overwhelmed by sheer weight of numbers. More than sixty were killed or wounded, the latter including Magniac and three yeomen. The rest were taken prisoner but were soon released because the Boers had nowhere to keep captives.

A skirmish at Klaarstroom in Cape Colony on 2 February typi-fied what was happening across South Africa even in areas once regarded as safe by the British. Situated in fertile mountains less than 50 miles from the southern coast, Klaarstroom was a town which had never been under threat during the Boer invasion early in the war. Yet on 1 February a force of eighty Imperial Yeomanry, all that was left of the 70th and 75th (Sharpshooters) Companies was sent from Prince Albert 35 miles away to see whether the Boers had occupied it.

On riding into Klaarstroom the Sharpshooters discovered that it was held by 300 Boers and beat a hasty retreat. "We had to bolt," said Sergeant-Major Thomas Jackson of the 70th Company, who had enlisted from the London Scottish. "We made a running fight for about nine miles and then we got to our main body and drove the enemy off. My horse was shot under me early in the fight and came down a rare 'purler' with me, sending my rifle and hat flying."[22] Jackson modestly failed to mention in his letter home that he and another man had already rescued their commanding officer, Lieutenant-Colonel R.K. Parke, covering him with rifle fire while he mounted his horse and escaped. Jackson was now stranded and as he made his way through a nearby farm found Lance Corporal Boyd, one of his comrades, lying dead. He took Boyd's rifle and bandolier and told the farmer to bury him. For several hours Jackson and another man lay on the top of a kopje looking down on the Boers and waiting for nightfall to shroud their escape. But a Boer patrol, perhaps alerted by the farmer, took them prisoner. "We were kindly treated by the Boers themselves, although I don't think much of their two commandants," continued Jackson. "They took us off with them when they moved off at about 2.30 the next morning and took to the hills. They looked after us very carefully for some 15 miles or so and then they either got careless or did not care whether we escaped or not, so we made a bolt for it and got off." After this indecisive enagement the Boer commando returned to the mountains, the yeomanry prisoners found the rest of the Sharpshooters two days later and Boyd and the one Boer killed in the skirmish were buried together.

Back in the south-western Transvaal Methuen embarked on a lengthy trek in February with a 1,500-strong force which included the remnants of the 5th and 10th Battalions Imperial Yeomanry. After venturing into Bechuanaland, where a rebellion had broken out, he crossed back into the Transvaal and headed for Klerksdorp through an area where British forces had never been before. Following a series of skirmishes, Methuen captured the laager of a Boer force led by De Villiers and De Beers, taking thirty-six prisoners and sixty-seven wagons. Two days later, on 19 February, he was confronted by 1,500 of the enemy at Hartebeestfontein on a plateau each side of a defile which led towards Klerksdorp. Methuen tried to take the left of the position but the 5th Battalion, from Shropshire, Worcestershire and Northumberland, could get no further than the spurs and flanks of the hill because of the ferocity of the Boer fire. He then sent the 10th Battalion to storm the right, supported by four field guns. The first crest was won with few casualties, but the Boers then retreated to the far edge of the plateau and the task of the yeomanry became much more formidable. They now had to face fire both from their front and from their left flank, the Boers on the unconquered western position having a clear view. At the same time there was danger from the rear when 500 Boers attacked the British convoy's escort.

The Official History of the war was lavish in its praise of the 10th Battalion and of the Australians who fought alongside it. "The yeomanry continued to gain ground, fighting like veteran troops from one cover to another," went its description of Hartebeestfontein. "Finally, greatly relieved by detached attacks which Lord Methuen launched against prominent parts of the Boer stronghold on either flank, the whole line charged against the southern edge of the plateau and tumbled the enemy on to the plain below where he was punished severely with a following fire."[23] Eighteen Boers were killed and Methuen's force lost sixteen dead and thirty-two wounded. Almost half were from the Imperial Yeomanry, the 10th Battalion suffering four dead and twelve wounded and the 5th Battalion one killed and three wounded. The 40th (Oxfordshire) Company, reduced to just twenty-nine men before the action began, suffered almost all the 10th Battalion's casualties and particularly distinguished itself during the five-hour fight. The road to Klerksdorp had been opened, although in a guerrilla war such an achievement was largely meaningless. But it did enable Methuen to march into the town later that day with an immense haul of captured stock and supplies and many Boer families who the British had forced to leave their farms.

De la Rey now seemed to be as omnipresent as De Wet and on 3 March he Smuts and Celliers, with 1,500 men attacked his home town of Lichtenburg far out in the hostile western Transvaal. The 600-strong British garrison consisted of the Northumberland Fusiliers, 100 men of Paget's Horse and forty from the 10th (Sherwood Rangers) Company Imperial Yeomanry. The Boers surrounded the town and, aided by sympathizers from within, some even managed to creep between the pickets and penetrate the streets. At 3.15am on the 3rd fire broke out on three sides of the town and from within it. The garrison defended the town stoutly all day, the pickets on the outskirts behaving with particular gallantry. The yeomanry saved its horses by stabling them in the town's Dutch church as the battle raged around it. At 5.30pm there was a two-hour ceasefire to enable both sides to remove their dead and wounded, but when fighting resumed the Boers had lost heart and they withdrew early next morning having lost fourteen killed and thirty-eight wounded. Among the British casualties of sixteen killed and twenty-four wounded, the two yeomanry units each lost one dead and two wounded. This time the Boers had been denied a victory by the courage and stubborness of the infantry and yeomanry and Captain Herbert Wilson of the Sherwood Rangers was awarded the DSO and three of his men the DCM.

In Cape Colony the first contingent of Imperial Yeomanry suffered one of its most embarrassing reverses just weeks before it was due to go home. In April the British launched a drive through the mountains between Aberdeen and Graff Reinet in an attempt to crush three groups of Boers still causing trouble in the area. On 6 April the Cape rebel leader Gideon Scheepers captured a party of the 5th Lancers and the 32nd (Lancashire) Company sent to watch the eastern passes of the mountains at Zeekoegat. The irony was that they should never have been there at all, having been sent by the commandant at Aberdeen because of a misunder-standing. The British horsemen were quickly overwhelmed, eight of the Lancers being wounded and twenty-three taken prisoner, while the yeomanry lost two dead, four wounded and thirty-three prisoners. The latter were near their discharge and perhaps it was too much to expect them to make a determined stand when they knew that the Boers would release them within days.

The war was now entering a new and even more ruthless phase as Kitchener's columns tried to flush out the commandos. Boer families forced from their farms were to be placed in concen-tration camps where thousands of them were to die. But the original contingent of Imperial Yeomanry would play little part in this. Except for the minority who chose to stay on in South Africa it was time for them to go home.

Political and military pressure to get the Imperial Yeomanry and Volunteer Service Companies sent home had been growing in Britain. As early as January Roberts, now back in London, had told Kitchener that he was worried about the effect on future Volunteer Force recruiting if the Service Companies were not repatriated.[24] By May Brodrick, the Secretary of State for War, admitted to Kitchener that some MPs who had served in the yeomanry "are pressing me and even raised a motion to force me to fix a date for the return of the original yeomanry". He added: "I gave them a very stiff answer but I imagine from your last letter you expect to release them shortly."[25] The message to Kitchener was clear.

The spring and summer of 1901 was a strange transitional period for the Imperial Yeomanry. Although most of the first contingent, now reduced to barely a third of its original strength of nearly 11,000, wanted to see the back of South Africa, the desire to come home was heavily tinged with guilt. Barbour had had enough of service with the Cheshire Imperial Yeomanry, but wrote apologetically to his family: "You must think it very un-patriotic of us not being anxious to stay out but what is making us all tired of being out is knowing that the authorities are making a convenience of the volunteers, especially of the old yeomanry."[26] In the 1st (Wiltshire) Company Lieutenant Awdry and Fowler, the latter newly promoted to captain, prepared to part company after a year of service. Awdry wrote to his father: "There are very few of us who want to stay really, though many like myself have a sort of half shamefaced feeling about going away with the war incomplete. Fowler has been promoted . . . and he will certainly stay but I don't think I shall unless you think I ought to or unless they find themselves very short of officers on amalgamating the new and old lots."[27]

The "new lot", as Awdry called them, were the second contingent of the Imperial Yeomanry who were now starting to arrive in South Africa. They were raised in Britain in early 1901 in very different circumstances from the volunteers who had gone out to South Africa a year previously. The story of their recruitment and experiences in South Africa will be told later in this book but there were few high born recruits in the ranks and little of the patriotic rush of blood to the nation's head which had characterized the period after Black Week. The New Yeomanry, as they were dubbed, were predominantly working class and more likely to be motivated by the recently introduced higher rate of pay or by the prospect of emigrating to South Africa. Many could not shoot, fewer still could ride and they had received no training at all before they arrived. The old yeomen regarded them with horror during the weeks in which the two contingents worked uneasily side by side. In June and July, 1901, what was left of the first contingent was finally withdrawn.

In theory the first contingent had no right to go home at all. The attestation papers which they had signed when they joined up stated that they had enlisted "for a term of one year, unless the war in South Africa lasts longer than one year, in which case you will be detained until the war is over." At the time it had seemed inconceivable that the Boers could defy the might of the British Empire for a year and the chief worry was that the war might be over before they got out there. But the recruits had scarcely bothered to read the small print in their rush to enlist and many had interpreted the clause to mean that they were joining up for a maximum of one year. The Army decided that it was better to go along with this mistaken belief than to force unwilling volunteers, many of whom had business and family commitments at home, to stay on in South Africa. Knight, the Imperial Yeomanry's Deputy Assistant Adjutant General, told the Royal Commission into the war: "There was no obligation with the first contingent to let them all go but it was generally understood at the time when we enlisted the men that it only meant for a year ... both men and officers certainly understood that a year was the limit for which they would be kept."[28]

In the Volunteer Service Companies discontent at being kept in South Africa had become rife. Some had been promised as long ago as October, when the CIV was sent home, that they too could return to their jobs and families. The volunteers serving with the South Staffordshire Regiment in the Orange Free State town of Reitz had been given a grand send off by the battalion, the band playing 'Auld Lang Syne' and 'When Johnny Comes Marching Home.' It soon turned out that Johnny was marching no further than the lines of communication that stretched up from Cape Town. Mackenzie and his comrades in the Green Howards Volunteer Service Company suffered the same fate. At the beginning of October he recorded triumphantly in his diary: "Grand news today, received orders to pack up and proceed down country on our way home. I need not attempt to describe the jubilation in my company."[29] The men travelled by train to Pretoria, where they were among sixteen Service Companies which took part in the official ceremony to annexe the Transvaal to the British Empire. But when the Green Howards arrived in Bloemfontein on 31 October the order sending them home was abruptly cancelled. Mackenzie wrote: "To our great disgust and annoyance had to entrain straight off and proceed to Kaffir River to stay on the lines of communication. We are sorry now that we left the regiment." Six months of tedium followed guarding the railway line just south of the Orange River, near Bethulie. Mackenzie lamented on New Year's Day: "Though there are not, I believe, many who regret coming out (I know I don't), we would all have preferred to begin the year as we expected – elsewhere."

93

At the beginning of May the Green Howards finally escaped from Bethulie and took a train south to a camp at De Aar, where eight other Service Companies were already waiting to go home. Just over a fortnight previously, on 18 April, there had been a near mutiny at the camp while Bryant and the Norfolk Regiment Volunteer Service Company were there. "The men had been for some time discontented with their lot," wrote Bryant. "A deputation composed of men from all companies called on each tent with the proposal that each company should call a parade for 8.30pm April 20th and that a deputation should wait on the officers of each company and inquire why we were being kept at De Aar having received orders for home and when we might expect to leave." The men "all agreed that they had been fooled about long enough."[30] This shocked the Army into action. These were no reluctant conscripts, every man was a part-time soldier at home who had volunteered to serve in South Africa. The following day the companies from the Norfolks, Hampshires, Suffolks, Lincolns, Bedfordshires, Black Watch, Oxfordshire and Buckinghamshire Light Infantry and the West Riding Regiment were told that they would leave for Cape Town on the 20th. This time the authorities were as good as their word. The Green Howards volunteers soon followed them and sailed from Cape Town on 16 May.

At home the return of the volunteers sparked a revival of the patriotic fervour which had accompanied their recruitment and departure but which had abated as the war dragged on. The Green Howards arrived back in Richmond, Yorkshire on 10 June where Mackenzie found that "our reception was most enthusiastic and we were splendidly and hospitably treated by the Mayor and Corporation and, indeed, by the whole of the inhabitants." When he and his comrades from Redcar arrived in their home town later that day the scenes were "wildly enthusiastic". Led by two military bands, they marched through cheering crowds to a platform where they were presented with an illuminated address to which was later added a new suit and an inscribed silver watch.

The Norfolk Regiment Volunteer Service Company was greeted by scenes which could have been celebrating some great victory rather than their return from a war which showed no sign of ending. As their train approached Norwich, small rural railway stations were packed with cheering crowds waving flags. For the last two miles the company's approach was announced by fog signals detonated on the line and in Norwich itself the men were played through the streets by massed bands to the Market Place, which was ablaze with torchlight. Each man was then summoned up to a platform where the Mayoress of Norwich gave him a silver medal inscribed "presented by the Mayor and citizens of Norwich" with a red, white and blue ribbon. "This day was more than compensation for all we have gone through," wrote Bryant.

Communities throughout Britain were determined to provide their volunteers with mementoes of their service. In the Wiltshire railway town of Swindon, a Yeomanry and Volunteers Reception Committee was set up to collect subscriptions and after some debate it was decided that each man should receive an illuminated address and a silver watch inscribed with his name. When the main body of men from the Imperial Yeomanry returned in July, the *North Wilts Herald* recorded that "the whole route from the railway station to the square in Old Swindon was one bewildering mass of fluttering flags" and that at one point "the sky was almost shut out with bunting". As the yeomen, led by four mounted police officers, rode through the streets "there was a continuous round of cheering which now and again broke into a tumultuous roar."[31] A month later twenty-five yeomen, twenty-three men from the Volunteer Service Company and six St John Ambulance Brigade volunteers received their gifts at a banquet at the town's Corn Exchange. The patriotic speeches by local dignitaries were typically long-winded and pompous. It took the presence of Sergeant-Major A.J. Lyford, who had had part of his jaw blown off by a Boer shell at the siege of Ladybrand, to remind them of the price that some had paid for going to South Africa.

Some of the smallest and unlikeliest places struck medals for their volunteers. The little town of Bedale in rural north Yorkshire, which had a population of just 1,100, gave a nine carat gold medal to nine local men who had volunteered for the war at a ceremony which would not have disgraced much larger communities. In Worcestershire the local council in Bewdley, with less than 3,000 inhabitants, presented handsome silver medals to sixteen volunteers and another seven to the families of those who had died in South Africa. Even in Dublin, where much of the population regarded the war as nothing more than British imperial bullying, a gold medal was struck for returning members of the 61st Company Imperial Yeomanry, which had been recruited in the Irish capital.[32]

The volunteers returned having won the general, if sometimes grudging, approval of their regular comrades in arms. As soldiers they had faults but given their hasty recruitment and lack of training this was hardly surprising. The CIV infantry battalion started off as an unfit collection of individualists with NCOs often unwilling to assert their authority and some officers of questionable quality. After a few weeks' training in South Africa followed by some hard marching and fighting during Roberts's advance across the Boer republics, they had improved out of all recognition. This was partly due to the high calibre of the recruits but also because of some intelligent leadership by Mackinnon, their commanding officer, and Bailey, their adjutant. As regular officers from the Guards they might have been expected to have taken an inflexible attitude towards their mixed band of gifted civilians but instead they chose to harness their men's intelligence rather than crush it. The result was the CIV's finest hour at Doornkop when intelligent use of cover enabled the regiment to advance with relatively few casualties.

The CIV attracted plenty of criticism for its early return home but very little for its performance on the battlefield. Mackinnon might not have been the most impartial witness when he told the Royal Commission that "no men could have been steadier than the City Imperial Volunteers were under fire"[33], but Ian Hamilton, under whom the regiment served for much of its time in South Africa, was equally complimentary. "They ripened very quickly," he said. "They improved before my eyes. The crossing of the Zand River was the first time I let them go at all and I was not quite sure of them but they were all right and then they did still better at Doornkop and at Diamond Hill they did very well indeed."[34] The Commission concluded that "the evidence given by officers who had the opportunity of seeing the work of this corps was unanimous in favour of their merit."[35]

The Volunteer Service Companies were also well thought of. They had the advantage of serving with the regulars of their regiments for months in South Africa and were usually intelligent enough to absorb the best ways of the latter while avoiding the worst. Buller, who had a number of the companies with the Army of Natal, commented that "they did very well indeed"[36] while Methuen remarked that they "seemed to me to do very good work."[37] Roberts said, "It was quite wonderful the way which the Volunteer Companies did when they joined the regular battalion. They fitted themselves into it and in a very few days they were excellent."[38] Regular officers felt able to support this very cautious experiment in using the Volunteer Force overseas but would never have backed the creation of large numbers of all-Volunteer units, such as the CIV, for the war. Some leading figures in the Volunteer movement favoured recruiting entire battalions from the best men in the Force in preference to the Volunteer Service Company system. Both groups agreed that the Volunteer Force as a whole was not fit for active service overseas.

The Imperial Yeomanry, with the surrender at Lindley and other lesser catastrophes still fresh in the military and public mind, attracted more mixed reviews. Their shooting was poor and the men's horsemastership surprisingly bad, although most could ride because they came from the country or from social backgrounds where they had learned to do so. Their failure to look after their animals was largely because they were not used to operating in a country where the harsh climate would quickly cripple or kill their horses unless they took good care of them. Both yeomen and colonial troops had a tendency to go everywhere at the gallop with fatal consequences for their mounts. Brabazon recalled that typically a man "if he rode into Pretoria to get a tooth pick or a glass of beer, would gallop his eight or ten miles there and back."[39] Rundle found that it was hard to get the Imperial Yeomanry to dismount from their horses when they halted and that "they

97

would sit upon them for half an hour unless somebody told them to get off".[40] Methuen, who commanded Imperial Yeomanry units throughout the war, discovered that in time they became fair horsemasters if he concentrated their minds by ordering them to march on foot. "They seemed at first to have an idea that I had an unlimited supply of horses always ready for them at a moment's notice," he recalled.[41] Many yeomen simply disliked the bad-tempered Argentinian and Hungarian animals they were given in South Africa and Rose-Innes accused the horses of spending "their leisure time in devising new means of exasperating those whose duty it is to attend them".[9] The result of all this was that frequently the yeomanry was stranded with sick or exhausted animals while the Boers, who normally had at least one spare horse per man, ran rings round them.

The officers of the first contingent of the Imperial Yeomanry were far superior to those of the second but were not an unqualified success. Some of those with titles and connections quickly found themselves jobs on Roberts's staff well away from any fighting while others drifted home within a few months if they were bored or if life had become too uncomfortable. Lord Scarborough, who had turned down the command of the 3rd Battalion in favour of the experienced Younghusband, said that the few commanding officers selected from the home yeomanry regiments were mostly not up to the job. By contrast the sub-alterns from these regiments were excellent. "It was simply a question of gaining experience," he said.[42] Some of the Imperial Yeomanry grumbled about being led by militia officers. Fowler told his family that the 1st (Wiltshire) Company "have been badly treated by having been put under militia or ex-militia officers who know nothing about cavalry or mounted infantry work" and complained that "this has lessened our chance of getting a show in the fighting."[10]

However, the Imperial Yeomanry at least had the advantage of having a ready supply of good replacement officers within its own ranks, which contained better raw material than any force which had ever left Britain. As far as possible the senior non-commissioned officers were recruited from the permanent staff of yeomanry regiments or from ex-regulars, but some of the latter had not served for many years and the battalion staffs proved woefully inadequate. The biggest problem among the rank and file was lack of experience which was not helped by the fact that the entire British Army was attempting to get to grips with a war which it had not been trained to fight. Methuen said: "They bought their experience rather expensively at first but I could place implicit reliance in them after a short time. This good result was due to their individual intelligence, their independence and the confidence they, with justice, placed in the leading of many of their officers."[43] Regular soldiers were frequently astounded by the yeomen's capacity for using their own initiative. Peel recalled being sent on outpost duty with two other men near Lindley. Finding it "to be a perfectly useless position" they moved on a mile or two to a better one which gave them a commanding view of the country. Shortly afterwards a party of regulars arrived who were astonished that the yeomen were without a sergeant to tell them what to do and that they had decided on the position themselves. "They thought the world was upside down," wrote Peel. A British cavalry officer told Peel that he would rather command Imperial Yeomanry than regular cavalry because "I don't say they are perfect soldiers but they are learning every day and they haven't had the common sense kicked out of them."[6]

The other side of the coin, the expense to which Methuen referred, was that the Imperial Yeomanry did not have the discipline and cohesion of regular soldiers. Roberts, although sometimes complimentary about the yeomanry, was nervous about them, referring to "the great anxiety I felt in regard to my communications being held in many places by partially trained troops such as the militia and the hastily raised yeomanry . . . the result was that our ill trained troops often led me into great difficulties." Disasters such as Lindley and Rhenoster River, he said, "showed what a danger it was to depend on troops who were not thoroughly disciplined and properly trained."[44] There is no doubt that the yeomanry often performed better if they were alongside the steadying influence of good regulars, as at

Ladybrand. But actions such as Hartebeestfontein showed that by the time they went home the best among them were capable of fighting well in any situation. A hastily raised citizen force operating in difficult circumstances against a formidable enemy had not disgraced itself.

CHAPTER FIVE

TRIUMPHS AND DISASTERS

BOSHOF. 5 April, 1900.

The Imperial Yeomanry fought its first action at Boshof, north-east of Kimberley, on 5 April, 1900. It faced a most unlikely opponent, a Frenchman who, like the yeomen, had volunteered to fight. The Count de Villebois-Mareuil had a quixotic nature, a passionate belief in the Boer cause and a love of military life undimmed since his retirement from the French army. He had at one time commanded the French Foreign Legion and, after leaving the army as a Colonel in 1896, made a living as a military writer. On the outbreak of the war he immediately went to South Africa, one of more than two thousand foreign volunteers who offered their services to the Boers. He was said to have been responsible for the disposition of the Boers when they repulsed the British at Colenso and later went from camp to camp criti-cizing the lack of initiative shown by their commanders at the sieges of Ladysmith and Kimberley.

The Boers decided to make him a General and asked him to organize all the foreign volunteers into one force. Instead of carrying out this task, the Count continued to do exactly as he liked and in March 1900 set off towards Boshof, a small town in the Orange Free State, 33 miles from Kimberley. He had with him about 100 foreign volunteers and some twenty-five Boers. His plan was to attack Boshof, which he believed to be lightly defended, and then continue south to dynamite the railway bridge over the River Modder, cutting Methuen's communications.

101

Had he not taken eleven days to cover the 80 miles from Brandfort to Tweefontein, just outside Boshof, he would have stood more chance of success. The reason for the Count's slow progress is unknown but, unfortunately for him, the day before he arrived Methuen had concentrated six and a half battalions of infantry, twenty-two artillery guns and 1,000 mounted men in Boshof.

Native scouts soon alerted Methuen to the presence of the Count's force on the morning of 5 April and the British force quickly stirred into action. The horses were out grazing when the news arrived, but within 35 minutes 500 Imperial Yeomanry under Chesham, 250 men of the Kimberley Mounted Corps and the 4th Battery Royal Field Artillery were galloping across the plain on which Boshof stood towards the Count's camp five miles to the south-east. The Yeomanry were from the 9th (Yorkshire Hussars), 10th (Sherwood Rangers), 11th (Yorkshire Dragoons), 12th (South Nottinghamshire Hussars) and 40th (Oxfordshire) companies. Peel, serving with the latter, scented action for the first time, but to his disgust found himself put in charge of the company water cart drawn by mules. Even so, as he struggled along trying to keep up, he found it an extraordinary and impressive sight, the troops advancing in a wide semi-circle. This was what so many of the yeomanry had joined for, going hell for leather towards an enemy who would stay to fight.

The native scouts kept the British force concealed behind some low hills until it was within 2,500 yards of the Count's position. But even when he realized that he was about to be attacked by a vastly superior force, the Frenchman's undoubted courage and sense of honour prevailed over Boer cunning and common sense. His force was on two kopjes, the foreign volunteers on one and the Boers with them on the other but the latter mounted their horses and retreated as the British started to outflank the position. Methuen sent some of the Imperial Yeomanry round to the left, the Kimberley Mounted Corps galloped to the right and the rest of the yeomen dismounted and took up positions in front. Peel managed to leave his cart with the ammunition column and hastened forwards towards the fray. Too late to be involved in the fighting but in time to be a spectator, he recalled: "The position held by the enemy was a sort of natural fortress, crowned with great boulders, behind which a man could stand secure from rifle fire. Behind it, uneven ground stretched away towards some hilly country in which pursuit would have been difficult."[1]

A four-hour fight followed, the Count completely surrounded, with the onset of darkness providing the only hope of escape. The Imperial Yeomanry moved cautiously forward. Methuen told Roberts in his despatch: "The order was intelligently carried out, care being taken to advance very slowly taking all advantage of the fine cover given by the bushes and boulders."[2] Inevitably there were casualties and Captain Cecil Boyle of the Oxfordshire Company became the first officer of the Imperial Yeomanry to be killed in the war. The British artillery opened fire but was of limited use because the two sides were now so close that the gunners had to take care to avoid hitting their own men. After the first shell one of the Count's volunteers rushed out towards their horses, apparently trying to escape, but was killed by a storm of rifle fire.[1] The defenders sent out a message saying that they intended to fight to the last, but at 6pm, as darkness was about to fall, they raised a white flag. The Count had just been killed by a shell, the loss of their leader causing a collapse in morale. They had also just heard the Imperial Yeomanry, now only 15 yards away in some places, being ordered to fix bayonets and storm the position. The prospect terrified them and the battle was almost over.

However, as the British troops rose to accept the surrender, a single shot rang out from the defenders killing 2nd Lieutenant Arthur Williams of the Sherwood Rangers Company. His angry comrades immediately shot dead the man responsible. For the most part the Count's motley band of volunteers, predominantly Frenchmen and Germans, with some Dutch and Russians, seemed relieved to be taken prisoner. A wounded Corsican asked Peel if he would be able to work in a British hospital and was amused when told that he was more likely to be sent to St Helena, where his compatriot Napoleon had been imprisoned. Given the ferocity of the fire, the casualties on both sides had been surprisingly light. The Boer volunteers had lost ten killed, including the Count, eleven wounded and fifty-one unwounded prisoners. A few had managed to escape. As well as the two officers who died, the Imperial Yeomanry lost one sergeant killed and eight men wounded, while the Kimberley colonial troops had two wounded. The dead, all of whom had come from overseas to fight in a war which did not directly affect them, were buried side by side in Boshof cemetery under the shadow of some Cypress trees. Villebois-Mareuil was buried with full military honours, a British bugler sounding the Last Post over the Frenchman's grave. One of the Russian prisoners, who claimed to be a prince, solemnly delivered an oration at the graveside. Methuen not only attended his funeral but had a headstone erected. It was a gesture of respect from one professional soldier to another, even if the Count's tactical grasp of the situation had not equalled his courage. He was buried on the day on which, according to the plans found on his body, he had intended to attack Boshof.

Boshof, although a small action, was a decisive and useful victory for the British, attracting much international publicity because of the Count's death. For the Imperial Yeomanry, it provided vital evidence that it was much better than its detractors had predicted. A *Times* war correspondent, who was present, praised the yeomen's performance. "Some people, both out here and at home, had ventured to declare that they would prove to be of very little use," wrote the unnamed journalist. "The event however has proved these critics to have been false prophets. Not only did the yeomanry show fine courage under fire, but they did their work throughout in exactly the fashion that should be followed in all operations similiar to that in which they found themselves engaged."[3] Roberts wrote to Lansdowne: "The troops seem to have behaved admirably and it is satisfactory to notice that the Imperial Yeomanry rendered valuable service."[2] It was an encouraging start and the yeomen had demonstrated a good eye for using ground but the problem was that the Boers would never have let themselves be trapped in the same way as the Count. The Imperial Yeomanry was to find time after time that the enemy had vanished and that often it would be defending rather than attacking in a war against a foe more skilled at mobile warfare than the yeomen were.

DOORNKOP 29 May, 1900.

Doornkop was a battle which should never have been fought, but which enabled the British to wipe a past humiliation off the slate. On this rocky ridge of hills south-west of Johannesburg, a few miles from the gold mines of the Rand, Dr Jameson's raiders had been cornered by the Boers in 1895. With no sign of the Transvaal Uitlanders rising to support them and having lost sixteen men killed, the raiders surrendered. Doornkop never evoked such a strong need for revenge as the British defeat by the Boers at Majuba in 1881, but Lieutenant-General Ian Hamilton seems to have felt that it was somewhere he ought to fight. There was certainly no convincing tactical reason for his decision to launch an all-out infantry assault against a position which he could have outflanked. Even the British order of battle at Doornkop on 29 May, 1900, was symbolic. Hamilton's force contained both the Gordon Highlanders, one of the regiments humiliated at Majuba, and the CIV, the City of London's own regiment, about to play its part in capturing the mines in which the City's financiers had invested so much.

Roberts's plan for capturing Johannesburg and the mines was simple. Twenty thousand men, French's cavalry and Hamilton's force, were to hook round to the west of Johannesburg, cutting the main road from the Rand towns to the city. To achieve this he had ordered Hamilton to move from his right flank to his left, west of the main railway line through the Transvaal. Meanwhile a second force of similar size would go straight up the railway and outflank Johannesburg from the east. The tactics had worked throughout Roberts's advance, often forcing the Boers back without a fight. This time, however, there was to be no walkover.

The Boers were spread out along a line of rocky hills east of the formidable kopje of Doornkop. Their front was about five miles long, the natural strength of the position making up for the fact that their forces were thinly stretched. They had set fire to the grass in front of the hills, leaving a blackened wasteland against which khaki uniforms were clearly and lethally visible. To the east another force of Transvaalers defended the hills of the Kliprivers Berg. At dawn on the 29th Hamilton's column marched north from its bivouac at Syferfontein and at 1pm reached the Klip River, which ran across the front of the Boer position. There they relieved Major-General John French, later commander of the British Expeditionary Force in 1914, whose mounted men had already clashed with the defenders and who then set off to outflank the Boers from the west. Despite the near certainty that French's move alone would have shifted the Boers from their defensive positions, Hamilton decided on a frontal attack. His reasons for not attacking the Boers on the Kliprivers Berg were

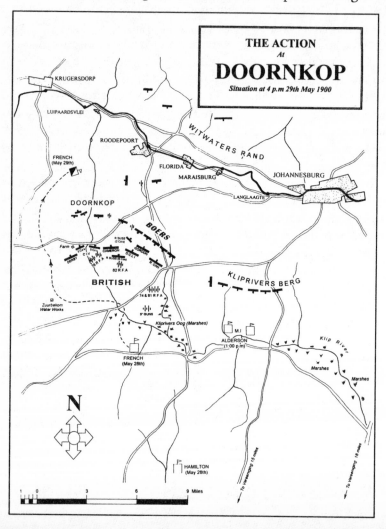

sound enough, the ground being difficult and the river at that point mostly impassable for guns, but his professed logic for the assault to the west is not convincing. He said that the enemy's extended line was weak, that his own men were short of rations and had to get to Florida, outside Johannesburg, to get supplies quickly and that he was afraid of taking his force too far away from the men guarding the hills behind him. In fact the Boer defences proved a tough nut to crack, he did not reach Florida until the next day despite the assault and the enemy was not in sufficient strength to have launched a serious attack on his rear. He had enough men to protect his flank while sending most of his force to follow French. But the prize of a victory at Doornkop appears to have been too great to resist. Something else may also have driven Hamilton to fight. He had a shattered wrist, smashed by a Boer bullet, to remind him constantly of his service with the Gordons at Majuba.

The British moved north-westwards and occupied positions opposite the Boers, whose defences stretched from Doornkop to the Potchefstroom road. The main attacking force consisted of the 19th Brigade, commanded by Major-General Horace Smith-Dorrien, which included the Gordons, and the 21st Brigade, of which the CIV was part, commanded, confusingly, by Major-General Bruce Hamilton. Smith-Dorrien took over command of all the infantry for the day, handing over his brigade to Lieutenant-Colonel James Spens of the King's Shropshire Light Infantry. The two brigades were to advance simultaneously, the 21st on the British left and the 19th on the right and it was decided, this being a day for symbolism, that the CIV and the Gordons should lead the way. The attack did not go according to plan, the 21st Brigade setting off at 2pm, half an hour before the 19th, and the British artillery not opening fire until 2.45pm, by which time the infantry was only 2,000 yards from the Boers.[4]

Smith-Dorrien had overruled Bruce Hamilton, who wanted to attack Doornkop itself, ordering him to avoid it and attack the kopjes to the east because he believed that it was impossible to assault both with the forces available. The CIV began its advance. It was an important day for the regiment, the first sizeable action in which an entire battalion of British volunteer infantry had been involved. Mackinnon led the men forward and after they had advanced for about 1,000 yards they halted as pom-pom fire poured in from a kopje to their left while they were simultaneously enfiladed by rifle fire from their right. Already their advance was being watched with interest by regular soldiers, the volunteers moving forward in short rushes, using all the little cover that was available, each group of men being given covering fire by their comrades. Although similar tactics had been devised on the Natal front, this was not the traditional way in which the British infantry had gone about its business. Ironically, the CIV had been drilled in the tactic by its regular Adjutant, Captain the Hon Joseph Bailey of the Grenadier Guards.[5]

Mackinnon led three companies of the CIV against the hill to their left while the five remaining companies, under Colonel Lord Albemarle, pushed north-eastwards towards a long spur which dominated the position. Both parts of the battalion were under constant heavy fire. Smith-Dorrien, worried that the 21st Brigade was moving too far to the left away from the 19th, ordered Mackinnon not to advance further but it was too late. Some of the CIV, under Captain Edward Trotter, Mackinnon's orderly officer, had rushed the hill and carried it after a sharp fight. About 500 Boers abandoned the kopje and galloped north towards Krugersdorp. As the chorus of the Boer Mausers grew ever louder, Albemarle's men halted for a time while the Cameron Highlanders came up on the right and preparations were made to storm the long spur. Smoke from the grass fires started by the Boers hung across the battlefield like a fog, making sighting difficult for the British artillery. Then the CIV and the Camerons, together with some men from the Royal Sussex Regiment, moved forward again in short rushes and by twilight the 21st Brigade was on the ridge. The Boers fell back to rocks in the rear before eventually fading away from the battlefield.

The CIV, exhausted but triumphant, had fired 9,500 rounds and taken two Boer strongholds without a single man being killed and with only one officer and eleven other ranks wounded. "This happy result is in great measure attributable to the intelligent manner in which the men had learned to take cover," wrote Mackinnon. "When one saw the bullets skipping through and in front of and behind the ranks one thought that not a man could escape being hit."[5] Lloyd recalled:"There is hardly a man in the regiment who was not within a yard or two of death that day."[6]

The Gordons had little use for such tactics, relying on *esprit de corps* and iron discipline rather than individual initiative. The position which the Highlanders had to assault on the British right was even more difficult than that which faced the CIV. It had the same blackened death zone of burnt grass but the gently undulating slope up to the Boer defences provided even less cover. However, it is by no means certain that the Gordons would have used cover even if there had been any. Instead of advancing as quickly as possible, each line of kilted soldiers rose and set off at a steady walk towards the Boers, 4,000 yards away. They were in open order, about 15 yards between each man and the lines well apart, but otherwise the tactics had changed little in fifty years. They remained absolutely silent and their discipline was so perfect that an order to change direction amid the most terrible rifle fire was obeyed as if they were on a parade ground. The Gordons only advanced at the double when they got close to the Boers and opened fire for the first time when they were within 200 yards. Fixing bayonets, they charged and took the first position, only to discover that it was a false crest, the real summit being 200 yards to the rear. Finally, soon after 5pm, they charged and evicted the Boers from their last defences. The Gordons had ninety-four casualties, twenty-one of whom were killed or died of their wounds. Their Volunteer Service Company had suffered badly with three killed and ten wounded. The Royal Canadian Regiment, advancing on the Gordons' right, used such cover as there was to good effect and had only seven men wounded. In the British lines men had watched in awestruck silence. When Winston Churchill interviewed one of the Gordons after the battle, his explanation for this astonishing display of unthinking courage was simple."It had to be done," he said.[7]

The Boers on Doornkop itself, increasingly unsettled by

French's successful flanking movement, abandoned their position, galloping across the front of the British infantry. But the exhausted troops mistook them for French's cavalry and they escaped into the darkness. The battle had been won at a cost to the British of twenty-eight dead and 134 wounded and the way to the Rand lay open. The CIV won high praise for its tactics. Ian Hamilton wrote in his despatch: "I think Colonel Mackinnon, Colonel Lord Albemarle and the CIV generally deserve the greatest credit for this fine performance which took place at the end of an 18-hour march during which both water and food had been hard to come by."[8] Smith-Dorrien said that the CIVs' performance "convinced me that this corps, at any rate, of our volunteers is as skilled as the most skilful of our regulars at skirmishing."[4] In fact they had proved themselves a great deal more skilled than most. The tragedy was that Churchill's Gordon Highlander was wrong. Taking the ridges next to Doornkop never "had to be done" at all.

LINDLEY 27–31 May, 1900.

The disaster suffered by the 13th Battalion at Lindley in May, 1900, marked the end of the Imperial Yeomanry dream. Wyndham, the creator of the Yeomanry, had wanted it to represent the cream of British manhood and the 13th Battalion took his scheme to its ultimate extreme. The 45th Company from Dublin had Masters of Foxhounds and the sons of much of Ireland's legal establishment in its ranks. The 47th, the Duke of Cambridge's Own, came from some of England's wealthiest families, and the 46th and 54th from Belfast represented Ulster Unionism's commitment to the Imperial cause. The battalion's officers included Lord Longford, Lord Ennismore, the Earl of Leitrim, James Craig, later Lord Craigavon, and Sir John Power of the Irish whiskey distilling family. Politics, money, patriotism and class, the combination was irresistible to the press and public, some of whom dubbed the battalion the 'Millionaires' Own'.

The DCOs, well connected as well as well heeled, only spent

a week in the unpleasant surroundings of the Imperial Yeomanry camp at Maitland. Admittedly their reward was weeks of training on the edge of the Karoo Desert north of Cape Town but life there was eased by the arrival of the Dublin men to keep them company and of a spectacular array of food, drink and other luxuries which had been sent out from England. On 15 May the two companies arrived in Bloemfontein to meet the Ulstermen, who had come straight from Maitland, and just a week later the newly assembled battalion was given its first orders for active service.

The first of the many controversies which characterized the entire Lindley fiasco now took place. Colvile had already been told by Roberts's headquarters that the 13th Battalion was to join his 9th Division, which was short of mounted troops. The intention had been that the yeomanry should link up with him at Ventersburg, south of Kroonstad, but because they were delayed waiting for forage they had not arrived by the time he left on the

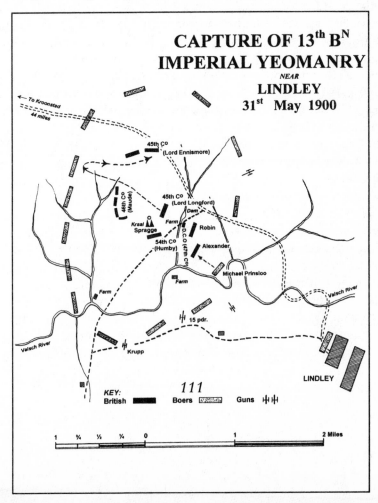

CAPTURE OF 13th B^N IMPERIAL YEOMANRY
NEAR
LINDLEY
31st May 1900

111

KEY:
British ▬▬ Boers ▨▨▨ Guns ┠┨ ┠┨

24th. Colvile's task was to march east to Lindley and then north to Heilbron, taking Hamilton's place on Roberts's right as the British advanced on Johannesburg. Having failed to meet up with him, the 13th was ordered to continue straight up the railway line to Kroonstad.

There the commanding officer of the battalion, Lieutenant-Colonel Basil Spragge, an experienced regular infantry officer, was handed a telegram, the origins of which are still a mystery. Spragge told the Court of Inquiry which investigated the Lindley affair: "I was shown a telegram to the Commandant Kroonstad from General Colvile directing me to join him with my regiment at Lindley."[9] Colvile denied ever having sent the telegram and his intelligence officer later claimed that it was addressed to Spragge by name. If that was the case it could not have come from Colvile, who did not know who the commander of the 13th was. If his name had been on it, Spragge should have been suspicious because such an order would not normally have been addressed to him personally but he remained adamant that it was not. There has been speculation that the Boers had tapped the telegraph lines and sent a bogus message to lure the yeomanry to destruction.[10] If so, it was a risky deception because Colvile was going to Lindley and might have stayed there long enough for Spragge to catch up with him. The addition of the yeomen, despite their inexperience, would have been a bonus for the under-strength 9th Division. The most likely explanation is that this was bad staff work by British headquarters who issued the order to Spragge but did not tell Colvile, who seems to have been genuinely unaware that the yeomanry were going to Lindley.

The 13th marched at daybreak on the 26th and that afternoon met a party of armed Boers. They claimed to be going to Kroonstad to surrender and Spragge naively disarmed them, invited them to lunch and then allowed them to go. The Boers promptly returned to Lindley with much valuable information. Private Maurice Fitzgibbon of the Dublin company, son of one of Ireland's most senior judges, recalled: "The scouts of the Boer commandos at Lindley had been permitted to enter our lines to find out our numbers, our armaments and the amount of our supplies, had even had lunch with us and all this information and hospitality at the expense of a few out-of-date rifles and a few perjured oaths."[11] Disaster had moved a step closer. The Boers now knew of the yeomanry's approach but Colvile did not.

When the yeomanry rode into Lindley the following afternoon it quickly became apparent that all was not well. Spragge told the inquiry: "I found General Colvile gone. No letter or message of any sort for me, the town ominously deserted and the people too frightened to give any information."[12] Private Norman Reckitt of the DCOs[10] thought that the woman serving food in the hotel was "suspiciously obliging" and within an hour the Boers opened fire from some of the houses. As Reckitt got his horse under cover "the bullets were whizzing pretty thickly across the square and little spurts of dust were to be seen all around." One of the Dublins gave a cry and fell, another man was hit in the knee. The yeomen were ordered to evacuate the town, which was commanded by hills and difficult to defend, and retreat to where they had left their baggage, three miles to the west on the Kroonstad road. After fighting a rearguard action they regrouped on the northern bank of the Valsch River.

Spragge now faced the most crucial decision of the entire Lindley affair. He could either make a run for it or set up his defences and send for help. His decision to do the latter was later heavily criticized, often by those with no detailed knowledge of his situation and no practical experience of the war in South Africa. Spragge could not have ordered a move that night, although there was a window of opportunity, albeit a brief and highly risky one, the following morning. By the time the entire battalion had regrouped outside Lindley it was about 5pm, the men were tired and so were the horses which had come 87 miles in three days. If Spragge had abandoned his baggage and tried to escape from the Boer noose that night the 13th Battalion would probably have met with disaster. These were inexperienced troops, still soft from too much good living in Britain and un-familiar with the country; to expect them to make a successful night march on exhausted horses was unrealistic. The only time that Spragge might have successfully withdrawn was early the following morning when his men and horses had got some rest and before the Boers had gathered around him in large numbers. But even then, if he had abandoned his baggage and ridden as fast as possible towards safety, it was a desperately dangerous course of action. The Boers loved nothing more than sweeping down on vulnerable British columns and the 13th, which had never fired a shot in anger before it rode into Lindley, would have been easy prey for the commandos. Furthermore Spragge knew that Rundle's 8th Division was in the area as well as Colvile and so his expectations of help were not unreasonable. His decision to stay where he was may have lacked the dash and drama of a gallop for safety but it was based on sound military common sense.

The Boers did not attack as the battalion prepared its defences on the night of the 27th. This gave Spragge the chance to send messages asking for help to both Rundle and Colvile. His message to the latter read: "Found no one in Lindley but Boers; have 500 men but only one day's food. Have stopped three miles back on Kroonstad road. I want help to get out without great loss." His message to Rundle was couched in similar terms. Both arrived safely but neither was to produce the assistance which he was asking for.

Colvile was already 18 miles north of Lindley and encountering resistance during his march to Heilbron. When two messengers from Spragge arrived at 7am on the 28th, Colvile did not get the impression that the yeomanry was in any immediate peril. Part of the problem lay with Spragge's wording "have 500 men but only one day's food". In his despatch to Roberts on 31 May Colvile wrote: "I gathered both from his report and in conversation with the despatch riders that his chief difficulty was that of supplies."[13] Most of Colvile's despatch, written on the day of the yeomanry's surrender but before the news had come through, is devoted to his fighting on the way to Heilbron. It is clear that Spragge's problems were far down his list of priorities. Colvile, who was already out of favour with Roberts, was under the impression that it was essential to the Commander-in-Chief's overall plan for him to get to Heilbron by the 29th. It later transpired that it would not have mattered if he had not arrived there for another week but his mind was firmly fixed on the big picture. Colvile's force was too weak to be divided and part of it sent back to Lindley so he decided to press on. He explained, "I did not feel justified in fighting my way back to the assistance of a mobile force which would in all probability be a day's march away by the time I reached Lindley." In a message to Spragge he wrote: "If you cannot join me by road to Heilbron you must retire on Kroonstad, living on country, and, if necessary, abandon your wagons." He sent the two yeomen and a native messenger back to Spragge by separate routes but, in an ominous development, they all returned after being unable to get through. Spragge was therefore unaware that no help would be forthcoming from Colvile. The latter did not tell headquarters what he knew about Spragge's situation for another 24 hours.

Rundle was further away, 40 miles to the south at Senekal. When Spragge's plea for help arrived he decided that as the latter had only one day's supplies he was too far away to help him directly. He therefore decided to try to draw Boer forces away from Lindley by mounting a diversionary attack eastwards towards Bethlehem. On the 30th Spragge sent another message to Rundle in which he predicted "can hold on unless they bring guns which they have sent for" and added, less accurately, "I can get out but shall lose in doing so." The messengers, a soldier called Smith and a native guide, were captured and Smith was shot on the spot by the Boers, probably because he was in civilian clothes.[14] The 13th Battalion was now completely encircled and the option of making a run for it was gone. No help was on the way and the Boers, fully aware of the prestige of those they had surrounded, had sent for reinforcements and artillery.

The position which Spragge had chosen was not a bad one, although the need to incorporate grazing for the horses and for a flock of sheep which the battalion had commandeered, meant that it was rather extended. Its centre was a 500-yard-wide valley running south from the Kroonstad road to the Valsch River. On the eastern side were two stony kopjes, the keys to the entire position, which were defended by the DCOs under Captain Clive Keith, a former officer in the 3rd Dragoon Guards. The valley was bounded to the north-west by a low plateau rising to a ridge with two conical kopjes. The 46th (Ulster) Company under Captain R.A.Maude occupied the south-western end of the plateau and the Irish Hunt Company, commanded by Captain Lord Longford, had outposts on the conical kopjes and the rest of its men at a kraal further back. The 54th (Ulster) Company, led by Captain James Humby, was kept in the valley as a reserve guarding the horses and transport. As well as pasture for the animals, there was a good water supply in the valley and the sheep supplemented the battalion's rations, although food was still short. They had plenty of ammunition and two small Colt guns but nothing which could counter Boer artillery.

Soon after sunrise on the 28th the yeomen heard the crack of the first Boer rifleshots. The ground was mostly too hard to dig trenches and they lacked the right tools but the British had managed to build a number of stone shelters during the night which provided some cover. Gradually the fire increased in intensity and Reckitt recalled: "The men on the kopjes under Captain Keith were having a hot time of it. They signalled that there was a heavy fire at them from three different points but they had managed to build breastworks and were keeping the Boers at a distance. It was evident that the enemy outnumbered us and were increasing in strength." That afternoon Keith, the DCO's popular commander, was killed by a bullet through the head. But, despite some casualties and gnawing hunger, on the 28th and 29th the British were not under serious pressure from the Boers.

However, on the evening of the 29th Piet De Wet arrived with reinforcements bringing the Boer forces up to about 2,500 men. More crucially, he brought with him four artillery pieces which were to seal the fate of the defenders. On the 30th the Boers drew the circle in more tightly and Spragge found that the grazing for his animals was becoming restricted. He sent Lieutenant Hugh Montgomery and sixteen men of the 46th Company to seize a ridge 2,000 yards to the west from which Boer marksmen were causing problems for the British. Five of the men hung back and although Montgomery got a foothold on the ridge he and his remaining force were surprised and taken prisoners that afternoon. Early the following morning Lord

1. An absent-minded beggar. Caton Woodville's 'gentleman in khaki' which illustrated the verses of Kipling's 'The Absent-Minded Beggar'. (National Army Museum.)

2. George Wyndham, Parliamentary Under-Secretary at the War Office, who first proposed raising the Imperial Yeomanry. (National Army Museum.)

3. Colonel Sir Howard Vincent MP, Commanding Officer of the Queen's Westminster Volunteers and a persistent campaigner for the auxiliary forces' involvement in the war. (National Army Museum.)

4. Brigadier-General Lord Chesham, one of the founders of the Imperial Yeomanry, who commanded the 10th Battalion in South Africa.

5. Sir Alfred Newton, the Lord Mayor of London, who was the driving force behind the raising of the CIV.

6. The CIV mounted infantry prior to its departure from London in 1900.

7. Farewell supper for some of the CIV held at the Mansion House in London on 26 January, 1900.

8. The first contingent of the CIV mobbed by enthusiastic crowds on its way to Nine Elms station in London on 13 January, 1900.

9. Men of the CIV aboard the *Garth Castle*, the ship which took them to South Africa in 1900.

10. Colonel Henry Mackinnon, Grenadier Guards, who commanded the CIV in South Africa.

11. Officers of the contingent of the 1st Hampshire Imperial Yeomanry.

12. The 48th (North Somerset) Company, Imperial Yeomanry, before leaving for South Africa in 1900.

13. Six brothers named Westley who enlisted in the 62nd (Middlesex) Company Imperial Yeomanry in 1900.

14. The Volunteer Service Company of the South Lancashire Regiment after boarding a troopship in Southampton in February, 1900.

15. British volunteers in action for the first time. The CIV mounted infantry advances on foot during its first action at Jacobsdaal, near Kimberley on 15 February, 1900.

16. The CIV infantry arrives at Orange River Station, February, 1900. (National Army Museum.)

17. 36th (West Kent) Company, Imperial Yeomanry, leaving camp on a reconnaissance, May, 1900. (National Army Museum.)

18. Lord Roberts, the British Commander-in-Chief in South Africa in 1900, who distrusted the volunteers but became Honorary Colonel of the CIV.

19. Lieutenant-General Lord Methuen, who commanded Imperial Yeomanry units for much of the war.

20. Major-General John Brabazon, Commanding Officer of the first contingent of Imperial Yeomanry in 1900, a post which quickly became meaningless.

21. Major Henry Dalbiac of the 34th (Middlesex) Company Imperial Yeomanry, whose recklessness led to his death in action at Senekal on 25 May, 1900.

22. Corporal Percy Ross of the 69th (Sussex) Company, Imperial Yeomanry.

23. Private Tom Brown of the 2nd (Wiltshire) Company, Imperial Yeomanry whose death in action on 20 August, 1900, left his brother Herbert grief-stricken. His family pinned his Queen's South Africa Medal to his photograph as a memorial.

24. The Volunteer Service Company of the Wiltshire Regiment in South Africa.

25. Lieutenant-General Sir Leslie Rundle inspects the first contingent men of the
11th Battalion, Imperial Yeomanry, at Harrismith, Orange Free State.
(National Army Museum.)

26. The return of the CIV to London. The parade passes through the Strand.

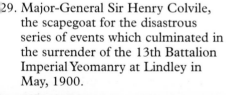

27. Percy Ross's cartoon illustrating the widespread bitterness in the Army about the early return of the CIV.

28. The Count de Villebois-Mareuil, the French volunteer killed fighting for the Boers in the Imperial Yeomanry's first action at Boshof on 5 April, 1900.

29. Major-General Sir Henry Colvile, the scapegoat for the disastrous series of events which culminated in the surrender of the 13th Battalion Imperial Yeomanry at Lindley in May, 1900.

30. Lieutenant-Colonel William Otter, the autocratic commanding officer of the 2nd Battalion Royal Canadian Regiment in South Africa.

31. Major George Williams, commanding officer at Tweefontein, who was killed and subsequently blamed for the capture of the camp.

32. Lieutenant Jack Watney, aged 20, of the 36th (West Kent) Company Imperial Yeomanry who was killed leading a charge at Tweefontein on Christmas Day, 1901.

33. Lieutenant-Colonel Basil Spragge, Commanding Officer of the 13th Battalion Imperial Yeomanry which surrendered at Lindley in May, 1900, with some of his officers. Spragge is at the head of the table on the right and second on his left is Captain C. M. Robin whose surrender left the battalion in a hopeless position. To Robin's left is Captain Lord Longford.

34. The first Tasmanian and Victorian contingents leave Melbourne, Australia, for South Africa in 1899.

35. From snow to the heat of the veldt. The guns of the Royal Canadian Field Artillery leave Ottawa, January, 1900.

36. 'De Wet's Own'. Men of the much-criticized second contingent of Imperial
Yeomanry in South Africa, 1901. (National Army Museum.)

37. Men of the second contingent Imperial Yeomanry serving in the 53rd (East Kent) Company. Several of those in the photograph were killed in the disaster at Tweefontein, on Christmas Day, 1901.

38. Men of the 100th (Northumberland) Company Imperial Yeomanry in 1902. By now many were barely distinguishable from the Boers they were fighting. (National Army Museum.)

Longford and forty men of the Dublin Hunt Company were sent to recapture the ridge which they did with great gallantry after a bayonet charge.

But by the morning of the 31st the writing was on the wall for the defenders, who had acquitted themselves well despite their lack of experience. During the night the Boers had brought three of their guns into position south of the Valsch and the fourth onto a flat-topped kopje about a mile north of the DCOs. Crouching in their positions the latter heard a boom followed by what Reckitt called "a peculiar shrieking in the air immediately above our heads" as the first shell came in. The DCOs on the two crucial kopjes took the brunt of the artillery fire. Reckitt recalled: "Another distant boom and a few moments of expectation. Someone had left a helmet and a greatcoat on a ledge of rock on the summit of the kopje a few yards in front. A few moments after the last boom there was a deafening crash and the piece of rock and the coat and helmet disappeared in a confused volcano of smoke and dust. They had got the range and our minutes were numbered." Another shell burst nearby where Lieutenant Aymer Lane, the son of a Major-General, had been directing his men. According to Reckitt: "After the cloud of dust had passed from around him, he appeared again uttering a peculiarly mild exclamation."

As matters reached a desperate climax outside Lindley, Rundle's attempt to draw the Boers away from the besieged yeomen came to nothing. On the 28th he marched eastwards from Senekal with 4,000 men, including the 4th Battalion and one company of the 11th Battalion Imperial Yeomanry. The Boers held positions on the Tafelberg and the Biddulphsberg, each side of the road. The next day Rundle decided to attack the northern face of the Biddulphsberg sending three companies of yeomanry to the north-east to guard his left flank while the other two remained south of the main assault. The latter, carried out by the Grenadier Guards, ran into heavy Boer fire which caused many casualties. This was made worse by the grass catching fire and burning to death some of the British wounded. The attack was called off when headquarters ordered Rundle to go south to

117

Ficksburg, having had little influence on the fate of Spragge's force.

Belatedly help was finally on its way to the 13th Battalion, although, as with almost everything in this sorry episode, this had its origins in a misunderstanding. On the 28th a message from Colvile explaining why he might not get to Heilbron by the following day was misinterpreted by headquarters as an appeal for help. Methuen was ordered to go to Colvile's assistance, picking up Spragge's force on the way. By the 30th, three days after the siege had begun, headquarters was still completely unaware of the seriousness of Spragge's plight. That day Methuen set off with a force which included the 3rd, 5th and 10th Battalions Imperial Yeomanry. In the afternoon Methuen heard that Colvile had arrived safely in Heilbron and later a messenger reached him with a telegram from Roberts. This told him that Spragge was "reported to be in a nasty place" and that, having relieved Colvile he should "then see what can be done for Spragge's Yeomanry". Knowing that Colvile was safe, Methuen hurried to the 13th Battalion's rescue.

But Spragge's situation was deteriorating quickly. Lord Longford, coming under shellfire in the position which he had captured only that morning, was ordered to leave it and join Lieutenant Lord Ennismore and the rest of the 45th Company on the more easterly of the two conical kopjes on the northern plateau. On the other side of the British position the DCOs were having an increasingly difficult time as more and more shells hit their position. Under cover of this fire, 200 Boers galloped up and ensconsed themselves among some boulders on the southernmost of the two stony kopjes.

Lieutenant Robert Alexander, in command on this kopje, said later that he received an order to retire which he believed to be from Captain C.M. Robin, who had taken charge of the DCOs after Keith was killed.[15] Others said that he received no such order,[16] but, whatever the truth , the DCOs abandoned the position and as they retreated towards the northern kopje a white flag was raised. The man responsible was Corporal Leonard Jacques of the DCOs, one of a small group manning a picquet

118

between the two hills. Jacques, doubtless panicked by the shell-fire, was immediately shot in the thigh by one of his comrades. Robin's inexperience and misplaced sense of honour then ensured disaster. He was under the mistaken impression that he was bound to respect his subordinate's surrender. Private Thomas McCrea of the 54th Company, one of a party of Ulstermen sent to re-inforce the kopje, heard Robin ordering the ceasefire. The distraught Robin said that he might as well blow out his brains but McCrea told him that he would prevent him from commit-ting suicide.[15] Robin moved off waving a white handkerchief and the kopje was surrendered. It commanded the whole British position and with its capture Spragge's situation became hopeless. Shortly afterwards at 2.30pm he ordered his force to surrender and although the gallant Longford fought on for a time eventu-ally he too had to give in. Longford had been badly wounded in the neck, face and wrist and had had a cigar removed from his mouth by a bullet. Fitzgibbon later recalled how, after the surrender, Boers approached the Dublin Hunt Company and "to our wonderment seized us by the hand saying, 'Well done, you fought well, right well'." One of the yeomen replied: "By George, you're sportsmen anyhow."[11]

The casualty list was a long one. Keith and sixteen other ranks had been killed, Sir John Power and three men died of their wounds and four officers and twenty-eight men had been wounded. Another fifteen officers and 367 men were captured unwounded bringing the total Boer bag of prisoners to more than 400. In Britain the news of the disaster was received with stunned incredulity. Questions were asked in the House of Commons and *The Times* called the surrender a "humiliating episode". In Ireland the fate of the Dublin Hunt Company and the Unionists was greeted with mirth by Nationalists but the Irish establishment was in mourning. The dead included Private Andrew Porter, son of the Irish Master of the Rolls, among the wounded was Sergeant Arthur Gray, son of a Senior Fellow of Trinity College, Dublin, and the prisoners included Corporal the Hon Victor Gibson, son of the Lord Chancellor of Ireland.

The final act had yet to be played. As the aristocracy and gentry of the 13th Battalion were taken away into captivity, Methuen's relief column was not far away. On the morning of the 31st a message reached them from Spragge saying that he could hold out until 2nd June. Methuen hurried on and on 1st June came up against a Boer force on a long low ridge at Paardeplaats, eight miles west of Lindley. As he did so he heard that Spragge had surrendered the previous day. The 5th Battalion Imperial Yeomanry attacked the Boers' right and centre, the 10th Battalion moved forward against their left and the 3rd Battalion galloped in a wide arc around their right to come in behind them. The ridge was quickly cleared and a party of men of the Sherwood Rangers and South Nottinghamshire Hussars, led by Lieutenant-Colonel Younghusband, pushed forward under artillery and rifle fire. As they did so they sighted the Boer convoy carrying the prisoners and booty from Lindley fleeing as fast as it could. Younghusband decided to intercept. "We suddenly came across a precipice, about a 25-foot drop, down which there was apparently no path and the face of which was fully exposed to the Boer fire," wrote Younghusband later. "Our blood was up and somehow or other thirty-six of us scrambled down the sheer wall on foot and had our horses shooed down after us."[17] They charged 400 yards into the convoy cutting off two guns and sixteen wagons, and were agonisingly close to rescuing the prisoners, two or three of whom managed to escape in the confusion. But the rescue party was too small and reinforcements failed to arrive because the rest of Methuen's force was too far away. Younghusband fought a brisk engagement with the Boer rearguard before being ordered to retire on Lindley, which he did with some difficulty. The yeomanry had lost five killed, sixteen wounded and ten men missing during the rescue attempt. Had Methuen's main force been able to get there in time then victory could have been snatched from the jaws of disaster.

Peel and his comrades in the Oxfordshire company of the 10th Battalion came across what he termed "a melancholy sight" as they reached the site of the surrender. "Several dead bodies of yeomen lay about; one poor fellow had taken out his first field dressing but had died before he could unroll it; another had tried to write a message but in his case too the pencil had slipped from his failing fingers," he wrote. "Deep anger and mortification filled our hearts as we gazed upon the pitiful scene and realized that we had come too late."[1] The rescue column at least had the satisfaction of finding the British wounded, who the Boers had left behind in the town. Among them was Longford who Peel had last seen on his lordship's wedding day not long before in London.

Inevitably a series of inquiries was held into the disaster. Astonishingly Jacques, whose raising of a white flag had fatally undermined the battalion's position, was not court-martialled. The twenty-three-year-old from Yorkshire, who had described his profession as "gentleman" when he joined the DCOs, was sent back to England in disgrace in June as soon as his wound had improved but kept his rank of Corporal until his discharge in December. The Army did later strip him of his medal and war gratuity[18] but no other action was taken although he was very publicly blamed in the inquiries into Lindley.

Spragge, Alexander and almost all the other key players at Lindley itself were exonerated. The only exception for a time was Robin, who, after initially being cleared by the Court of Inquiry, had his medal and war gratuity withheld by headquarters. He appealed against this and it was decided "considering his want of military knowledge and his subsequent good service" that both should be restored.[15] The principal scapegoat was Colvile, who Roberts already disliked for his failure to catch the Boers after the British were ambushed at Sannah's Post in March. Roberts sacked Colvile from his command and he returned to England. In a despatch to the British Government Roberts said that the arrival of the 9th Division at Heilbron by the 29th "was obviously a matter of minor importance compared to the relief of the 13th Battalion Imperial Yeomanry." He continued: "In my opinion Lieutenant-General Colvile displayed a want of military instinct in deciding to continue his march instead of returning to the assistance of the yeomanry." Colvile was sent to Gibraltar to command an infantry brigade but in December, 1900, Brodrick, the new Secretary of State for War, announced that he agreed with Roberts that Colvile was "mainly responsible" for the surrender at Lindley. Colvile was told to resign but refused and so was sacked for the second time and forced into retirement.

Significantly the Royal Commission which investigated the war did not condemn Colvile. The Commission's relatively neutral stance was fair as, although Colvile was an arrogant man who did not cover himself with glory, neither was he entirely to blame. His principal failure was that he did not immediately tell headquarters of Spragge's request for help and ask whether it was essential to reach Heilbron by the 29th. This failure was symptomatic of the entire Lindley affair. The real culprit was chaotic British staff work and lack of communications between different parts of the Army and for that Roberts must bear some responsibility. Add to this an extraordinary run of bad luck and all the ingredients for a disaster were present. Lindley provided those who were sceptical about the Imperial Yeomanry with plenty of ammunition, including Roberts himself, who commented: "Disciplined troops have much more confidence in each other and I think that is the reason why the yeomanry probably had to give in so quickly."[19] As a judgement on the speed of the final surrender there was some truth in this but the principal reason for what happened at Lindley was that the 13th Battalion had been let down by an inadequate command system.

NOOITGEDACHT 13 December, 1900.

The battle at Nooitgedacht in the Magaliesberg mountains west of Pretoria brought 1900 to a dismal end for the British. Here in the troublesome heart of the western Transvaal a Boer force of about 3,000 men gave a British column of 1,500 commanded by Major-General Ralph Clements a bloody nose and came close to destroying it. Clements, a veteran of campaigns in Africa and Burma, should have known better than to choose this site to camp his force of 652 mounted troops and 863 infantry. They included about 200 Imperial Yeomanry from the 20th (Fife and Forfar Light Horse), 26th (Dorset) and 27th (Devon) Companies. Ironically the name Nooitgedacht means 'never expected' and certainly Clements never expected that three Boer commanders, Smuts, De la Rey and Beyers, would combine to attack him in such force. Camping there had two advantages for Clements, a good supply of fresh water and a mountain crest from which to heliograph to Major-General Robert Broadwood at Rustenburg, twenty miles to the north-west. But that same mountain, rising almost sheer for a thousand feet, also dominated his camp. The Boers quickly saw that if they could overwhelm the 300 men of the 2nd Battalion Northumberland Fusiliers placed on the mountain as pickets then they would command Clements's position.

The Boer plan was for Beyers to attack the pickets on the mountain while Commandant Badenhorst would advance on the camp in the valley from the west and Smuts and De la Rey attacked from the south. A plan for a synchronized dawn assault by three columns after a night march was almost bound to go wrong and Badenhorst advanced too quickly. He came up against the British pickets in the valley at 3.40am on 13 December, attacking before the other Boer forces were in position and at first swept all before him. But then reinforcements from the British mounted infantry arrived and, with heavy casualties on both sides, pushed him back.

Scarcely had the shots from this fight died away when more gunfire was heard from the mountain as the Boer attack on the pickets began. The Northumberland Fusiliers fought well but they were outnumbered, outflanked and each man had only the normal field supply of ammunition in his pouch. The battle there went on for almost two and a half hours, the Boers advancing with the steadiness of veteran British infantry but using the buffalo horns formation favoured by their Zulu enemies. Finally at 6.45am the last twenty men of the Fusiliers surrendered.

About 100 men from the Fife and Devon Companies of the Imperial Yeomanry were sucked into the fighting on the mountain as it reached its crescendo. There is confusion as to whether they were ordered to block the bottom of the ravine, which was the only route from the valley to the top of the mountain, whether they were told to hold a position near the top or whether their task was to relieve the beleaguered Northumberlands. The yeomen were certainly under the impression that the latter was their task and struggled up the ravine, called Nooitgedacht Nek, for a thousand feet with their rifles and bandoliers. Their timing could not have been more unfortunate for they reached the top just as the Boers swept forward to the edge of the plateau, where they commanded the exit from the ravine. As men dashed out to try to find cover they were shot down, Captain R.W. Purvis of the Fifes and Captain W.E.J. Bolitho of the Devons falling wounded. Other yeomen leapt over their bodies and made for a small trench where Lieutenant Alfred Campbell of the Fifes, the son of a former commander of the Royal Yacht, was shot dead. Out of twenty-seven men of the Fife Company, six were killed and seven wounded. The Devons lost five killed and ten wounded and more than twenty men from both companies who could not escape back down the ravine surrendered.

The Boer fire now rained down unchecked from the mountain on the British in the valley. Among the mounting casualties was the tiny pet monkey kept as a mascot by the Imperial Yeomanry which was hit three times, although somehow it survived the battle. Clements, although to blame for the predicament in which his men found themselves, now proved their saviour. Leaving a fringe of yeomanry, mounted infantry and Kitchener's Horse to defend the bottom of the ravine down which the Boers were now climbing he began to withdraw his forces to a kopje to the south-east called Yeomanry Hill. This had been occupied by a small force of yeomen since before the action began and there they could regroup and make a stand out of range of the Boers on the mountain. The withdrawal was covered by the Dorset Imperial Yeomanry under Captain Sir Elliott Lees, who had six men wounded, and at one point Lees and his orderly Ingram rode back and rescued two dismounted yeomen who had been left behind.

The guns and the transport had to be saved and the rescue of one artillery piece, a six ton 4.7 inch naval gun, proved particularly dramatic. It said everything about Clements's defensive preparations that this gun was pointing the wrong way when the

Boers attacked. No field of fire had been cleared on the side towards the mountain but this enabled its commander, Major Inglefield, to creep back through the undergrowth with his men to prise it from its position. The gun then rolled down the valley, gathering speed like some juggernaut as it passed through the British camp and out the other side. A triumphant Inglefield then hooked it up behind a team of oxen and dragged it to Yeomanry Hill. The rest of the guns had already been evacuated and last back to the hill were 250 men of the 2nd Mounted Infantry, which had distinguished itself throughout the battle.

A new danger then appeared from the south-west. De la Rey's and Smuts's advance had been held up by a gallant stand by some men of Kitchener's Horse but they were now advancing towards Yeomanry Hill. Their two artillery pieces fired some shells into the already frightened British transport animals before being put out of action by Clements's guns. The whole baggage train careered in panic towards Rietfontein to the south. Clements was a good horseman as well as a quick-thinking leader and with a few others galloped after it. Helped by volunteers, including Sergeant Pullar of the Fife Imperial Yeomanry, he rescued the transport just before it blundered into the Boers.

Clements now heard belatedly from the Intelligence Department that Beyers was advancing on him with 2,000 men. Late as it was, this information made him realize the size of the Boer force now gathering around him and abandon any attempt to stage a stand on Yeomanry Hill. He realized that he must get out of the valley as soon as possible and in this he was helped by the indiscipline of the Boers and their inability to push home their advantage. Tired after a night march and a long day's fighting, the Boers lingered to loot the supplies left behind in the British camp. Clements again seized his chance and at 2.30pm ordered a retreat to Rietfontein, twenty miles away, which was carried out successfully with the Imperial Yeomanry forming the rearguard.

At Rietfontein the British counted their losses. Out of 1,515 men, eighty-eight had been killed or died of wounds, another 172 had been wounded and 368 taken prisoner, a total of 638. The Imperial Yeomanry lost fifty-seven, one officer and ten men killed or died of wounds, two officers and twenty-one men wounded and one officer and twenty-two men taken captive. Although there had been much individual heroism, Sergeant Donald Farmer of the 1st Battalion Cameron Highlanders winning the Victoria Cross for rescuing an officer under fire, the British knew that they had been lucky to escape at all. It was the worst reverse since Sannah's Post the previous March. Boer casualties had been about 100.

In Britain there were demands that heads should roll over such an embarrassing episode. When the House of Commons reassembled after the Christmas recess Brodrick promised to deal severely with those responsible for this and other setbacks in the war. He told the House: "Wherever the result of a court of inquiry establishes a *prima facie* case, I shall insist that the officer be brought to a court martial."[20] Roberts and Kitchener both dug their heels in. Roberts believed that officers would be reluctant to assume responsibility if the threat of a court martial was hanging over them every time they made a mistake and told Kitchener: "I have pointed out to Brodrick the danger of allowing the House of Commons to deal with questions regarding the conduct of officers."[21] French took over command in the Magaliesberg region and although Clements continued to operate in the area until mid-January he was then sent to a less demanding command at Pretoria. His skill in extricating himself from a mess of his own making saved him from a worse fate. Kitchener told Brodrick: "I am very glad you did not press matters against Clements. He is a fine gallant soldier but made a serious mistake of judgement as regards what a defensible position should be. Many have made similar mistakes in the war."[22]

CHAPTER SIX

THE MEDICAL VOLUNTEERS

The resources of the infant Royal Army Medical Corps were soon overwhelmed by the scale of the conflict in South Africa. The Corps had only been set up in 1898 after years of criticism of the Army's medical arrangements and was an amalgamation of the officers of the Medical Staff and the rank and file of the Medical Staff Corps. When the South African war broke out less than 18 months after Lansdowne announced the formation of the RAMC, the Corps had an establishment of 540 officers and 2,792 other ranks to tend the Army's sick and wounded throughout the Empire. The strength of the RAMC in South Africa quickly swelled from thirty-four officers and 263 men at the outbreak of war in October to 379 officers and 2,235 rank and file by the New Year. Reservists and retired officers were soon back in uniform, but, despite their recall, the Army Medical Department admitted that after the first two Army Corps had been sent to South Africa "the home establishment of the Royal Army Medical Corps was practically exhausted".[1] Volunteers were desperately needed to serve both in South Africa and in Britain, where military hospitals had to be maintained and where many of the sick and wounded from the war were sent.

Unlike the manpower crisis which resulted in the raising of volunteer forces such as the Imperial Yeomanry, the Army had anticipated that it would need to use and co-ordinate civilian medical help in a major conflict. After the bloodshed of the Franco-Prussian War had shocked British public opinion, the National Society for Aid to Sick and Wounded in War was set up in 1870. But there was still no central organization to co-ordinate civilian assistance and to try to avoid the chaos which unorganized and unrealistic offers of help could cause. In 1898 a conference was held at the War Office which resulted in the formation of the Central British Red Cross Committee. The Deputy Director General of the Army Medical Department became a member of the committee, along with representatives from the main civilian organizations. It was decided that in wartime two hospital trains and a hospital ship should be fitted out by civilian groups and and an agreement on who should deal with offers of help from doctors, nursing sisters and male nursing orderlies was reached. But the committee's formation was only announced in April 1899 and, like the RAMC itself, it was still in its early days when it was put to the severest of tests by the war in South Africa.

Public donations for voluntary medical assistance poured in as soon as war was declared, the National Society for Aid receiving £65,000 within two months and just under £179,000 by May 1901. The Borough of Windsor gave £6,100 which enabled the Central British Red Cross Committee to authorize the building of a hospital train a week after the conflict began. The train was named after Princess Christian, one of Queen Victoria's daughters who gave £650 towards it, and was completed in just ten weeks.[2] The following March it became the first train to arrive in Ladysmith after the lifting of the siege. The committee also pushed ahead quickly with plans for a hospital ship, selecting the 3,200-ton yachting cruiser the *Midnight Sun* because it could be rapidly converted. After two and a half weeks in a Tyne shipyard and having been renamed after the committee's president, the *Princess of Wales*, the ship was ready to leave. However, its departure was delayed by a boiler breakdown and it finally sailed for South Africa on 8 December, the first of three voyages in the next year during which it treated 728 men and travelled over 40,000 miles. Some sections of the press criticized conditions aboard the ship but the Central British Red Cross Committee rejected the claims after an investigation.[3] A second ship, the *Maine*, was donated by an American transport company and converted into a hospital with funds raised by a committee of American women led by Lady Randolph Churchill, mother of Winston Churchill. Staffed mainly by Americans, the 2,228-ton iron screw steamer made two trips to South Africa. After arriving back in Britain in July, 1900, the ship sailed to China, where the Boxer Rebellion had broken out, to help the sick and wounded of all the nations involved in that conflict.

Representatives of the British Red Cross Society began work in South Africa a month after the outbreak of war supplying hospital beds and equipment and clothing for the sick and wounded as well as distributing the first of thousands of parcels sent by wellwishers throughout the Empire. The society also later funded a second train, known simply as Number 4 Hospital Train, which began work in June 1900. After a year the society handed over its work in South Africa to the local Red Cross organization.

The pressing need for more medical staff was partly met through a pre-war agreement between the War Office and the St John Ambulance Brigade to supply medical orderlies to swell the ranks of the RAMC. The men of the SJAB had become a familiar sight at public events in Britain since the organization was founded in 1883 and had earned widespread praise when they turned out to help at two railway disasters in 1898. Their training was limited, covering only first aid and stretcher bearing, but even with no experience of hospital and nursing work they were badly needed in South Africa. The response to the SJAB's call for volunteers was remarkable, about 1,900 men, approximately one fifth of its total strength, eventually serving in South Africa. In some areas the proportion was much higher, Oldham sending 128 men from a strength of 226, Blackpool thirty-three out of fifty-seven and Kendal sixteen out of forty.[4] The earliest Kendal volunteers were William Inder and Harry Hunter who travelled to Preston in Lancashire where they and other SJAB orderlies were given the sort of send off later experienced by the CIV and the Imperial Yeomanry. Inder recalled: "Preceded by the band and accompanied by the local SJAB men, police and fire brigade we marched to the railway station through the Preston streets which were lined by thousands of people."[5]

There were similar scenes as they left London after a few days at the SJAB headquarters in Clerkenwell where they were drilled, given a crash course in nursing duties and kitted out with their new uniforms. When Inder and Hunter, who were both serving in the 2nd Volunteer Battalion Border regiment as well as the SJAB, landed in Cape Town on 18 December they were probably the first members of the Volunteer Force to arrive in South Africa. The SJAB also supplied about half the forty orderlies serving aboard the *Princess of Wales* and by June, 1900, nearly 1,100 men from the Brigade were serving alongside the RAMC in South Africa with many more in private hospitals. Many of them found leaving Britain for the first time a nerve-wracking experience. William Blundell, from Blackpool, confessed in his diary: "Perhaps I should never return, who knows? My feelings at leaving my home and friends can be better imagined than described."[6]

The War Office turned to every possible source to build up the medical services in South Africa. As well as calling for men from the small Militia Medical Staff Corps, it asked members of the Volunteer Force to come forward for overseas service for the first time. The medical element of the Force consisted of fourteen companies of the Volunteer Medical Staff Corps, bearer companies of the Volunteer infantry brigades and a large number of regimental medical officers, some battalions having as many as six of the latter. The men were asked to enlist into the RAMC for a year or for the duration of the war and more than 600 came forward, including Thomas Wetton, his brother and seven others from the 1st Sussex Volunteer Infantry Brigade Bearer Company in Brighton. They joined up because they were, as Wetton put it, "infected with the general patriotic enthusiasm" and sent to Aldershot where they stood for hours in the freezing cold while their kit was handed out in instalments over a period of several days. They joined the 23rd Field Hospital which consisted of five officers and men from the RAMC, two civilian surgeons, four specially enlisted civilian pharmacists, nine Volunteer Force men and eighteen SJAB orderlies.[7]

This mix illustrated the measures the Army was having to take to get medical units up to strength. The War Office employed an increasing number of civil surgeons and by July, 1900, 377 of these were in South Africa who, together with the 104 in private hospitals, almost outnumbered the 497 RAMC officers.[1] By 1902 56 per cent of the medical officers in South Africa were civilians.[8] An appeal for civilian pharmacists to work in South Africa produced 170 suitable recruits. Many women volunteered to serve as nurses and either worked in British hospitals or went to South Africa, although there was much prejudice against them doing the latter. Nearly 1,300 applied to join the tiny Army Nursing Service Reserve, which was only 100 strong before the war, although more than a quarter were rejected as being insufficiently qualified. The rules on nursing qualifications were mostly strictly enforced but on at least one occasion the Red Cross and the ANSR had to bow to outside pressure. The Princess of Wales, later Queen Alexandra, personally selected twelve nurses to go to South Africa and, as the Red Cross report into voluntary medical organizations in the war dryly observed, the organization "at once recognized the value of nursing sisters selected in this manner".[2]

Another source of medical personnel from overseas was the New South Wales Army Medical Corps in Australia which sent seven officers and eighty-five men to South Africa. They arrived in December, 1899, forming half a bearer company, half a field hospital and manning a dressing station and ambulance wagons. This mobile unit proved so good that reinforcements were requested by the British and a second contingent of eleven officers and 109 men arrived in February, 1900, followed later by a small thirty-five-strong draft. Further medical units came from Australia and Canada just before the war ended in 1902.

But away from the corridors of the War Office and the head-quarters of the main voluntary organizations, an extraordinary development took place. It had its origins in a letter to *The Times* by Dr George Stoker, a London throat specialist who had once served in the Turkish army, advocating independent flying hospitals as the most useful form of voluntary aid in South

Africa.[9] His suggestion was taken up by Captain Josceline Bagot, a Conservative MP who was also an officer in the Westmorland and Cumberland Yeomanry, who set up a committee with his wife and friends. The Bagots and the Central British Red Cross Committee quickly agreed that Stoker's proposal was impractical and instead it was decided to provide a 104-bed stationary hospital which would be attached to one of the larger military hospitals in South Africa. A total of more than £13,600 was subscribed by private donors, the largest sum of £5,000 coming from the Duke of Portland after whom the hospital was named.[10] The Portland Hospital was the first such organization to serve with the British Army and the first of nine private hospitals which went to South Africa and which at one stage were treating about 12 per cent of the sick and wounded there.[11] Like so many of the Boer War volunteer organizations, it was a miracle of rapid deployment, the committee starting work on 22 November and the first staff sailing for South Africa on 9 December. By just after Christmas forty-nine staff, including Captain Bagot, Lord Henry Bentinck, its treasurer, and a Swiss chef, and forty-one tons of equipment were in Cape Town. It opened for business at Rondebosch in Cape Colony on 8 January, remaining there for three months and treating nearly 500 patients.[12]

The same need to do something towards the war effort that fuelled the formation of the CIV and the Imperial Yeomanry now seized those whose inclination was towards healing rather than fighting. John Langman, who had been treasurer of the Portland Hospital before it left England, now decided to go one better and donate an entire hospital himself. He and his son Archibald, a lieutenant in the Middlesex Yeomanry, organized a 100-bed hospital in eight weeks and he agreed to pay the forty-four staff and fund the upkeep of the hospital for six months or until its return to England. It is not known how much this generous gesture cost Mr Langman but it must have made a considerable dent in his inherited wealth. The hospital, whose surgeons included the writer Arthur Conan Doyle, creator of Sherlock Holmes and the author of a history of the Boer War, arrived in South Africa in late March and was the first private hospital to get to Bloemfontein during the typhoid epidemic.

In similar vein Lord Iveagh of the Guinness brewing dynasty offered to spend some of his vast fortune on equipping an Irish Hospital for service in South Africa. The British Central Red Cross Committee, which was vetting all such proposals, turned down his suggestion that it should be a mobile unit and instead asked him to form a 100-bed stationary hospital, although as a compromise he was allowed to select and take his own transport. Among its surgeons, who embarked in February, 1900, was the Irish-born Stoker, whose letter had started the fashion for private hospitals, which had now spread beyond Britain. A wealthy American, Mr J. Van Alen, provided the smallest of these, a 25-bed section of a field hospital, which the donor accompanied when it left England in February. It was later expanded to 100 beds and served with Methuen during his operations near Kimberley in April. The last of the hospitals donated by individuals was the Princess Christian, the gift of Alfred Mosely, who had spent most of his life in South Africa, and which was increased from 100 to 200 beds during its service in Natal.

Scotland provided two hospitals and Wales one. The Edinburgh and East of Scotland Hospital was organized by the city's Lord Provost and financed by subscriptions totalling more than £12,300 from the area. While most of the private hospitals recruited orderlies from the SJAB, this one obtained as many as possible from the Edinburgh and Aberdeen companies of the Volunteer Medical Staff Corps.[2] The hospital arrived in Cape Town in April and remained in South Africa for seven months. The Scottish National Red Cross Hospital was set up by the St Andrew's Ambulance Association, the Scottish equivalent of the St John organization, with the aid of more than £45,000 subscribed mostly in the west of Scotland. It served at Kroonstad in the Orange Free State throughout its five months in South Africa. In Wales subscriptions of more than £12,000 financed the Welsh Hospital organized by a committee of leading citizens from the principality. After arriving in South Africa in May its site was clearly marked by a magnificent flag with a red dragon on a yellow

133

background made by the ladies of the Cape Cambrian Society.[13]

Of all the private ventures, the Imperial Yeomanry Hospital was the largest, best organized and most lavishly equipped. It was entirely separate from the Imperial Yeomanry's military organization but was founded specifically to look after the yeomen who, as the Red Cross report put it, "were likely to be drawn from a social class accustomed to greater comforts than the regular soldier." Even before it left for South Africa it was agreed that this was impractical and that it should treat all soldiers, but the hospital always nursed as many of the yeomanry as possible. The organizing committee, led by Countess Howe and Lady Chesham, whose husband was serving with the Imperial Yeomanry, read like a roll call of Debrett's having in its ranks seven Duchesses, four Marchionesses and forty-three other titled ladies. Several of them were the wives of yeomanry colonels and, with an unrivalled range of rich contacts, they raised £127,000 within four months.[14] A scheme to name wards and beds proved especially popular. People in Surrey preferred to give money to the Home Counties Ward, while others were named after the Sherwood Rangers Yeomanry and the City of Sheffield. A gift of £50 entitled the donor to name a bed, the Devon and Somerset Staghounds securing three for £150.

The formidable clout of the Imperial Yeomanry Hospital Committee enabled it to set up a 500-bed Base Hospital with a staff of 190, including nineteen doctors led by Alfred Fripp, surgeon to the Prince of Wales, within six weeks. The equipment was of a sort which other hospitals could only dream about. Surgeon-General Sir William Wilson, Roberts's Principal Medical Officer, later observed tartly: "They were equipped and maintained on a scale which it would be impossible, as it is unnecessary, for our service hospitals to imitate."[15] On 17 March the hospital opened at Deelfontein, a healthy spot 4,600 feet above sea level near De Aar, 500 miles north of Cape Town. The soldiers who were lucky enough to be treated there were so impressed that they nicknamed it 'The Haven of Rest' and at the end of May it was expanded to more than 1,000 beds.

The coffers of the committee were so full that it was decided

134

to expand its original plans and set up a Field Hospital and Bearer Company, which became the only civilian unit of its kind operating in South Africa. The Field Hospital's senior surgeon was Charles Stonham, a leading consultant at Westminster Hospital and a Surgeon Captain in the Middlesex Yeomanry, and the majority of its 169 staff were recruited from the Volunteer Medical Staff Corps. The unit arrived in Cape Town on 7 April and two months later was to find itself in the front line.

Some of the first medical volunteers arrived just as they were needed most after the British reverses of Black Week. Inder and his fellow SJAB orderly Hunter were sent straight to No 2 General Hospital at Wynberg, Cape Town, where they were shocked by what they saw. "What a sight," wrote Inder. "Eighty of the Highland Brigade wounded last Monday at Magersfontein. Poor fellows all cut up, stern looking warriors with legs, arms and heads covered with blood, kilts clotted and caked with it."[5] The SJAB orderlies found themselves working night and day to cope with about 1,200 wounded who had been brought to the hospital in the shadow of Table Mountain, but some, including one man who had been hit by ten bullets, were beyond help. Inder described how "the perspiration ran off me when raising the patients accompanied by shrieks and painful moaning."

The staff at Wynberg celebrated Christmas as best they could but on Boxing Day Inder was finally reduced to tears by the death of a patient who had been shot in the spine. He recalled: "I cheered him to smile by telling him he would be safe in the morning. For an hour and a half I stood there holding his hand, then quite suddenly his quick breathing ceased and with a low vibrating gurgle he quietly died. He was gone. Then I broke down." Despite such graphic evidence of the horrors of war, Inder did not like being so far from the front line. He confessed: "My idea in volunteering was as a field stretcher bearer and first aid man at the firing line where the bullets were spitting and to treat my comrades in arms when they most needed help, that is where they fell, and here we are at the base." James Crook, an SJAB man from Blackpool, was sent further up the line to De Aar in Cape Colony, to join Number 5 Stationary Hospital. He wrote home: "The British soldier who came from the front is not the fine stalwart man of gentlemanly appearance that you read about, for a good many of them have long beards and long hair and several came down minus shirts, shoes and with their clothing all torn."[6]

Few of those who had volunteered to come to South Africa to treat the sick and wounded found themselves near the fighting, most being sent to general hospitals or to stationary hospitals along the lines of communication. One exception was the Imperial Yeomanry Field Hospital and Bearer Company which on 7 June, 1900, found itself near Roodewal and Rhenoster, in the Orange Free State, where the Boers had snapped up the inexperienced Derbyshire Militia and captured the Imperial Yeomanry head-quarters baggage. After being shot at by the Boers, who later apologized when they realized that they were a hospital unit, they were taken prisoner. This at least gave them the chance to help the wounded British prisoners while the Boers looted a mountain of captured baggage and post. "The scene at the station at Roodewal will live in our memories for ever and is beyond my descriptive powers," wrote Stonham. "Our first care was, of course, for the wounded. We found fourteen of them lying in the station sheds or propped up against the extemporised defences. Poor chaps, many of them had been hard hit."[14]

Later, at the camp by the Rhenoster River where the prisoners were taken, the Imperial Yeomanry Hospital's surgeons operated without a break from 4pm until after midnight, amputating limbs, repairing fractures and dealing with many serious neck, chest and abdominal wounds. It was a surreal, nightmarish scene, the surgeons operating by flickering lamplight as around them a stockpile of captured British ammunition was being blown up by the Boers providing a huge fireworks display. "A Tommy, partially under the influence of chloroform, would sing a snatch of a comic song, another indulged in language of more force than purity and yet a third would incoherently call on those at home," remembered Stonham. It was, he said, "a weird and gruesome night" and the doctors and orderlies lay down exhausted after their first experience of dealing with the damage inflicted on flesh and bone by Mauser bullets. Four days later they were released from captivity, ironically by men of the Yorkshire Imperial Yeomanry. Shortly afterwards Lord Chesham, whose wife had played such a key role in organizing the hospital, trotted up with men of the Buckinghamshire Imperial Yeomanry to see how they were faring.

The 23rd Field Hospital with its mixture of regular soldiers, volunteers, SJAB orderlies and civilians was sent to join Rundle's 8th Division in the Orange Free State after disembarking at Port Elizabeth in March. After weeks of trekking the hospital for a time established itself at Thaba 'Nchu where its tents were soon overcrowded with more than 100 sick and wounded and the local chapel and schoolroom were commandeered to provide extra space. With rations having to be brought from Bloemfontein by convoys which were frequently attacked by the Boers, the men soon became poorly nourished and sickness became far more of a problem than battle casualties. Diarrhoea, dysentery and enteric, today called typhoid, were the most common diseases, needing a milk diet and careful nursing, but fresh milk was almost unobtainable and the tinned variety hard for the sick men to stomach. "The men lay in tents upon the hard ground, wrapped in their single blanket with a waterproof sheet between their bodies and Mother Earth," wrote Wetton. For the Sussex Volunteers looking after them it was hard, unrelenting and unglamorous work.[7]

Typhoid was by now taking a terrible toll of the British throughout much of South Africa. "This fever is a terror," said Inder, who nursed some of the victims brought down to Cape Town. "I have two of the 2nd Dragoons who are almost too long for their beds and must have weighed more than 13 stones each when in good health. Now they can hardly lift their hands being practically reduced to skeletons." But it was in the Orange Free State capital of Bloemfontein, captured by the British in mid-March, that the epidemic was at its worst. Typhoid feeds on poor hygiene and overcrowding and with the arrival of Roberts's army the population of the town had soared from 4,000 to 40,000 in a month. Some of the soldiers had already picked up the sickness

137

from drinking polluted water to stave off the thirst that perpetually gripped the British troops in the blasting heat of South Africa. Swarms of flies spread the disease, aided by a lack of even the most elementary hygiene in the British camps which sprung up around Bloemfontein. Roberts, with other matters on his mind, was largely indifferent to the problem. When he resumed his march to Pretoria at the beginning of May he left 4,500 sick and wounded behind him in Bloemfontein and by the end of the month there were 11,000 men unfit for duty in the town. Not a day went past without funerals. The conditions in the Army's hospitals, overcrowded and short of medicine and other supplies, were denounced by William Burdett-Coutts, a Conservative MP who visited them, in an emotive article in *The Times* which caused a sensation in Britain.

It was during the epidemic from April to June, 1900, that the private hospitals played their most important role. The Langman Hospital was the first to arrive in Bloemfontein on 8 April, followed shortly afterwards by the Irish and Portland Hospitals. Some staff from the Welsh and Scottish National Red Cross Hospitals were also sent to Bloemfontein to help deal with the crisis as was the twenty-two-strong Southampton Ambulance Corps, raised by the people of the Hampshire port. The volunteers lives were at risk as they worked in the hospitals and twenty-three of them were buried in Bloemfontein by the time the epidemic ended.[16] Of the Portland's twenty-four orderlies, nine went down with typhoid of whom one died. Anthony Bowlby, the Portland's senior surgeon, was impressed by their conduct: "In the face of these risks the behaviour of our orderlies was beyond all praise. They were all St John Ambulance men and had had no previous experience of hospitals or sick people. They proved a most excellent lot and were most keen to learn to nurse. It was quite surprising to us to see how little they seemed to fear being attacked although they could not help knowing that the risks were very considerable."[12]

In late May the cold nights killed the flies, by mid-June the epidemic was under control and by early July there were few fresh typhoid cases. Bowlby said that with July "came empty beds and empty tents and it seemed difficult to believe that the whole of the sickness and overcrowding should have come and gone in three short months." The private hospitals had won a fine reputation at Bloemfontein and unlike the Army hospitals never ran out of medicines or supplies even at the height of the epidemic. Conan Doyle, serving with the Portland, even found time to write some of his history of the Boer War. The Army's hospitals were investigated by a special Royal Commission which tamely concluded that "there has been nothing in the nature of a scandal with regard to the sick and wounded." Not everyone was so generous. The civilian surgeons attached to the RAMC were astonished by its bureaucratic inflexibility and among the soldiers who were its patients the Corps was fast becoming detested.

Some of the private hospitals followed Roberts's advance to Pretoria, the Scottish National Red Cross Hospital setting up in Kroonstad and the Langman, Irish and Welsh Hospitals moving to the Transvaal capital in July and August. There the Irish Hospital moved into the Palace of Justice, providing 500 beds by the end of July. But the era of the private hospitals was drawing to a close. The Portland, under-employed since the end of the epidemic and with its staff's contracts due to run out in August, told the Army that it was prepared to stay until September but that three doctors had to be back in England by October. Bowlby said: "We heard in reply that it had been decided not to send any more hospitals to the Transvaal and that there was no present need for the maintenance of so many beds as had hitherto been required." The Portland, the first of the private hospitals, closed on 12 July having treated more than 1,000 patients. Between July and November seven more of these hospitals followed suit, their beds and equipment being donated in most cases to the Government. The RAMC had expanded and was still recruiting in Britain and nearly 4,700 doctors, nurses and other medical staff had been taken on in South Africa.[17] The Government was no longer in such dire need of charitable help.

There was one exception to these closures. The marvellously equipped Imperial Yeomanry Hospital was too fine an asset to lose and instead expanded its operations. A 100-bed hospital was opened at the Imperial Yeomanry's Base Camp at Maitland, near Cape Town, and a small convalescent home for officers founded in Johannesburg but the main project was a new hospital in Pretoria. In June the indefatigable Countess Howe went to see Lansdowne to suggest setting up a base hospital in the newly conquered Transvaal capital and he contacted Roberts who approved the plan. Two months later, after an opening ceremony performed by Roberts himself, it began work in a large house in Pretoria, quickly increasing the number of beds from 400 to 530. The final project was a 140-bed branch hospital at Elandsfontein, near Johannesburg, the base of the second contingent of the Imperial Yeomanry which arrived in 1901. To finance these the Imperial Yeomanry Hospital Committee raised another £15,000 through an appeal in Britain and sold its Deelfontein hospital to the British Government and the Maitland branch to the Cape Colony authorities for a total of £17,000 in April 1901.[14] That month the men of the organization's Field Hospital and Bearer Company returned to Britain after months of trekking in South Africa. After their baptism of fire at Roodewal, they had followed the British advance across the eastern Transvaal, arriving at Komati Poort on the frontier with Portuguese East Africa in September. As some Boers crossed the border and threw their weapons away, Stonham said: "The news made us fondly think the end was at hand." Instead by October they were back in Pretoria and in December marched to Rietfontein to deal with the casualties from the British near-disaster at Nooitgedacht.

The Pretoria hospital closed at the end of September 1901 and the smaller one at Elandsfontein only survived until December, although the committee was prepared to carry on running it. Countess Howe said that Surgeon-General Wilson "intimated that the military authorities required no further assistance from private hospitals". So the largest of these ventures came to an end five months before peace was signed in South Africa. It had raised more money than any of the others and treated more patients, a total of over 20,000, of whom more than one-third were yeomen, in nearly 2,000 beds. Eighteen of its 711 staff died in South Africa and were commemorated on memorials in Deelfontein and

Pretoria. It had also demonstrated the powerful influence and fearsome organizational skills possessed by ladies of the British upper class.

The soldiers treated by the private hospitals were under no doubt that they had done good work in South Africa. The average British Tommy loathed the RAMC, which, it was said, stood for 'Rob All My Comrades' because of the number of thefts from patients. Not all the criticism was fair, it being hardly surprising that a recently formed and poorly trained Corps should struggle to cope with such a large number of patients. But by comparison the private hospitals were mostly better equipped and often staffed by the best doctors. The patients knew where they would rather be. Ross, of the Sussex Imperial Yeomanry, was slightly wounded in December, 1900, and "in spite of protests" was sent to an RAMC hospital. "The damned RAMC, I seldom, if ever, have heard it alluded to without the big, big D's," he wrote. After waiting for several hours without being treated he limped on to the Imperial Yeomanry Field Hospital which was only a mile away. "Every consideration was shown to us," he recalled. " In a few minutes we were lying down in a fine tent of the marquee brand and drinking excellent cafe au lait and eating bully and biscuit." After being treated Ross lay smoking a Turkish cigarette which one of the orderlies had given him and "fervently swore that the grandest institution in South Africa was the IY Field Hospital".[18]

The facilities at the Imperial Yeomanry Hospital in Pretoria were so good that Bryant's comrades in the Norfolk Regiment Volunteer Service Company all wanted to be sent there. "This hospital was a picture, the management marvellous and the attention to patients perfect," he wrote. His praise extended to all the private hospitals: "One thing which the Irish Hospital showed up was the rottenness of our own medical staff, for had not this, Langman's, the Imperial Yeomanry and other private hospitals been in Pretoria during the first few months it is too awful to contemplate what would have been the result and the death toll."[19]

The Army authorities, and Wilson in particular, never entirely liked the private hospitals, although they recognized the necessity of harnessing the patriotic public mood of 1900 and the need for extra resources early in the war. Wilson's report into the medical arrangements in South Africa criticized some of the private hospitals for "having equipment that was quite unsuited for field service". He said that the Imperial Yeomanry Field Hospital and Bearer Company would have been more useful if it had had its own transport, criticized the Edinburgh and East of Scotland Hospital for its bulky equipment and the Scottish National Red Cross Hospital for having equipment "unsuited for camp life". Although he praised the Portland for being "the model of what a small, civil hospital should be" the overall impression is of a man trying to suppress his irritation. He criticized the private hospitals' doctors for not carrying out jobs such as inspecting cooking and sanitary arrangements and was scathing about their initial reluctance to increase the number of beds. "It is quite possible to combine every consideration for these gentlemen, who sacrifice much for the benefit of the Army, with the real requirements of the service which are, as a whole, better understood by the professional than the volunteer," he wrote.[15]

Wilson's temper snapped after Conan Doyle told the Royal Commission into the war that there would have been a "disastrous breakdown" of the medical arrangements in South Africa had it not been for the private hospitals. He wrote an irate letter to the Commission pointing out that during the Bloemfontein typhoid epidemic the three private hospitals treated an average 6.6 per cent of the patients and 11.5 per cent at the height of their involvement. "Assistance to the extent of even 10 or 11 per cent which these hospitals gave during two weeks at the worst period did not amount to the prevention of a 'disastrous breakdown'," he wrote. He said that at the end of July, 1900, 88 per cent of the sick in South Africa were in military hospitals, 5 per cent in the Imperial Yeomanry Hospital and 7 per cent in other private hospitals and concluded: "I do not wish to diminish the importance of the work done by these hospitals but they formed a very small part of the medical organization."[11]

The Principal Medical Officer also had doubts about the

recruits from the Volunteer Force and the SJAB who served alongside the RAMC. He said: "The emergency personnel . . . were, as a rule, willing and anxious to do their best but for want of training their efficiency was far short of what was necessary and the duty of instructing these men in the ordinary work of a military hospital fell on the officers and NCO's of the permanent establishment. That the results were as good as they proved to be says much for the zeal, energy and efficiency of that permanent establishment." Wilson believed that in future it would be better to use such recruits in field units rather than in general or stationary hospitals where their basic training fitted them only for less responsible duties. But he admitted: "They improved in nursing duties, after prolonged instruction, especially the Volunteer Corps, who are recruited from a higher and more intelligent class."[15] The Royal Commission on the Care and Treatment of the Sick and Wounded said that the SJAB orderlies worked well but "were to a great extent untrained and quite unused to hospital work and some of them appear to have been rough and unfitted for the purpose of tending sick men."

The medical volunteers themselves criticized the RAMC less than other British soldiers. Wetton wrote an impassioned defence of the Corps concluding: "Although individual cases sometimes unfortunately did occur of those who were no credit to their uniform, I consider such were comparatively rare and the Corps as a whole was above reproach." There was occasionally friction between civil surgeons and RAMC doctors and one such case at No 8 General Hospital at Bloemfontein was investigated by the Royal Commission into the medical services. The RAMC said that the civilians had "neglected their duty and were rowdy and not teetotal" while the accusation in the other direction was that the Army officers were "inattentive and inexperienced". The Commission, which seems to have been keen to avoid controversy wherever possible, concluded that "there were in fact some faults on both sides." But mostly, despite civilian bewilderment at the RAMC's obsession with form-filling, the two sets of doctors co-existed amicably.

It was as well that they did because, despite the closure of the private hospitals and Wilson's criticisms of all the volunteers, the Army continued to need civilian recruits. Some volunteered for a second term of service, including Inder who had another enthusiastic send off in England. He survived the hospital wards but died of pneumonia in South Africa in 1902 after having left the SJAB to join the Imperial Military Railways. In March, 1901. there was a further appeal for volunteers in Britain which produced just over 1,000 recruits, including another 400 from the SJAB and others from the medical units of the Volunteer Force. Doctors from civilian life and the auxiliary forces continued to be recruited throughout the war and by 1902 the RAMC provided only 40 per cent of the medical officers in South Africa. The Official History of the War said that "the civil surgeons sent out from England at the beginning of the war were on the whole more efficient than the majority of those who came out later, the latter being for the most part young men fresh from the hospitals."[8]

Co-ordinating this difficult blend of soldiers, qualified civilians and well-meaning amateurs was never an easy task. The latter, some of whom arrived individually in South Africa determined to do something but without a clear or realistic plan, were a particular problem. In October, 1900, Sir John Furley, the Special Red Cross Commissioner in South Africa, wrote an angry letter to Lord Wantage, who served on the Central British Red Cross Committee responsible for co-ordinating voluntary help. Furley claimed that the rules by which voluntary aid was supposed to be directed through the committee were being blatantly flouted and blamed the War Office for not issuing instructions to the military authorities in South Africa. He complained: "We all know now what a scramble there was for costly and unorganized assistance sent out under more or less authority and how funds were collected, some for the purpose of aiding the hospitals, while others having less defined limits only increased the waste and confusion. Men and women, especially the latter, went out to South Africa all wishing to do something for the soldiers but with no practical idea as to where and how they were to do it . . . Every man and woman who thought they could do something determined to run his or her own show, the result in waste and overlapping was truly appalling whilst self-advertisment was carried on to an extent which was the envy of traders."[2]

Despite all the criticism of freelance do-gooders, heavy-handed orderlies and unsuitable equipment, the volunteers brought desperately needed aid to the Army Medical Department at a time when it was under the greatest pressure. Without the hundreds of civilian doctors and more than 2,000 men from the SJAB and the Volunteer Force who came forward in the early months of 1900 it is doubtful that the RAMC would have had enough men to cope. The private hospitals were less essential but still helped ease the pressure and the Imperial Yeomanry Hospital played a significant role in treating the sick and wounded. They also saved the Government a great deal of money and several donated the Army much valuable equipment when they went home. The total value of voluntary medical aid to the British war effort has been estimated at £1 million while the funds raised for the private hospitals alone came to £300,000.[2]

As with the volunteer military units in the Boer War, the raising and equipping of the medical volunteers allowed people to get involved at a time of national crisis and women to play a direct role. The volunteers themselves felt that it had been worthwhile. Stonham wrote after he returned to Britain: "So ended what to all of us must ever remain a most enjoyable experience, not only on account of the varied scenes we had witnessed and new experiences we gained but also, let us hope, from the higher and better feeling that we did our best to relieve many suffering men who were striving and enduring so much for their country."[14]

CHAPTER SEVEN

COLONIAL VOLUNTEERS

As the 19th century drew to a close the belief that the British Empire was a family was not solely the preserve of imperial ideologists. It was the view of ordinary people, the product of shared blood, common experience and a perceived mutual self-interest stretching across the oceans. The Boers living in Cape Colony did not share it and most French Canadians were luke-warm, but for the rest of Queen Victoria's white subjects the Empire was a source of both intense pride and reassuring strength. The Boer War, coming just two years after the old Queen had celebrated her Diamond Jubilee, provided ample evidence of this loyalty. It also gave the fledgling countries of Australia, New Zealand and Canada a chance to take a step along the road to nationhood and gain useful experience for their small military forces. As Dr Frederick Borden, the Canadian Minister of Militia, put it: "Canada has thrown off the swaddling clothes – she is a full grown member of the family which makes the Empire."[1] Many colonists also sympathized with the Uitlanders because they too had emigrated to a far-off land chancing harsh conditions in search of a better life. Australians had swelled the ranks of the Uitlanders during the 1890s when an economic depression at home prompted them to move to the Rand and some had taken a leading part in the Jameson Raid. In Australia there were also fears that a British defeat in South Africa would endanger one of the two sea routes from Europe. But such cold global calculations as this were mostly those of politicians. The colonial reaction to the war was a matter of gut instinct, the

146

imperial family closing ranks against what was seen as Boer impudence.

The first offers of military help came from the colonies before the war even started. In Australia, which did not become federated until 1901, the Government of Queensland offered to send 250 mounted infantry and a machine-gun section to South Africa in July, 1899. Soon every Australian colony had offered troops and public enthusiasm was intense, 1,900 men putting their names down for enlistment in New South Wales. Chamberlain thanked them on behalf of the British Government and said that he hoped that the need for their services would not arise. At the end of September the Victorian Government convened a conference in Melbourne attended by senior military officers from all the Australian colonies which proposed a combined contingent of 2,500 men, more than half of them mounted. In New Zealand there was also solid support for a war against the Boers, but in Canada matters were more complicated. Prime Minister Sir Wilfred Laurier's Liberal Government had its power base in Quebec, where French Canadian feelings about the conflict varied from the mixed to the downright hostile. The Canadian Government passed a resolution of support for the Uitlanders but Laurier discouraged participation in the war.

Eight days before war broke out Chamberlain sent a telegram to the Governors of the colonies asking for military assistance. Sloppily worded, complacent and arrogant, it became a source of immense controversy. The words which constantly came back to haunt the British Government were "in view of numbers already available, infantry most, cavalry least, serviceable." This was widely and unsurprisingly interpreted as encouraging the sending of infantry and discouraging the despatch of mounted infantry and cavalry against an enemy who moved everywhere on horseback. Lansdowne wriggled furiously on the hook and told the House of Lords: "The reason infantry were asked for was that it was proposed that we should attach small bodies of colonial soldiers to the units of imperial soldiers already at the Cape."[2] This explanation confirmed what was already apparent from the telegram. The British wanted a token colonial presence not effective military help and the Royal Commission into the War later accused Whitehall of an "unfortunate propensity to belittle" colonial troops.[3] The Australian colonies, which had offered 2,500 men, were asked to send 1,000 and the New Zealanders were requested to send 200. All immediately signified acceptance but in Canada the Government dithered until the outbreak of war on 11 October triggered a wave of patriotic fervour in the English-speaking provinces and Laurier offered 1,000 infantry.

Recruiting throughout the colonies was accompanied by the same enthusiasm which later characterized the raising of the Imperial Yeomanry, the CIV and the Volunteer Service Companies in Britain. It was part of the same phenomenon and there was no difficulty in finding the men. Both New South Wales and Victoria managed to persuade the Imperial Government to increase their contingents slightly and eventually 1,271 Australians embarked, of whom 156 were cavalry, 444 infantry and eighty-five from the New South Wales Medical Staff Corps. Some common sense had by now prevailed and 465 of the Australians were mounted infantry as were the 203 Zealanders.[4] On 28 October the first Australian troops, mostly recruited from the militia, marched through Sydney in pouring rain which failed to dampen the enthusiasm of the huge crowd which had assembled. There was spontaneous singing as the bands struck up 'Rule Britannia' and 'Soldiers of the Queen' and among the patriotic slogans displayed was "The Lion and the Kangaroo will put old Kruger through."[5] At the end of November the first contingents from Australia and New Zealand sailed for South Africa from Albany Harbour in Western Australia.

The force raised in Canada was designated the 2nd (Special Service) Battalion, Royal Canadian Regiment of Infantry, and was recruited and despatched to South Africa in just two weeks after Laurier had told Chamberlain of his Government's decision to help. It was commanded by Lieutenant-Colonel William Otter, an autocratic officer from the small Canadian permanent force, which supplied about 15 per cent of the contingent. Half came from the militia and about one-third had no previous military experience. Eight companies, each of 125 men, were recruited at different centres across the country and the response was strong everywhere except in the French-speaking heartland of eastern Quebec. On 30 October the battalion, capable of doing little more than forming ranks and sometimes marching in step, sailed down the St Lawrence River towards South Africa.[6]

The first overseas colonial troops to land in South Africa travelled from Britain. A squadron of two officers and 100 men of the New South Wales Lancers had left Sydney in March, 1899, and sailed to Britain to take part in the annual military tournament at Islington, followed by training at Aldershot. When war broke out some of them volunteered for active service in South Africa and they left England in October amid much popular acclaim. On arrival in Cape Town on 2 November the two officers and sixty-nine men disembarked while thirty-one men returned to Australia for a variety of reasons, where they received much abuse from politicians, press and the public. In most cases this was hardly fair as some were medically unfit and others were minors who had been ordered home.[7] In South Africa a detachment of twenty-eight men under Second Lieutenant S.F. Osborne was temporarily attached to Methuen's command and first saw action at the Battle of Belmont on 23 November. They then fought at Graspan, Modder River and Magersfontein and were dubbed 'The Fighting Twenty-Nine' by British troops. The reverse at Magersfontein on 11 December was a sobering experience for the Lancers. "The Boers have a class of sharpshooters and when any of us showed in the least degree you would hear the ping of a bullet," wrote Trooper Charles Webster. "No drink and the heat was terrible, this was no joke."[5]

By now the first contingents from Canada, New Zealand and Australia had all arrived in South Africa, but until the New Year none, except the Lancers, saw action beyond a few shots fired on patrol. They found themselves on the line of communication, chafing at the bit as the news of Black Week sent shock waves through the Empire. One of the solutions to the military crisis was glaringly obvious. "They are sadly in want of mounted troops and are sighing for mounted rifles," wrote Captain J.M. Antill, commanding the New South Wales Mounted Rifles on

15 December. "We could do with a few more thousand."[5] The same conclusion was belatedly being reached by the British military authorities who gratefully accepted further offers of help, particularly mounted troops, from the colonies.

Britain had turned down the offer of a second Canadian contingent on 2 November, but on 16 December this decision was reversed. Canada set about recruiting two battalions of Canadian Mounted Rifles, one drawn mainly from the militia and the other from the North West Mounted Police, and three batteries of artillery. More than 5,000 recruits came forward for less than 1,300 places. At the end of the month, after discussions with Chamberlain, Lord Strathcona, the Canadian High Commissioner in London, told Laurier that he planned to raise and equip a regiment of mounted scouts at his own expense. Strathcona's Horse, which cost his lordship £200,000, was a British regiment in theory but a Canadian one in practice, its men recruited from the cowboys and frontiersmen of the West. Canada's second contingent had far too many gunners, more than 500, but the 700 men of the Canadian Mounted Rifles and nearly 600 from Lord Strathcona's Horse were troops capable of taking on the Boers on their own terms.

Australia, like Canada, sent a mixture of publicly and privately raised units. The official second contingent from the Australian colonies numbered just under 1,500, more than 1,000 of them mounted troops with an artillery battery, medical staff and only about 150 infantry. Everywhere recruits came forward and throughout Australia they were cheered through the streets as they marched to their ships, the last embarking on 3 February. At the same time a private committee, backed by subscriptions in Australia and London, was set up to raise a corps of Australian Bushmen for South Africa. The idea was that this should be recruited from men used to the rough and tumble of life in the Australian bush, although inevitably the 1,400 who left for South Africa by the middle of March 1900 included adventurers and patriots who were not real bushmen. In March Chamberlain asked if the Australian authorities could raise more men of the Bushmen's stamp at the Imperial Government's expense. Some

2,400 of these Imperial Bushmen, as they became known, sailed by the beginning of May and there would have been no difficulty in obtaining four or five times that number.

The enthusiasm was as great in New Zealand. Frank Perham, who joined up early in 1900, recalled: "Like a lot of other young men, my brother Luke and I became infected with the adventure bug and were eager to take part."[8] The second New Zealand force consisted of just over 200 men of the Mounted Rifles and thirty-eight from a machine-gun battery and over the next few months five more contingents, some privately financed, were sent to South Africa, where they won a reputation as some of the best mounted troops. India and Ceylon also sent small contingents which, because of the British Government's decision that the conflict should in theory at least be a white man's war, could not include native troops. Ceylon sent 122 mounted infantry recruited from white tea planters, while in India Lieutenant Colonel Dougald Lumsden raised nearly 300 mounted troops from the European volunteer corps.

New Year's Day, 1900, saw the Australians and Canadians in action together in a minor but successful foray to Douglas, south-west of Kimberley, where Cape rebels had been causing problems for the British. A column including 250 Queensland Mounted Infantry and 100 men from the Royal Canadian Regiment set off westwards from Belmont to attack a laager at Sunnyside, near Douglas. At 11am on the first day of the new century the British began shelling the laager while the Queenslanders worked their way round to the left and 'C' Company of the RCR, recruited from southern Ontario, doubled across open ground to a kopje 1,200 yards from the enemy position. From there they advanced in rushes, using cover well, until a final bayonet charge took the Boer laager. The Canadians escaped unscathed, but the Queenslanders had lost two men killed in a brush with Boer pickets before the main action began. Troopers McLeod and Jones became the first Australian enlisted soldiers to die in battle and later the nation's first military memorial was erected on the battlefield. Six Boers were killed, twelve wounded and thirty-five captured in this audacious sideshow.

Many of the colonial troops found themselves under the command of Major-General John French, whose task was to check the enemy on the central front in Cape Colony and protect the railway system which was so vital to the British. There were constant minor actions in the area in early 1900. On 15 January sixty men of the New Zealand Mounted Rifles under Captain Maddocks drove off a Boer attack at Slingersfontein with a gallant bayonet charge which so impressed the British that they renamed the kopje New Zealand Hill. The next day a patrol from the New South Wales Lancers and the Australian Horse was ambushed in the same area, losing one man killed and a dozen taken prisoner. On 9 February twenty West Australians trapped by 400 Boers on a hill three miles east of Slingersfontein mounted a determined resistance which astonished their attackers before escaping at nightfall. Three days later at Hobkirk's Farm the Victorian Mounted Rifles lost seven dead, including their commander Major G.A. Eddy, and fourteen wounded, covering the retirement of some British infantry.

When Roberts arrived in South Africa in January he converted the remaining Australian infantry into mounted units before setting off for the border with the Orange Free State where his invasion force was assembling. His mounted troops included men from the New South Wales Lancers, New South Wales Mounted Rifles, Queensland Mounted Infantry and the New Zealand Mounted Rifles, while the Royal Canadian Regiment was one of the infantry battalions of Colvile's 9th Division. The Lancers found themselves in the van of this mighty imperial force which set off on 11 February. "As far as you could see, behind and to the left, was nothing but troops," wrote Trooper A.A. Burgin.[5] It was an impressive scene but greater drama was to follow. Roberts planned to relieve Kimberley quickly before marching east to seize Bloemfontein and French's mounted men were given the task of getting to the besieged mining town. French found a gap in the Boer defences at Abon's Dam and in one of the most awe-inspiring sights of the war 6,000 men from British cavalry regiments, two mounted infantry corps and supporting artillery burst through at the gallop and vanished into a cloud of dust towards Kimberley. On 15 February French and his staff entered the town ending a siege which had lasted four months. The Australian war correspondent 'Banjo' Paterson, who rode in with them, wrote: "The people simply hurled themselves at the horses and cried and wept for joy."[5] Some of the overseas colonials with French had little time to enjoy their status as conquering heros, the Queenslanders and New Zealanders clearing the enemy from Dronfield, 11 miles to the north, the following day.

The main enemy army under Cronje had now done what the cannier Boer leaders always avoided and dug itself into a well-defended position from which there was no escape. More than 4,000 of them, hopelessly encumbered with families and baggage wagons, were entrenched on the north bank of the River Modder near Paardeberg. Cronje expected to be relieved but instead the British noose around him grew stronger. On 18 February The Royal Canadian Regiment forded the river to the north bank west of the Boer laager and swung right behind a hill. Led by 'A' Company they advanced over the ridge and down the long, open forward slope where they came under fire and where Private James Findlay from Ontario became the first member of the battalion to be killed in action. As casualties mounted the Canadians halted several hundred yards from the Boer positions and opened fire. There they lay for several hours in the baking heat with little cover, vulnerable to Boer marksmen. The RCR's position was difficult but not desperate until Kitchener intervened. The Boers were surrounded and common sense suggested that the best policy was to shell them into submission. But Kitchener, more used to dealing with the relatively poorly armed Dervishes of the Sudan, wanted to finish the battle quickly with the bayonet and ordered a series of charges during the day. Without consulting Smith-Dorrien, commander of the 19th Brigade of which the RCR was part, Kitchener ordered the Duke of Cornwall's Light Infantry to cross the river and attack along the north bank.

Lieutenant-Colonel William Aldworth, commanding the DCLI, had a heated discussion with Otter about the situation before ordering a general charge just after 5pm. As the DCLI passed through their lines, the Canadians leapt to their feet and joined in, running across the 600 yards which separated them from the Boer lines. The Mausers wreaked efficient havoc, Aldworth, his adjutant and his bugler all being killed along with many of his men and the Canadians suffering terribly. The charge faltered after 300 yards, although a few men made it further and two Canadian bodies were found in the Boer trenches. Smith-Dorrien, who had not ordered the charge, was appalled and at first believed that the Canadians had launched an unsupported attack until he discovered the truth about Kitchener's rash intervention.

When night fell on the 18th the Canadians set about recovering their dead and wounded and counting the cost. They had lost eighteen killed, three mortally wounded, and sixty wounded, nearly 10 per cent of their strength, in an attack which should never have been ordered. For the next nine days they licked their wounds in the British trenches around Cronje's army. Early on the morning of 27 February, Majuba Day, a day on which the British badly wanted a Boer surrender in revenge for the humiliation of 1881, the RCR was ordered to attack again. The assault ended in a chaotic retreat in circumstances which are still not entirely clear. A voice was heard to call "retire" and a lieutenant then repeated the order and ran to the rear. Amid confusion and mounting casualties the attack quickly unravelled and the men retreated to their trenches. Whatever the truth about what happened it made no difference to the outcome of the Battle of Paardeberg as within a few hours the Boers surrendered and the British had a propaganda triumph as well as their first major victory of the war. Otter agonised about the Canadian retreat for hours afterwards but it appears to have gone largely unnoticed by the British high command. The RCR's commanding officer, a haughty disciplinarian, was not popular with his men but his courage was never in doubt. Two months after Paardeberg he was wounded by a bullet through the neck at Thaba 'Nchu in the Orange Free State as he stood in the open steadying his men. His temporary loss was greeted with mixed emotions in the Canadian ranks, some men being glad to see the back of him for a time.[6]

Throughout the early months of 1900 more and more overseas

colonial troops arrived in South Africa. The Canadian second contingent sailed into Cape Town in February, the westerners of the 2nd Canadian Mounted Rifles with their cowboy hats and strange saddles fascinating the local population. The following month most of the Canadians were ordered to help suppress a renewed rebellion in Griqualand, nominally British territory in the northern Cape but in reality mostly populated by Boer farmers. They had a dull time of it there except for 'E' Battery of the Royal Canadian Field Artillery which took part in the sharp fight at Faber's Put alongside the Imperial Yeomanry at the end of May. The Canadians lost one man killed and eleven wounded during the action in which an attack on the British camp by 600 Boers was driven off. Roberts had a policy of using newly-raised troops such as the yeomanry and the colonials on the fringes of the conflict, freeing regular troops to fight the main Boer forces and so units from both the Imperial Yeomanry and the Bushmen raised in Australia were sent to join Carrington's force in Rhodesia, where the only enemies which most of them encountered were malaria, typhoid and dysentery.

Since the start of the war the Boers had been besieging a small British force in Mafeking, a dull little stop on the western railway in Cape Province's northern extremity. Although it was of no strategic value, relieving the town had become an obsession with the British, a matter of imperial prestige. Two forces set out to reach Mafeking, one a flying column from Kimberley commanded by Colonel Bryan Mahon, the other from the Rhodesian Field Force led by Colonel Herbert Plumer. The latter included the 3rd Queensland Mounted Infantry and 'C' Battery of the Royal Canadian Field Artillery, who thereby escaped from the heat and boredom of Rhodesia where so many of their colonial comrades were stranded. Seven hours after joining Plumer's force they marched to link up with Mahon's men 20 miles west of Mafeking. On 16 May the combined relief force drove back the Boers in a four-hour action near the Malopom River, the Canadian artillery firing 180 rounds and silencing the Boer guns. The Queenslanders, frustrated at being told to remain in the rear, disregarded their orders and joined the small British infantry force with the column in a wild bayonet charge which took the Boer position. "It was funny to see the fellows duck when a shell came along but they did not seem to mind the Mauser bullets," said Trooper Norman Cowley. "It was the pom-pom which made us think of home and mother."[5] The next day Mafeking was relieved, unleashing scenes of hysterical celebration throughout the Empire. The Prime Minister of Queensland received a telegram from Baden-Powell, commander of the Mafeking garrison, thanking him "for invaluable assistance by Queenslanders".

By the time Mafeking was relieved, Roberts had already begun his march to take Johannesburg and then Pretoria, the great prize. His army deliberately included representatives from the entire imperial war effort, Royal Navy bluejackets as well as British regular soldiers, Canadian infantry and mounted troops, Australians from every state, New Zealanders, even Ceylon's tiny contingent of tea planters. The RCR, part of the 19th Brigade in Ian Hamilton's force, marched 327 miles in thirty days, fighting on twenty-one of them, the Boers always falling back as soon as they were likely to be outflanked. At Doornkop, just outside Johannesburg, on 29 May the Canadian infantry stormed a position on the right of the line losing eight men wounded. To their left the CIV won praise for its skill in advancing in short rushes and the Gordon Highlanders' respect for its inflexible gallantry as together they took the main position. A week later Roberts was in Pretoria. As the British approached Lieutenant W.W.R. Watson of the New South Wales Mounted Rifles was sent forward with a flag of truce to demand the surrender of the Transvaal capital. The young officer was taken to General Botha's home where, as the Boer leaders gathered, Mrs Botha made him tea and sandwiches. Watson said: "After an hour's chat they drew up a letter and Botha informed me that if I would conduct the Governor of the city to Lord Roberts, terms and conditions could be arranged. So they all shook hands with me and said I ought to be pleased at meeting their greatest statesmen and generals."[5] The next day Roberts marched into Pretoria with 26,000 troops, an occasion which Canadian infantryman Corporal William

Hart-McHarg described as the greatest moment of his life.[6] For Watson it was a disappointment. The men from New South Wales had been promised that they would form Roberts's bodyguard but the order was countermanded and they found themselves relegated to marching through the outskirts of Pretoria.

Of seventy-eight Victoria Crosses awarded for supreme gallantry during the Boer War, ten were won by men serving with units from Australia, Canada and New Zealand. The first was awarded to Sergeant Arthur Richardson of Strathcona's Horse, which had arrived in South Africa in April 1900 and been sent to join Buller's forces on the Natal front. Richardson was with a thirty-eight-strong party from the regiment when it was attacked by an enemy force twice its size at Wolve Spruit, 15 miles north of Standerton on 5 July. Private McArthur, whose horse had been killed and who was himself wounded, was in danger of being captured by the Boers when Richardson rode back and rescued him under heavy fire. On 24 July Captain Neville Howse of the New South Wales Medical Staff Corps became the first man serving with an Australian unit to win the VC when he rescued a wounded trumpeter during an action at Vredefort, just south of the Vaal River in the Orange Free State. A few weeks later two Tasmanian Imperial Bushmen, Lieutenant Guy Wylly and Trooper John Bisdee, were also awarded VC's for rescuing wounded men after they were ambushed near Warm Bad in the Transvaal.

The reputation of the overseas colonial volunteers was further enhanced by the defence of Elands River post in the western Transvaal for twelve days in August. Now largely forgotten, the action was a minor Victorian military classic. By August De la Rey's commandos were starting to cause trouble in the region as the conflict moved towards guerrilla warfare. The British decided to withdraw from a number of smaller posts including the one at Elands River, 40 miles west of Rustenburg. But before they could do so the Boers, tempted by a huge mountain of stores worth £100,000 which had built up at Elands River, laid siege to the post. The 500-strong garrison, including 105 New South Wales

Citizens Bushmen, 141 of the 3rd Queensland Mounted Infantry, forty-two Victorian Bushmen and 201 Rhodesian Volunteers, commanded by Colonel Hore of the 5th Dragoon Guards, came under heavy Boer shell fire on 4 August. The camp was quickly in chaos, many of the garrison's 1,500 horses and mules being killed or maimed by De la Rey's artillery. On the first day the defenders suffered thirty-two casualties and that night the Australians and Rhodesians desperately dug trenches with every tool they could lay their hands on including bayonets. Picks were so scarce that some men paid others £3 for half an hour's use. The following day Carrington, who had already been on his way from Zeerust to pick up the supplies and evacuate the post, drew near with a 650-strong column including some New Zealand gunners and the New South Wales Imperial Bushmen. By the afternoon of the 5th Carrington was only two miles away and his scouts could be seen by the defenders. But resistance from the much stronger Boer force was so vigorous that he retreated. The next day Baden-Powell, who had marched from Rustenburg with 1,000 men to help Hore, heard Carrington's gunfire receding and wrongly assumed that he must have evacuated the garrison.

Carrington telegraphed Roberts telling him that the defenders at Elands River would have no alternative but to surrender. Although now on their own and surrounded by between 2,000 and 3,000 Boers, no such notion entered the heads of Hore's garrison. They fought back as best they could with their only artillery piece, an old seven pound muzzle loader, launched a series of raids on the snipers who constantly plagued them and rejected an offer from De la Rey to be allowed to go to the nearest British base if they surrendered. The Boers were not interested in prisoners, they were after the stores. But as ever the burghers were inneffective besiegers, unwilling to incur heavy casualties by launching an all-out assault on the post. When they did attack an outlying kopje they drove sheep and goats in front of them to provide cover but animals and men alike fell to some well-directed rifle fire.

After ten days the British, who had assumed that the post had fallen, discovered their mistake when they intercepted an African carrying a message from De la Rey to De Wet. Roberts was furious. In a telegram to several senior officers he said: "I am greatly distressed that Hore should have been left so long without help."[9] His rage immediately galvanized them into action and by the following day five columns with a total of 25,000 men were on their way to Elands River. The first the garrison knew of it was when the Boer riflemen failed to reply to their shooting as the besiegers melted away. At 3am on 16 August pickets challenged two horsemen who turned out to be scouts from the relieving forces and four hours later Kitchener and his staff rode in. Amid the stench of the rotting animal carcases and the debris of stores smashed apart by Boer shells, the garrison rose and cheered them. They had suffered eighty casualties, twenty of them dead, and earned much deserved praise for their stubborn courage.[5] Neither Carrington nor Baden-Powell had covered themselves with glory and the creaking, ill co-ordinated British staff system had been found wanting once more. Nobody had taken a grip on the situation and ensured that a force was sent to Elands River to find out what had happened.

By October the year's service for which the men of the Royal Canadian Regiment had enlisted was up. In the months since the fall of Pretoria they had seen little action, first guarding some coal mines and then fruitlessly joining in the first great hunt for the elusive De Wet. Most of the men wanted to go home but unknown to them Otter had raised the subject of them extending their service and after discussions involving the Earl of Minto, Governor-General of Canada, and the War Office, Roberts asked the RCR to stay until the end of the war, which he believed was drawing near. Otter, never one of nature's democrats, consulted his officers but not the rank and file before agreeing to the Commander-in-Chief's request. Utter confusion followed. The men received Otter's order announcing their extension of service at the same time as they received a telegram from the officer commanding the line of communications on which they were serving telling them that they could go home. They realized that Otter had volunteered their services without their consent and most refused to stay on in South Africa, forcing their embarrassed

159

commanding officer to tell Roberts that they wanted to go home. Roberts was annoyed but bowed to the inevitable and on 1 October 400 officers and men of the RCR sailed for Canada. The rest served on for a few weeks before returning home in time for Christmas via Britain, where they were received as heroes.[6]

The second contingent of Canadians was also preparing to go home but before it did so won three VCs during a desperate rearguard action to protect a column at Leliefontein near Van Wyk's Vlei in the eastern Transvaal on 7 November. The 1st Canadian Mounted Rifles had by now been renamed the Royal Canadian Dragoons, leaving the 2nd to continue with the CMR title. The Dragoons and two guns of 'D' Battery, Royal Canadian Field Artillery, were given the task of protecting the rear of the cumbersome column commanded by Smith-Dorrien which was trying to get back to Belfast. Hundreds of Boers swarmed around the rearguard, at one stage launching a mounted charge, a tactic which they were to use with increasing frequency during the guerrilla war. The RCD and the Canadian gunners fought unflinchingly during the withdrawal, Lieutenant Hampden Cockburn being awarded the VC for sacrificing his handful of men to enable the guns to get away. Every man in the party was killed, wounded or captured, Cockburn himself being slightly wounded. Sergeant Edward Holland kept the Boers away from the artillery with his Colt gun and when he saw that the enemy was too near for him to escape with the carriage he calmly lifted the gun off it and galloped away with it under his arm. He too was awarded the VC, as was Lieutenant Richard Turner who, although twice wounded, dismounted with his men and drove off the enemy. Turner later commanded the 2nd Canadian Division during the First World War and added an impressive string of further awards and decorations to his VC. Given the ferocity of the fighting which enabled the column to get away, the RCD's losses of three killed, eleven wounded and sixteen taken prisoner could have been much worse and the gunners escaped without casualties. The column eventually reached Belfast on 17 November and soon afterwards the Canadian mounted troops and artillerymen sailed from Cape Town directly to Canada.

Strathcona's Horse followed them via England in early 1901 and in theory this ended Canada's part in the conflict until the final months of the war. In practice many Canadians served in British and South African units, more than 1,200 enlisted in the newly formed South African Constabulary and a small number in the Canadian Scouts. Despite its name the Scouts, commanded by Major Gat Howard, who had won the Distinguished Service Order with the RCD, contained a mixture of colonial troops and was not formally a Canadian unit.[6]

The early Australian and New Zealand contingents also went home at the end of 1900 and the beginning of 1901. They received an ecstatic welcome, some communities struck medals to present to the men and Edmund Barton, first Prime Minister of the newly-federated Australia, told the returned soldiers that "united Australia could never forget" deeds such as the defence of Elands River post. Perham's return to New Zealand was delayed by being captured by the Boers while escorting some officers on a sightseeing trip to Paardeberg. "My rifle and bayonet were seized, also bandolier, leggings, watch and all valuables," he recalled. "A photo of a New Zealand lassie in my breast pocket was handed round for all to have a look at and then, with a grin, was handed back to me. One Boer made an attempt to remove my tunic but I protested so he did not persist." Later in the war such protestations would be ignored by the ill-clad Boers. Perham was well treated and eventually released with a pass signed by the Boer commandant to ensure that he walked unmolested to Kimberley. Ten days later he left for Cape Town where 400 New Zealanders rebelled against an order forbidding them from going into the centre and "marched to the town in a body and quite enoyed themselves too". The authorities decide to placate rather than punish men who were so near to embarkation and it was not long before Perham was home. "Invercargill was all out to give us a right royal welcome, the decorations were wonderful and there were cheering crowds everywhere," wrote Perham. But his return was tinged with sadness because his brother Luke had been killed in action with the New Zealanders in South Africa the previous August.[8]

Kitchener's urgent need for mounted troops led to the British Government agreeing to the despatch of 30,000 men, including 17,000 Imperial Yeomanry and 8,000 South African Constabulary, in the early months of 1901. Fresh contingents were requested from the colonies to provide the rest and between February and April Australia sent 5,219 men and New Zealand 1,118, while a further draft of 321 Australians sailed in August.[4] When the Canadians suggested sending another contingent in early 1901 the British at first hesitated before telling the Ottawa Government that further troops were not needed, although recruiting for the SAC in Canada continued.

Among the overseas colonials who arrived in South Africa in early 1901 were the 5th Victorian Mounted Rifles who by June found themselves in the eastern Transvaal. They were part of a column commanded by Major-General S.B. Beatson, an Indian Army cavalry officer whose relationship with his Australian troops was soon to provoke a political row. On 10 June 350 Victorians commanded by Major Morris of the Royal Artillery were sent south of Middelburg to sweep through the country. Two days later they received an order from Beatson not to go any further south and they camped near a farm called Wilmansrust. Morris ordered that at night rifles should be stacked according to regulations rather than retained by the men, an unwise move during a guerrilla war. Pickets were placed too far apart and positioned in daylight, when their location was noted by local Boer farmers. That night 150 Boers evaded the pickets and attacked the camp, completely surprising the Australians. "The Boers went through the camp, shooting men down and yelling like madmen," said Trooper Frank Halsall. Unable to get to their rifles quickly, the Victorians lost fourteen killed and forty-six wounded of whom four later died. Another eighty were taken prisoner but released that night.

The survivors rejoined the column where Beatson condemned the Australians as a "a lot of white-livered curs". This resulted in a near-mutiny in early July when some men discussed whether they should refuse to march with Beatson. Three of the alleged ringleaders Troopers James Steele, Arthur Richards and Herbert

Parry were court-martialled and sentenced to be shot, although this was commuted to imprisonment and they were sent to serve their sentences in England. Australians living in London petitioned King Edward VII for their release while the Australian Government took the issue up with its British counterpart. The three men were released soon afterwards, allegedly because they had been tried under the wrong section of the Army Act but more probably because the whole matter had become politically embarrasing.[5]

Many of the details of the Beatson affair, including his comments about the Australians, were hushed up at the time. Much secrecy also surrounded the fate of Lieutenants Morant and Handcock, who were executed in 1902. Harry 'Breaker' Morant and Peter Handcock were serving in a South African irregular unit called the Bushveldt Carbineers, which was mainly comprised of Australians, in a remote part of the northern Transvaal. In 1901 the two Australian officers were accused of murdering Boer prisoners and after conviction were executed by firing squad. They claimed that they were obeying orders and that shooting prisoners had become accepted practice and to this day many aspects of the case are still unclear. Kitchener, who could have commuted their death sentences, chose not to exercise his prerogative of mercy and the case was kept secret until after they were shot. Both this case and that of the three troopers from the Victorian Mounted Rifles sowed discord in the imperial family, contributing to a long legacy of anti-British feeling in Australia.

In November, 1901, the British Government changed its mind about further Canadian volunteers and requested a corps of yeomanry, which would be paid for by Britain but be clearly a Canadian unit. It was named the 2nd Regiment Canadian Mounted Rifles and 900 officers and men were recruited, a quarter of whom had already seen service in South Africa. The sixty-one-strong 10th Canadian Field Hospital was recruited at the same time but the two units did not arrive in South Africa until February, 1902. The Canadian Government, which still had mixed feelings about the conflict, unwillingly agreed to raise another 2,000 men for the Mounted Rifles but they did not get to South Africa until the war was over. In 1902 the new Australian federal administration despatched more than 4,000 men in what was now called the Australian Commonwealth Horse, while New Zealand sent another 3,284 men to help meet the continuing need for mounted troops. Kitchener had a high opinion of the overseas colonials and used many of them in the vast drives he was organizing to ensnare the remaining commandos.

The Boers still in the field continued to give Kitchener's forces a bloody nose at every opportunity. The 5th Queensland Imperial Bushmen suffered heavily at Onverwacht in the eastern Tranvaal on 4 January when a British column was surprised by 500 Boers, most of whom had been hiding in a deep hollow. The Queenslanders and the Hampshire Regiment Mounted Infantry made a brave stand on a small ridge with little cover, the Australians losing thirteen dead and eighteen wounded before being overwhelmed. At the end of February De Wet, twisting and turning like a hunted animal to avoid a drive in the eastern Orange Free State, decided to break through the advancing line at Langverwacht. In his path were seventy-six men of the 7th New Zealand Mounted Rifles who lost twenty-three killed and forty-three wounded as De Wet, swinging his sjambok to encourage his less committed burghers, forced his way through.

On 31 March the Canadians had their heaviest casualties since Paardeberg at Boschbult in the south-west Transvaal. A column commanded by Lieutenant-Colonel George Cookson of the Bengal Lancers, which included some of the 2nd Canadian Mounted Rifles, set off on a reconnaissance. The column was led by a decoy Boer force into the arms of a larger one and Cookson established his defences in a farm. During the fighting which lasted all afternoon a small party of the CMR, led by Lieutenant Bruce Carruthers, was almost wiped out while defending an outlying position. Faced by overwhelming odds and with little cover the twenty-one Canadians fought to the end, seventeen being killed or wounded, the dead including Carruthers. One mortally wounded man broke his rifle as the Boers approached to ensure it would not be captured, another who had been hit in six places kept firing until the attackers got to within 25 yards and then threw the bolt away. The Boers called off their attack on the main British position having inflicted 178 casualties, the Canadians losing eleven dead and forty-three wounded. It was the Canadian third contingent's first and last major action of the war.[10]

Almost 30,000 overseas colonials served in South Africa, but although they formed only a small part of the overall imperial war effort they had a usefulness out of all proportion to the size of the contingent. This was partly because, except for some medical staff and the Canadian infantry and gunners, they were virtually all mounted troops. They were also the sort of independently minded resourceful soldiers who were ideal for taking on the Boers. The British war correspondent Edgar Wallace was impressed by an Australian scout operating with a column. "He tells the officer commanding that force many things, there are Boers on a farm three miles ahead or a Boer convoy is five miles to the front," wrote Wallace. "He is not a soldier as we in London know soldiers. He doesn't like shouldering arms by numbers and he votes squad drill damn silly."[5] The British Army was constantly amazed by the free and easy ways of the colonials. The Queensland Imperial Bushmen taught the volunteers from the London Scottish that the best way to clean a rifle barrel was to fire a bullet first thing in the morning.[11] One British regular officer attached to a column complained to its colonial commander that his men never saluted him. "Neither do they me," replied the colonel, "but they can fight."[12]

The other side of the coin was that some of the colonial officers, particularly those with the later contingents, were not up to scratch, whilst among their men discipline sometimes broke down altogether. They were usually well behaved out on the veldt where there was nothing to do but hunt Boers but all hell could let loose once they were near a railway or a town. One unit of Bushmen had to be locked in a barbed wire compound for 24 hours after firing from the open railway trucks in which they were travelling at almost anything that moved.[5] Rice of the Wiltshire Imperial Yeomanry described an anarchic scene in Cape Town. "I remember seeing a mounted policeman riding up to a group of Aussies in Adderly Street and telling them to get back to camp," he wrote. "They simply surrounded his horse and at a given signal his feet were taken out of the stirrups, he was hoisted up by a heave under his boots, at the same time another chap hit the horse by his tail and away he went, the policeman sitting down hard in the road. They went into the bars for a drink but all the pubs were forbidden to serve them so they shot at the bottles on the shelf behind the counter, the barman fled, then they helped themselves."[13]

Although at the time the colonial contribution was hailed as a triumph for imperial unity, in fact it helped set in motion a move towards a greater sense of nationhood which was to continue for the rest of the 20th century. At first the War Office in London patronisingly wanted a token colonial presence until it discovered that it needed these contingents urgently after Black Week. At the same time the overseas colonials, volunteering for the usual mixture of reasons which included patriotism and a sense of adventure, discovered an identity of their own. By the First World War Canada, Australia and New Zealand had laid the foundations of their own modern armies and wanted their own military formations. The imperial family was growing up fast and the Boer War had proved to be an important catalyst in this process.

CHAPTER EIGHT

THE SECOND CONTINGENT

The chaos at Aldershot was more than the unfortunate Lieutenant-Colonel Hew Fanshawe of the 2nd Dragoon Guards could cope with. The recruits for the second contingent of the Imperial Yeomanry, soon popularly known as the New Yeomanry, poured in by the thousand filling the Wellington and Stanhope Lines at the Hampshire Army base and spilling over into the Marlborough Lines. Some arrived without any warning, others drifted in drunk in ones and twos, while many turned up without anyone in charge of them. A few of those on the official rolls handed in were missing altogether. The first batch arrived on 24 January, 1901, and within a week 1,500 men needed feeding and kitting out. Fanshawe had been given the task of dealing with them but his resources were completely inadequate, the first 1,100 men arriving before an adjutant had been appointed. As another 10,000 men came in during February, the Imperial Yeomanry depot had only seven officers to handle them. Experience soon taught them that only about 450 a day could be clothed and often the yeomen waited several days before they got their uniforms and equipment.[1] "Paraded four times altogether but each time dismissed without anything being done," wrote Robert Hay, from Edinburgh, in his diary on 7 February.[2] The workload overwhelmed Fanshawe and by the end of February it was decided that a more senior officer was needed to take charge. The man chosen was Major-General Henry Mackinnon, who had commanded the CIV infantry in South Africa with such distinction. Even after he arrived the confusion at Aldershot was so great that Mackinnon later admitted: "After shipping out 13,000 or 14,000 yeomen to South Africa, we discovered that we had seventy officers still left who had not even joined at Aldershot, although we had shipped off the whole of the men."[3] The fact that almost one in seven of the officers of the second contingent had not been sent out with the men they were to command says everything about the hurried and disorganized way in which the force was raised. It was a farcical episode.

War Office intransigence over providing drafts for the Imperial Yeomanry was partly to blame. Kitchener, too often ready to cut corners without thinking through the consequences of his orders, must also take his share of responsibility. The second contingent was raised because of the urgent need for more mounted troops in South Africa. By late 1900 there were estimated to be only 20,000 Boers in the field but they had been winnowed down to the very best and hardest men. The half-hearted, the lazy and the cowardly had already returned to their farms or surrendered. On paper Kitchener's superiority was overwhelming, with more than 200,000 men now in South Africa, but most of these were tied up in garrisons or on the lines of communication. More mounted men were needed to hunt down the remaining commandos and protect convoys, but there was already a shortage and the situation was getting worse. Some of the colonial troops, their term of service over, were heading for home, the much improved mounted infantry had been ground down by constant campaigning and the first contingent of the Imperial Yeomanry was reduced to little more than a third of its original strength of nearly 11,000. The yeomanry's shrinkage was unnecessary, indeed scandalous, because Lucas and the other senior officers who had created it had constantly urged that they should be allowed to recruit drafts to keep it up to strength. The War Office refused all such requests, claiming that it would raise men itself through the existing Regular Army system but in fact doing nothing. In December, 1900, just after Clements had come so close to disaster at Nooitgedacht, Lucas tried again, proposing to raise 5,000 reinforcements, but once more he was turned down.

Kitchener, with typical forcefulness, set about solving his

shortage of mounted troops and had a powerful ally in Roberts, now back in Whitehall. New recruits for the Imperial Yeomanry were on Kitchener's shopping list, along with more colonial troops, a couple of regiments of regular cavalry still in England and 1,000 mounted infantry who had just finished training at Aldershot. But he did not want to resurrect the Imperial Yeomanry organization of 1900 with its committees of landed gentry and independent procurement organization. In early January the Commander-in-Chief wrote to Brodrick, the new Secretary of State for War: "I hope you will be able to send out some yeomanry drafts as they are a very useful body of men. Lord Chesham has written a memo which I have forwarded with the object of doing away with any cumbrous organization in England for getting recruits for the yeomanry."[4] A couple of weeks later Roberts wrote to Kitchener assuring him that, after his return to Britain, "almost the first thing I did was to submit a memo pointing out the necessity of sending you more mounted troops." Soon afterwards Roberts told Kitchener that the Government "took my advice about sending you as many mounted men as possible and as soon as possible and we have got leave to despatch 30,000."[5] Of these 5,000 were yeomanry to be sent out before the end of February with another 5,000 yeomen to be despatched later. Most of the rest were colonial troops and from the new South African Constabulary, which was being raised in Britain and the colonies by Baden-Powell, the hero of Mafeking.

The New Yeomanry had little in common with the first contingent and reflected the change in public attitudes to the war since those emotional days in the wake of Black Week. The incentives now were money and the chance to emigrate, not patriotism or the prospect of adventure. The second contingent was to be paid five shillings a day, four times the standard cavalry rate earned by the first Imperial Yeomanry and the same as colonial troops. This removed a grievance over differentials which had caused much discontent among the first contingent until their pay had been increased to five shillings in January. Brodrick begrudged the expense of the New Yeomanry, complaining to Kitchener that "they are the most costly force who ever left these islands".[4] In 1900 married men had been discouraged from joining. A year later they were not only encouraged but the Government promised that it would help their families to join them in South Africa if they decided to stay there after the war. Milner's long-term imperial game plan was to anglicize South Africa with thousands of loyal British settlers. Only that way, he believed, would the Boers finally be crushed. One of the greatest strengths of the first contingent had been the raising of local units frequently led by officers well known to their men and the subject of much pride in the counties where they were recruited. With a few exceptions, this system was swept away and although the home yeomanry regiments were once again given the task of recruiting, the men had to be sent to Aldershot within six days of being signed up. There they were formed into sections of 110 and bundled off to South Africa, each draft under the command of a 2nd Lieutenant, whom they had usually never met before. Although the men had been asked which company they wanted to join, this pretence of keeping county units intact was quickly abandoned. Enlistments were for the Imperial Yeomanry generally and Hampshiremen were mixed up with men from Hertfordshire, Yorkshiremen sailed alongside Scottish recruits and Cockneys were despatched with men from Devon.

The new scheme made the raising of the first contingent seem almost leisurely by comparison. On 15 January Roberts asked two officers to prepare a plan for the New Yeomanry and appointed Lucas as Deputy Adjutant General of the force. The Army Order outlining the scheme was published two days later and recruiting began immediately. The War Office was doubtful that enough men would come forward but Lucas was confident that the new terms, particularly the high pay, would attract between 15,000 and 25,000 recruits. He was soon proved right, thousands of men turning up at the fifty-one recruiting centres, thirty-eight of them run by the yeomanry regiments and most of the rest by a small number of authorized Special Corps. By 9 February the initial target of 5,000 men had been reached and the War Office announced that up to12,000 could be recruited. Roberts was optimistic about the force, telling Kitchener on 15 February:

"The yeomanry enlistment progresses satisfactorily, over 7,000 were passed up to last night, good men on the whole I am told."[5] Soon more than 10,000 men had been accepted and as more were still coming forward the ceiling was raised to 15,000. By 4 March 13,644 had joined up and 300 more were expected from Ireland and with the annual drill season of the yeomanry regiments approaching it was felt that they should stop recruiting. The following day it was announced that all recruiting should cease except for the few units being allowed to go out fully formed and men who had already been promised that they could enlist.[6] Recruiting was also allowed to continue in Ireland, where the war was dividing the country along sectarian lines. There were plenty of recruits in the Unionist north but less enthusiasm in Dublin and none at all in the rest of the south. Of the 748 men who joined in Ireland, 582 enlisted in Belfast, all the Irish recruits being sent to the Curragh instead of Aldershot. Across the whole of Britain 16,431 men out of 39,045 who had come forward in less than two months had been accepted. The War Office's limit of 15,000 had been breached but all were sent to South Africa. The New Yeomanry, the subject of much controversy and ridicule in the months to come, had been born.

Some yeomanry regiments were impressed by their new men, the South Nottinghamshire Hussars reporting that "all recruits were equal in every respect to those previously raised for the Imperial Yeomanry" and the Royal Wiltshire Yeomanry describing its men as being of "as good a stamp as those raised last year". But mostly the recruits were very different from those who had joined the Imperial Yeomanry in 1900. Gone were most of the gentlemen rankers and prosperous farmers who had enlisted in the first contingent. The New Yeomanry was predominantly urban and overwhelmingly working class, many of them being skilled men. The Hampshire Carabiniers reported that the ninety-two men it had selected out of 356 who applied were "nothing like the class of last year in any way" and added snootily that they were "not the class of men from which Hampshire Carabiniers are recruited". The Queen's Own West Kent Yeomanry said that the recruits were "inferior to those enlisted last year both physically and socially". Whereas in 1900 the men of Kent would have enlisted without any pay at all, in 1901 "the increased temptation in the way of pay for the most part only attracted idle, loafing unemployed youths who are not so likely to settle down to a steady colonial life." Despite this criticism the West Kents were remarkably undiscriminating, accepting 198 of the 230 men who made their way to the drill hall in Maidstone. By comparison the Duke of Lancaster's Own Yeomanry enlisted only 315 of its 1,503 applicants in Manchester, Liverpool and the the industrial towns of Lancashire. The regiment said that "large numbers were rejected at preliminary inspection as not being of the right stamp, being undersized, weedy and loafers evidently attracted by the pay."[7] In Ireland, which the previous year had raised the prestigious Dublin Hunt Company, there were problems with absenteeism and drunkenness among the 1901 recruits.

Vincent, that most persistent campaigner for the involvement of the auxiliary forces in the war, was horrified by what he saw. "Duke Street, Piccadilly was taken up with the most extraordinary looking out-at elbow crowds trying to enlist into the yeomanry," he told the Royal Commission.[8] Curiously, the scenes he witnessed were at the offices of the Duke of Cambridge's Own, which in 1900 had recruited a select company of gentlemen prepared to pay their own passage to South Africa, but a year later became notorious for the large number and poor quality of its recruits. Many of the 2,424 men its committee enlisted were among those later sent home from South Africa because they were medically unfit or poor soldiers. Lucas visited Duke Street and "told them that their recruits were not in my opinion up to the standard."[9] However, the DCOs, apparently motivated by the desire to find potential settlers rather than good soldiers, persisted in signing up men who had already been rejected by other recruiting offices. Knight described the quality of the DCO's recruits as "disgraceful" and said that they were even worse than the second contingent men enlisted at Leicester and Reading, who were also notoriously bad.[10] The DCO's committee had originally planned to send two complete battalions to South Africa but soon decided that it would be better to send all their recruits to the Imperial Yeomanry's melting pot in Aldershot because they could not find the right officers. It was as well they did so, for had their 1901 recruits gone out as a unit, they would probably have suffered a far worse disaster than the surrender at Lindley.

The re-emergence of the DCO's committee, even if its recruitment standards had been dramatically lowered, showed that the spirit which had characterized the raising of the first contingent was not entirely dead. Paget's Horse raised another 448 men and was praised for the quality of its recruits but like the DCOs did not go out to South Africa as a battalion. Only a few ready formed units were allowed by the War Office, which shared Kitchener's aversion to reviving the original Imperial Yeomanry organization. The Sharpshooters, their committee once again led by the Earl of Dunraven and Henry Seton-Karr MP, raised two whole battalions, the 21st and the 23rd. As in 1900 their shooting test was tougher than that in the Imperial Yeomanry generally which probably explains why half the 1,205 men they recruited came from the Volunteer Force and almost one in six were former regulars. The men were mostly earning good money in civilian life as clerks, grooms, merchant seamen, electrical engineers and farmers and were far better raw material than most of the second contingent. They came from all over Britain and the best were recruited in northern England and Scotland.

The Rough Riders also shook the dust off their 1900 organization and recruited 509 men at their offices near Victoria station in London although they admitted that they were "not socially of so high a standard as last year". These recruits, two-thirds of whom had no previous military experience, were formed into the 22nd Battalion, drilling on Horse Guards Parade before sailing together on 1st April. The last of the four fully formed battalions was the 24th (Metropolitan Mounted Rifles), who were mostly Volunteer Force men from London. This new unit was the brainchild of Colonel Henry Byrne, commanding the 21st Middlesex Volunteer Rifle Corps, and was based at the latter's barracks in Pentonville, north London. Byrne, who commanded the battalion in South Africa, found experienced officers to lead it and his men were at least given plenty of drill before they left even if their training was sketchy. The War Office also sanctioned three companies of Imperial Yeomanry, the 88th and 89th raised in Wales by Sir Watkin Williams-Wynn, and the 98th, recruited from Volunteer Force gunners in North Yorkshire.[11] The rest of the second contingent had to take its chance in the chaos developing at Aldershot.

Even these few units had to fight hard to avoid being sent out to South Africa piecemeal. Lieutenant-Colonel Alexander Weston Jarvis, who commanded the 21st Battalion, successfully resisted War Office pressure to have it broken up and his men eventually left England together. "I felt that if they were sent out in drafts of 110 I should never see the regiment again," he explained.[12] The Sharpshooters, the Metropolitan Mounted Rifles and the Welsh companies were allowed to clothe and equip themselves as the first contingent had done. But the War Office was against too many local initiatives and a request from the Rough Riders Committee that its battalion should be allowed to wear a distinctive badge and belt buckle was turned down.

But for all the curled lips and raised eyebrows among those who remembered the superior class of 1900, the men who enlisted the following year were still of a far better quality than Regular Army recruits. One third of those who enlisted in the Metropolitan Mounted Rifles were mechanics, engineers and skilled workmen and another third were clerks. The new Derbyshire contingent contained railwaymen, clerks, foundrymen and mechanics while many of the 609 men selected by the Queen's Own Royal Glasgow Yeomanry were from "a superior class of tradesmen".[7] This was what Milner dreamed of, skilled men in search of a better life who would outnumber the Boers and make South Africa safe for the Empire. The men may not have shared his grandiose dream but their motivation for joining, where it was not high pay or to escape from unemployment, was frequently emigration. Many believed that the war was almost over and that at the worst they would have to do only a little fighting before they could begin a new life having travelled out at the Government's expense. Scottish recruits were particularly keen to move to South

Africa, the Imperial Yeomanry office in Edinburgh reporting that 60 per cent of the men it enlisted would settle there while Colonel Sir John Gilmour of the Fife and Forfar Light Horse wrote: "It was evident that the great majority of applicants desired to reach South Africa more with the personal object of doing well for themselves as settlers rather than as fighting men."[13] Lucas, who knew the contingent better than most, summed the men up well. "The second contingent may have been a little inferior socially to the first but they were a superior class of men to the ordinary Army recruits," he said. "They were not men who were going to adopt the Army as a profession, they were mechanics and workmen who, owing to slackness of labour, thought it was a good opportunity to earn five shillings a day. There was no doubt that was a great inducement and they also wanted to go out to South Africa with the idea of settling out there."[14]

The problem was that the New Yeomanry was very raw material indeed and the men had little time to learn their new trade. Roughly two-thirds of them, 10,407 out of the 16,431 who joined, came straight from civilian life. Of the 6,000 with some sort of previous military experience just under 4,000 were from the Volunteer Force while the yeomanry, which had provided almost one fifth of the first contingent, contributed only 622 men. There were 846 ex-regulars and 597 from other military forces, some of whom had already served in South Africa in the Imperial Yeomanry or locally raised forces.[7] However, this was a force consisting overwhelmingly of Volunteer Force recruits who could shoot but not ride and civilians who could do neither. These were not Wyndham's foxhunters and farmers, indeed the only time some of them had previously been astride a saddle was on a beach donkey ride in Margate or Blackpool. Chesham later admitted: "I suppose out of the new lot, the 1901 Yeomanry, 75 per cent had never been on a horse before they passed the test in riding at home and about 25 per cent had ridden very little."[15] Although 3,629 men, almost ten per cent of those who applied to join, were rejected because they could not ride, the tests were often a farce. The Duke of Cambridge's Own turned away just ten men out of more than 4,700 applicants for lack of riding skill.

The West Kent Yeomanry admitted that "had as strict a test been applied as last year the percentage of men rejected for riding would have been double." The North Somerset Yeomanry insisted on higher standards, failing one third of its applicants on the riding test, but said that "there was great difficulty in obtaining men who could ride even a quiet horse around a riding school". The shooting of the recruits from the Volunteer Force was mostly good but was woefully bad among those who had not had the advantage of being 'Saturday Night Soldiers'. In all 3,162 applicants failed the shooting test but the standards applied varied dramatically from area to area. In Dorset the yeomanry admitted that the men's shooting was "inferior" but rejected only one out of 153 potential recruits while in Derbyshire where "many candidates had no idea of shooting" 248 out of 652 failed the test.[7] In some counties there were allegations that men only passed by bribery or by getting somebody else who could shoot to impersonate them at the ranges. The War Office, which was spending so much on the men's pay, decided parsimoniously to restrict the issue of ammunition to twenty-one rounds per man. Yeomanry commanding officers argued that this was inadequate but appeals to increase the allocation were turned down. For many of the New Yeomanry these were the only shots they fired before they found themselves fighting the veteran Boer commandos in South Africa.

As he struggled to cope at Aldershot, Fanshawe saw at first hand the consequences of the men's failings having been ignored. "I consider the riding and shooting tests as carried out in most cases were quite useless," he wrote. "The majority of the men had no idea of riding and the shooting which I saw would have been considered very bad for a bunch of infantry or cavalry recruits." He and his hard-pressed staff had little time to do anything about this. The men were instructed in the care and handling of rifles but the ranges at Aldershot were so far away and the winter weather so bad that it was impossible to do much target practice. Every day 180 men out of the thousands now milling around the base were given some riding instruction on horses lent by the regular cavalry. After riding, the men were sent to the regiment which supplied the horses to groom the animals and clean their saddlery.[1] Most of the men had no riding training at all and when they arrived at their base camp in South Africa had the greatest difficulty in even getting on and off their horses. The training given to the first contingent of Imperial Yeomanry had been poor but compared to that received by its successors a year later it seemed a marvel of thoroughness and care.

In its desperate haste to recruit men the War Office also relaxed the medical tests for the New Yeomanry. It was decided that a recruit need not be up to the physical standard required for the Regular Army and would be accepted provided that he was "free from organic disease or other defect likely to prevent him from doing his work during the duration of the present war".[16] The decision did not take into account the realities of the conflict in South Africa, where punishingly hot days, freezing nights and long hours in the saddle exacted a terrible physical toll on mounted troops. Tougher men were needed, not those who would normally have been rejected. Even this reduced standard of fitness was not always enforced. Although 5,501 applicants for the new force were rejected on medical grounds, many doctors were overwhelmed by the large numbers to be examined in such a short time and did not carry out the tests rigorously. Some almost certainly turned a blind eye to the physical shortcomings of the men they approved. When they were given a further examination in South Africa hundreds of the men were found to be unfit. Of the 724 men of the second contingent sent home because they were unlikely to become efficient soldiers, most were rejected for medical reasons. Some of them had heart or lung problems, others had varicose veins, bronchitis, hernias, dental problems or general debility. All should have been weeded out in England. The War Office was only saved from further em- barrassment by the fact that most of the recruits came from manual jobs which ensured a basic level of fitness and they quickly adapted to the harsh conditions in South Africa.

The greatest scandal surrounding the second contingent was its recruitment of some of the most incompetent officers ever sent overseas by the British Army. Like almost everything connected with the raising of the force this was a direct result of the speed and lack of forethought with which it was organized. By this stage of the war there was also a serious shortage of good, experienced officers available. The War Office had imposed restrictions on applications for commissions in the Imperial Yeomanry. Regular officers and those in militia battalions which had been called up were banned from applying and most of those in the Reserve of Officers were required for the regular forces. This left the posts to be filled by officers of unembodied militia battalions, the Volunteer Force and the yeomanry, together with men who had already served in the ranks in South Africa. The best of the yeomanry officers had gone out with the first contingent and few came forward to join the second. Militia and Volunteer Force officers usually had no experience of active service and no training in mounted warfare. Many were indifferent horsemen and did not have a good eye for ground. Men who had already served in South Africa sometimes made excellent officers but many lacked the right leadership qualities and others turned out to be scoundrels and drunkards utterly unfitted for a commission.

More than 3,000 men applied for just over 500 commissions available in the new force. There was supposed to be a proper vetting procedure, the applicant filling in a form stating his previous service and attaching a recommendation from his former commanding officer or someone else who could give a valid opinion as to his abilities. In theory all applicants then had to be interviewed by the officers given the responsibility for raising the new force before final selections were made. Because the second contingent was hastily scrambled together in a few weeks this did not happen. "In some cases these candidates for commissions did not see any responsible officer," Knight admitted to the Royal Commission. "In some cases they saw the hall porter who gave them a form to fill up. In other cases they only wrote and had a form sent to fill up in which they were asked to give two references and they were told they had to be medically examined."[17] The references usually went unchecked and some were undoubtedly bogus. Lucas conceded that many references "were found to have been made without suf-

178

ficient acquaintance with the qualifications of the individual concerned."[18]

The second contingent was sent to South Africa so rapidly that the full extent of the problem did not become obvious until the officers began arriving with the drafts they were commanding at the new Imperial Yeomanry depot at Elandsfontein, near Johannesburg. Knight recalled: "The result, as seen in South Africa, was startling. Some had never ridden, some had never been in decent society before, some had indifferent records as privates in the first contingent. As an instance, Sir John Sinclair, commanding one of the old squadrons, wrote to me when they arrived in the country and said, 'I see with disgust that three of my most inefficient privates have been given commissions in the yeomanry'." Of this trio one "was unable to hold his water when he saw a Boer", while another suffered from fits. They were not untypical. Knight added: "We had one man who was a Maltese. The only thing we were ever able to find out he could do was to play the piano. He refused to get on a horse at all. He is now taking money at the door at one of the principal hotels at Pretoria."

It was not uncommon for officers who had been put in charge of drafts of yeomen sent out from Britain to arrive drunk at Elandsfontein. Knight asked one such drunkard about his previous military service. On being told that he had been in the Imperial Light Horse, Knight sent for Major Karri Davies, one of the ILH's senior officers, who was nearby, and asked for his opinion of the newly commissioned man. Davies did not mince his words, describing him as an "impertinent, incompetent coward". Knight continued: "This man had served as a saddler in the 16th Lancers, he served as saddler sergeant in the Imperial Light Horse, he had never held any executive rank, he could not speak the King's English properly, his only comment when Major Davies's report was read to him was, 'Well, he didn't ought to have said that'. He was one of very many who were like that."[19]

Chesham was equally horrified by what he saw and later cited the case of one officer who was initially rejected in South Africa because his English was so bad that he could not control his men.

179

Further investigations revealed that he had an extremely colourful past. He had been jailed for two years for diamond stealing in Cape Town, had also served in the Bechuanaland police and had taken part in the defence of Mafeking. When Baden-Powell, who had commanded the Mafeking garrison, was asked for his view of him he described the man as "very plucky" but "such a hopeless drunkard that we had to reduce him from the rank of corporal". With the help of a persuasive tongue and a couple of medal ribbons this officer came very close to commanding his men in action.[15]

Much of the burden of dealing with these officers was shouldered by Major Arthur Poynter, who took over command of the new depot at Elandsfontein. Among those who Poynter encountered were Lieutenant Leyland-Naylor, whom he described as "a really low class adventurer and quite unsuitable", Lieutenant Mamo, rejected "because of his absolute want of power of command over men and because he was a hopeless rider" and Lieutenant Samson, another "hopeless drunkard". Perhaps the most bizarre of these incompetents was Lieutenant Stroud. "All he thought of when he arrived was advertising his embrocation," snapped Poynter. "The status of a yeomanry officer ranks lower than that of an officer of any of the irregulars who are recruited from the scum of South Africa."[9] The attitude of many of them towards paying bills was certainly irregular. The Field Force canteen in South Africa eventually refused to cash any more cheques from Imperial Yeomanry officers because so many had bounced.[20]

Out of 506 officers commissioned into the New Yeomanry forty-two were thrown out of the Army altogether as being beyond salvation. Many of them arrived back in Britain protesting furiously that they had been treated unfairly and that they had not been given a chance to prove themselves. They formed 8 per cent of the officers of the second contingent, but this figure concealed the true extent of the problem. The actual total of those rejected by the Imperial Yeomanry after they were commissioned was nearer 100, about 20 per cent of the total. Almost sixty were found jobs as railway staff officers or filling other harmless posts on the lines of communication where they would be less likely to put lives at risk.[21] To replace them dozens of regular officers already serving in South Africa and experienced in fighting the Boers were drafted into the Imperial Yeomanry and a few officers of the first contingent agreed to stay on. It was their knowledge which was to prove crucial in forging the second contingent into an effective fighting force after many trials and tribulations.

An internal inquiry ordered by the War Office said that the rejected officers were "mainly of three classes; those socially unfitted who did not secure the necessary respect of their men, those who proved unreliable owing to inebriety or monetary difficulties and those who were unable to ride and had not sufficient training to be entrusted with the command of men." The latter were the most numerous and the report argued that many of them would have become competent officers if there had been time to train them. It pointed out that regular officers usually learn their jobs from experienced NCOs and men, while the raw Imperial Yeomanry officers had been put in charge of completely untrained troops.[22]

It was not long before Parliament, the press and the public were asking questions about the raising of the second contingent in general and its officers in particular. Brodrick took the escape route traditionally favoured by governments at times of controversy and appointed a committee, chaired by General Sir Reginald Gipps, to look into the matter. The Gipps Report not surprisingly concluded that "the primary cause of any shortcomings in the quality of officers and men selected appears to have been the urgent demand for the recruitment of a very large number of troops in an unprecedentedly short space of time." It agreed that part of the problem was that Kitchener had asked for the new force to be sent to South Africa as soon as possible. Gipps and his colleagues were scathing about the selection of officers and concluded: "Many were granted commissions without a personal interview with a member of the Imperial Yeomanry Committee or any preliminary test of their capabilities in horsemanship. Moreover, of the candidates who had seen previous service, the majority were approved without reference to their former commanding officers, whose reports upon their character and capacity should have been called for in every instance."[9]

The Royal Commission said that "a little more care and forethought on the part of military authorities in this country would have induced them to prevent the despatch of this force in a state of disorganization which was the direct cause of the defects which became manifest on its landing in South Africa."[23] It was an extraordinary mess, the more so because it was completely unnecessary. Had regular drafts been sent to the first contingent after proper training in Britain the Imperial Yeomanry could have been kept up to strength without any of the dramas which marked its history throughout much of 1901.

The Scottish Horse, which was also recruiting men in Britain at this time, was neither part of the Imperial Yeomanry nor did it manage to remain entirely free of it. It was originally raised from Scots in South Africa in November, 1900, to act as a town guard in Johannesburg. Major the Marquess of Tullibardine of the Royal Horse Guards, son of the Duke of Atholl, felt that the Scots-born population of South Africa could be put to better use and wrote to Kitchener saying so. Tullibardine had no plans to join the regiment himself but as a result of his letter was told to take over command and raise four squadrons for active service. With the help of local Scottish societies, he soon had his men, about half of them Scots or of Scottish descent, the rest, as he later admitted, "being from anywhere", although he at first banned Boers, foreigners and half-castes. He got 200 of his best recruits from the Volunteer Service Companies of various Scottish regiments. Tullibardine said: "Whenever I heard that any of these companies were time-expired having finished their year in South Africa, I used to go down and interview them and get any of those who wished to stay on to see the end of the war or to get experience of mounted work or to settle in the country." They were used to discipline and excellent shots, and the Marquess praised them as the "best men I ever had in the regiment".[24]

In addition to recruiting in South Africa and later raising more than 500 men in Australia, Tullibardine also started casting his net in Scotland. Having got authority from Kitchener to recruit in

182

Britain, he wired the Highland Society of London for help. Unfortunately this enmeshed the enterprising aristocrat in the War Office's bureaucracy. In order to get permission to raise the men, the society had to agree that the Scottish Horse should be affiliated to the Imperial Yeomanry although in South Africa Tullibardine had already been given the go-ahead to organize it as an independent corps. Having made this concession the society then raised nearly 400 officers and men. But before they sailed in February and March, 1901, they were sent to Aldershot where they were caught up in the Imperial Yeomanry's shambolic organization. Instead of being allowed to wait until they were ready to go out as a complete unit, they were mixed up in various drafts and it took considerable initiative by Tullibardine to rescue them. "Having had their names privately sent to me, I boarded the ships containing drafts from home," he said. "On one ship containing about two or three hundred of the Duke of Cambridge's Yeomanry, I picked out eleven of my men and on another ship containing yeomanry, four. These men were included on the strength of the yeomanry squadrons to which they were attached." He then had the greatest difficulty in extricating them from this bureaucratic muddle despite the fact that "the only condition I made when I offered to raise the above men from home was that they should be directly under me in South Africa and not subject to the Imperial Yeomanry authorities."[24] It was months before problems about the men's pay were finally resolved.

Kitchener then told the Marquess to recruit a second regiment of Scottish Horse and he wrote to his father, who used his considerable influence to get the required men. Between June, 1901, and the end of the war more than 800 officers and men recruited in Edinburgh, Aberdeen, Perth, Stirling and Inverness were sent to South Africa, the Scottish capital providing the largest contingent. Altogether fifteen officers and 1,235 men were sent out from Britain to join the Scottish Horse. They were almost exclusively Scottish, only ninety-seven Englishmen, fifteen Irishmen, two Welshmen and eleven colonials being permitted to enter their ranks.[25] The same could not be said of the Scottish Horse in

South Africa which gradually abandoned its policy of refusing to recruit foreigners and Boers. Several Swedes living in South Africa were allowed to join and Boer scouts served with the regiment proving highly effective against their compatriots. As well as his Australians, Tullibardine also later tried to recruit Canadians but was refused permission by the Government in Ottawa. Even in a war where irregular units were commonplace, Tullibardine's scheme was highly eccentric. But he provided Kitchener with nearly 3,500 mounted men, most of whom proved good soldiers in this demanding guerrilla war.

Although the most pressing need was to recruit mounted troops for South Africa, the Government also decided to replace the original Volunteer Service Companies which returned to Britain in 1901. But the decision to pay the New Yeomanry the colonial rate of five shillings a day had a disastrous effect on recruiting for the new companies which were still paid at the normal infantry rate of one shilling. In 1900, when war fever was at its height, pay had not been so important for the volunteers but in the more mercenary atmosphere of the following year it was crucial. "The number of men was very much shorter than was anticipated but the reason was very obvious indeed, that the yeomanry were getting five shillings a day," said Vincent. "The volunteers desiring to serve their country in the field in 1901 and 1902 naturally therefore went to the five shillings a day service instead of to the one shilling a day."[26] The Imperial Yeomanry also provided opportunities for promotion to non-commissioned or commissioned ranks which were few and far between in the Volunteer Service Companies. Almost all Vincent's men from the Queen's Westminster Volunteers who joined the second contingent of the Imperial Yeomanry were immediately promoted to sergeant and some later received commissions. Because of this only forty-three new Volunteer Service Companies were raised and many of them were under strength, only 5,432 men embarking for South Africa.[27] The Green Howards, whose first company had numbered 115, had just thirty-five in 1901, the South Lancashires were down from 140 to thirty-two and the Bedfords from 137 to twenty-three.[28]

The men of the new Volunteer Service Company of the Royal Sussex Regiment embarked from Southampton at the end of April, 1901, alongside 800 newly recruited members of Baden-Powell's South African Constabulary, who were also on five shillings a day. An amusing incident showed that the SAC men were feeling financially flush. "Just as we were about to cast off one of these men tossed a telegram with a coin wrapped in it to a gentleman on the quayside, shouting, 'Send this off for me please, you can keep the change'," recalled Private John MacDonald of the Sussex company. "The gentleman caught it, gravely nodded and raised his hat and walked away. I do not know what the member said when he was later informed that he had chosen for his messenger the Duke of Norfolk, who was at that time Postmaster-General." As the Duke had previously served in South Africa with the Sussex Imperial Yeomanry he would have been familiar with the emotions of men leaving for the war and may even have obeyed his instructions. The Sussex volunteers did not feel capable of such largesse.[29]

A request from Kitchener that 1,000 cyclists be raised in Britain to speed across the veldt as a new mobile force fell on similarly stony ground. Only two of the eight planned companies, totalling 218 men, were raised. Another 325 men came forward from the Royal Engineers Volunteers along with a battery of gunners but the overall message was clear. From now on if the Government wanted men from the auxiliary forces or from civilian life to serve in South Africa it was going to have to pay for them. In just a year the mood of the British public, tired of a war which showed no sign of ending, had undergone a sea change.

CHAPTER NINE

DE WET'S OWN

The remnants of the 1900 Imperial Yeomanry looked on aghast as their replacements from the second contingent arrived. "Oh what fun they are," Lieutenant Barbour of the 21st (Cheshire) Company told his family. "They have done two marches but there are rarely more than three-quarters of them in the saddle at the same moment. On picket at night they started by firing at anything and everything, always imaginary."[1] The newcomers's inexperience caused endless extra work for Barbour, while Rice, still serving with the 2nd (Wiltshire) Company, was glad to board a train to Cape Town after a short spell with them. "They were of more use to the Boers than to the British as they let their horses go constantly," he recalled. "We had to go after them and bring them back but I am sure that some fell into the Boers' hands."[2] The colonial troops were equally contemptuous. A Canadian scout with a convoy being escorted through a dangerous area by the New Yeomanry remarked: "The Boers in this part of the world are not hungry or they would have taken us all long ago."[3] Trooper Waine of the New South Wales Mounted Rifles wrote home that the second contingent were such an invaluable source of rifles and remounts for the commandos that they had been dubbed 'De Wet's Own'.[4]

Even before they fired a shot in anger Brodrick was worried about the usefulness of a force raised in such haste. "I am glad you think the yeomanry draft will be useful though their rawness rather frightened me," he wrote to Kitchener.[5] All his fears were quickly justified, although it was hardly the fault of the hapless yeomen themselves. So urgent was the need for mounted troops and so insistent was Kitchener that they must be used immediately that some never got as far as the Imperial Yeomanry depot at Elandsfontein. Despite being ignorant of even the most basic rudiments of soldiering, they were ordered off trains taking them up from Cape Town and immediately sent into the field.

Those who got to Elandsfontein did not find it an enlightening experience. The camp itself was far better than the Imperial Yeomanry's first base at Maitland, situated on a gentle slope behind a kopje overlooking a valley near the mines of the Rand, with a healthy climate and a good water supply. In theory, after training, drafts of fifty men at a time were to be sent to the existing Imperial Yeomanry companies until all the first contingent had been replaced. In practice many of the new men were sent straight off from Elandsfontein and few were sent to the companies which they had asked to join back in England. The Cheshires' new men were Londoners who had signed on for the Duke of Cambridge's Own, while the Wiltshires received Scotsmen, including Hay and his comrades from Edinburgh, and the Glamorgans mainly Leicestershire men. The training for those who did stay at Elandsfontein was as sketchy as it had been at Aldershot. There were only 250 horses available for riding practice in a camp which by the end of April contained more than 5,000 men.[6] Most of these animals were so worn out that they were useless for active service which at least had the advantage of giving their inexperienced riders an easy start. The staff at the camp were in any case much too busy weeding out those who were medically unfit and getting rid of incompetent officers to have much time for instruction. They were also unclear as to who many of their men were because the yeomen had been sent out without being given individual service numbers and many had no papers and no record of when they had last been paid. "Owing to the way the country drafts had been mixed up at Aldershot and the incompetency of some of the officers placed in charge of them, it was exceedingly difficult to trace some men at all," admitted Knight.[7] Some of the documents had still not arrived by the end of the war.

On paper the second contingent comprised ninety-six

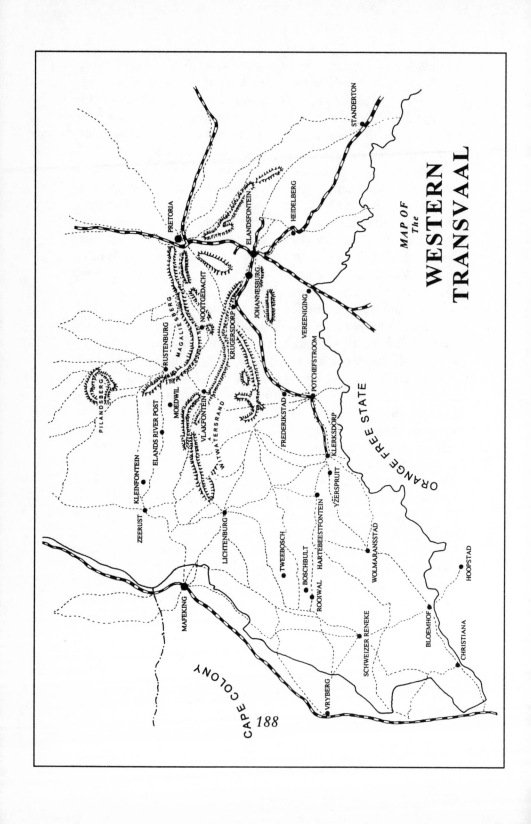

MAP OF
The

WESTERN
TRANSVAAL

STANDERTON

PRETORIA

ELANDSFONTEIN

HEIDELBERG

RUSTENBURG

NOOITGEDACHT

MAGALIESBERG

KRUGERSDORP

JOHANNESBURG

VEREENIGING

PILANDSBERG

ELANDS RIVER POST

MOEDWIL

VLAKFONTEIN

WITWATERSRAND

FREDERIKSTAD

POTCHEFSTROOM

KLERKSDORP

ORANGE FREE STATE

KLEINFONTEIN

VZERSPRUIT

ZEERUST

LICHTENBURG

TWEEBOSCH

HARTEBEESTFONTEIN

WOLMARANSSTAD

HOOPSTAD

BOSCHBULT

ROOIWAL

MAFEKING

SCHWEIZER RENEKE

BLOEMHOF

CHRISTIANA

CAPE COLONY

VRYBERG

188

companies, formed into seventeen battalions, some of the latter having four companies and others double that number. As with the first contingent, they were quickly scattered throughout the country wherever they were most urgently needed and many battalions became purely administrative units. The companies, increasingly referred to as squadrons, were attached to the various columns hunting the commandos between Pretoria and Graff Reinet, as well as to the west of Johannesburg and from Elandsfontein eastwards to the north-eastern Orange Free State. They also garrisoned towns such as Kimberley, Mafeking and Zeerust, theoretically ready to sally forth when required. The official strength of the companies was increased from 121 to 155, which had the advantage of requiring less officers for the whole force because the number of the latter in each company remained the same. This eased the problems caused by 20 per cent of the original officers having to be sacked or transferred to less demanding jobs.

The commanders to whom the second contingent was attached had to start from scratch giving them the training which they should have received at Aldershot and Elandsfontein. Rundle, who was given 3,000 yeomen, sent back 20 per cent of them, including most of the officers, because they were so useless. He then set about reorganizing the rest into three battalions, the 1st, the 4th and the 11th, with fresh officers and began to teach them the basics of their new occupation. However, when Rundle took 500 yeomanry on a march through the Brandwater Basin at the beginning of May, they were helpless in the wild ravines of the Wittebergen. The operation in a region which had produced such a rich harvest of prisoners the year before led to the capture of only one Boer and the deaths of a handful of others. In Kroonstad Major-General Edward Locke Elliot took a more realistic view of his new charges. When he organized an operation to flush out Boers he chose an area of flat country to the west of the railway between Kroonstad and the Vaal River. Three columns marched through the district without encountering any opposition but it at least gave the yeomanry some riding practice in easy terrain.[8]

The yeomen were shocked by the tough life for which they had so blithely volunteered. A month after arriving in South Africa, Private Joe Duncalf of the 22nd (Cheshire) Company wrote home: "All our men say they wish they were at home. They say they will never join the yeomanry again and I am sure I shall not. I have had enough but we have to make the best of it now and we laugh about it and talk about what fools we have been to give comfortable homes up." Duncalf, a devout Christian, found the destruction of Boer farms particularly shocking. "It makes my heart ache to see good things broken and homes broken up which had at one time been happy and peaceful," he told his family. "I say now 'curse war', I am sure God never meant war to be."[9]

The need for mounted troops was so great that some of the new Volunteer Service Companies found themselves in the saddle. The men of the 2nd Volunteer Company of the Royal Sussex Regiment were at first used as infantry escorts to convoys, but soon, MacDonald recalled, "practically the whole company had taken horses or bicycles and became mounted infantry." Unlike the first contingent of volunteers, MacDonald and his comrades were split up among the regular companies of the regiment rather than remaining as a separate entity. He wrote: "The life was that common to all mounted troops at this period, sudden moves, long marches by day or night and sometimes both in every sort of weather."[10] Many of the volunteer infantry found themselves guarding the lines of blockhouses which began to snake their way across South Africa in 1901. The Hampshires were in charge of a fever-plagued stretch of railway near Komati Poort in the eastern Transvaal where many of them went down with malaria as they built thirty blockhouses along the line. Some volunteers escorted trains, a dangerous occupation as men from the London Scottish attached to the Gordon Highlanders discovered when theirs was blown up by the Boers in the Transvaal. "We did not have time to recover from the shock before they fired a volley into us," said one of them. "It did not sound and feel nice, about eighty bullets striking the train at once." But the Gordons' armoured carriage stayed upright and they sallied out, driving off their attackers.[11]

The New Yeomanry had a shaky start in its first major action at Vlakfontein in the south-western Transvaal, on 29 May. The 230 yeomen of the 7th Battalion who had set off from Naauwpoort under Brigadier-General Henry Dixon three days earlier, were a mixture of first contingent men in their last days of service and newcomers from the second contingent. As was usual for the Imperial Yeomanry, they were not a complete battalion, only the 27th (Devonshire), 48th (North Somerset) and 69th (Sussex) Companies being present. Dixon also had 200 men of the Scottish Horse, six companies of infantry from the Derbyshire Regiment and the King's Own Scottish Borderers and seven artillery pieces. His task was to search for hidden guns and ammunition to the west of Naauwpoort, but, unknown to him, a 3,000 strong Boer force under the guerrilla leader Christoffel Kemp had assembled in the area. On the 29th Dixon reached Vlakfontein sixteen miles west of Naauwpoort where he left some of his infantry in camp and marched out in three detachments with the yeomanry on his left and the Scottish Horse on the right. A search for guns in the valley proved fruitless and at midday Dixon took the centre detachment back to a nearby farm where a cache of ammunition was found. Dixon decided that it was too late in the day to remove this hoard and ordered the whole force to return to camp. The yeomanry, together with 100 men of the Derbyshires and two guns, was to act as rearguard during the withdrawal.

Kemp was about to launch an ambitious strike against the rearguard. The Boers had already experimented with using mounted charges when attacking British columns but at Vlakfontein they added a new refinement to this tactic. At 1.30pm, just as the rearguard under Major Harry Chance of the Royal Artillery was preparing to retire, Kemp's men set fire to the nearby grass. Using the dense smoke as cover they began to drive in the yeomanry screen whilst simultaneously launching a feint attack on the Scottish Horse and the rest of the British detachment on the right. Chance pulled back his infantry and sent the guns after them, but the grass fire rapidly gained on the yeomanry with the Boers advancing just behind it. Suddenly the situation developed into a crisis. Masked by the smoke and aided by a yeomanry picket which had retreated without orders, the Boers outflanked Chance on his left and out of the flames burst 500 men, some firing from horseback, others shooting as they led their mounts at the run. The yeomanry suffered heavily, six of its sixteen officers being killed or mortally wounded. Among the dead were Captain Henry Armstrong, who had been commissioned into the Devon company a year previously, and Lieutenant Charles Campion of the Sussex company, an old Etonian and the nephew of an earl. Seventy of their men were killed or wounded and the rest panicked and galloped past the guns to the rear. The artillery was captured as the gunners were shot down and the Derbyshires in the rearguard almost annihilated, leaving Kemp in control of the ridge on which the fight had taken place.

By 2pm Dixon and Lieutenant-Colonel Charles Duff, commanding the Scottish Horse, who were both retiring towards the British camp, realized that Chance was in trouble although the scale of the problem was not yet apparent. Dixon galloped forward, ordering another company of the Derbyshires to mount a counter-attack, while Duff sent two companies of the KOSB to help. The Boers began to waver and when the British bayonets came close they galloped away. The infantry, joined by some of the yeomanry who had recovered their nerve, recaptured the guns and the ridge. The casualties in an hour and a half's fighting had been the heaviest since Nooitgedacht five months previously. The Boers lost forty-one killed while the British casualties were sixty-two dead and 118 wounded. The Scottish Horse escaped lightly but the Imperial Yeomanry lost more than a third of its number killed or wounded. Vlakfontein did little for its reputation although at this stage the Army was still inclined to be tolerant. Dixon, who had been caught with a divided force by an enemy whom he had not realized was there, refrained from criticizing the yeomanry in his report on the action. Kitchener told Brodrick: "I am afraid some of the New Yeomanry were somewhat wild but that must be expected at first."[12]

Such tolerance did not last and over the next few months the New Yeomanry was heavily criticized for its incompetence and willingness to surrender in a series of minor actions. Major Edmund Allenby, later to command the British forces in Palestine during the First World War, wrote scathingly: "These yeomen are useless. After being some months in the field they learn a bit but by the time they are of any use, they have probably been captured two or three times, presenting the Boers on each occasion with a horse, rifle and 150 rounds of ammunition per man."[4] Questions were asked about the second contingent in the House of Commons and there was derisive comment in some newspapers. Kitchener soon lost patience and as early as July suggested that the whole of the Imperial Yeomanry should be sent home. Both Roberts and Brodrick opposed this characteristically drastic solution. "You talk of sending back all the New Yeomanry," wrote Brodrick. "I am sorry they are doing so much less well than you hoped but I trust you will not get rid of them all at once. Surely the training of the winter must have given them some experience and it would be a little difficult here if they were discharged and you found yourself short of mounted troops." Roberts took the same line, telling the Commander-in-Chief, "I don't see how the strength of your mounted troops can be kept up, if the war lasts much longer, without yeomanry."[13]

However, Kitchener's rage began to subside and the willingness of the best of the second contingent to learn quickly was starting to win friends among the mainly Regular Army officers who commanded them. "The yeomanry have been doing better lately," Kitchener admitted to Brodrick in August. "We have got rid of a good many that were not worth five shillings a day and though there are still some that I cannot trust in the field, I am now getting more value out of the best of them."[5] The criticism in Parliament and the press angered some of those who saw the yeomanry's work at first hand. Lieutenant-Colonel John Keir, commanding the 1st Battalion, wrote in September: "Much indignation in 1st Imperial Yeomanry at reports in papers about new yeomen. Most unjust. In my opinion my men are very good indeed." The 12th Battalion's commander, Lieutenant-Colonel Cecil De Rougemont, asked: "Can you enlighten me as to why everyone crabs the New Yeomanry? I consider they are extremely good and brave as lions." Lieutenant-Colonel William Hickie, whose column included the 103rd (Warwickshire) and 107th

(Lanarkshire) Companies, joined this supportive chorus. "I see that they have been asking questions in the House about the New Yeomanry," he wrote. "I would not change these two companies for an equal number of men from any corps in South Africa."[14]

The gallant defence of a convoy at Rooikopjes, outside Griquatown, by men of the 74th (Dublin) Company on 24 August was one of a series of actions which began to change the Army's views in South Africa although public opinion in Britain proved harder to shift. The two-mile-long convoy was taking food to this remote town in the north-western Cape which was surrounded by Boer commandos and in urgent need of supplies. It was escorted by 100 men of the 74th Company, commanded by Major James Humby, who had been taken prisoner at Lindley the previous year, and some Northumberland Fusiliers and local troops. When the convoy was attacked by several hundred Boers 15 miles outside Griquatown, Humby quickly laagered the wagons. As he did so, the Irish Yeomanry seized a ridge which commanded the convoy and held it during fierce close-quarters fighting through an entire night, losing seven killed, and twenty-five wounded of whom seven later died. Three of them, Privates Oliffe, McLean and Bonynge, who had grown up as children together, were shot side by side and afterwards buried in the same grave. The Boers, who had between thirty and forty casualties, were beaten off and the convoy continued to Griquatown.[15]

The severest test for the New Yeomanry since Vlakfontein came in a two-day action in the Marico River Valley, near Rustenburg in the western Tranvaal, in early September. Kemp, reinforced by De la Rey, attacked Methuen's column on its way to Zeerust. The thickly bushed valley was full of Boer riflemen who poured in fire while the ox transport slowed the British to a crawl and the column was halted for four hours by a gun stuck in a spruit. The escort included men of the 5th and 9th Battalions Imperial Yeomanry who suffered most of the casualties, losing twelve dead and twenty wounded. Methuen pushed on to his destination, the yeomanry matching his determination with a toughness that would have been unthinkable a couple of months previously.[16]

The most graphic illustration of the New Yeomanry's improvement came at Moedwil, one of those short but bloody actions which were increasingly a feature of the guerrilla war. The engagement at Moedwil, fought in the early hours of 30 September, involved many of the same British troops who had come so close to disaster at nearby Vlakfontein four months previously. Dixon had been replaced by Colonel Robert Kekewich, who had commanded the defenders of Kimberley, and who had with him 370 men of the Derbyshire Regiment, 400 of the 1st Scottish Horse, 160 of the 7th Battalion Imperial Yeomanry and a few gunners. By the end of September most of the British columns had temporarily withdrawn from the cauldron of commando activity around the Magaliesberg to reorganize leaving only Kekewich still trekking. Like vultures drawn towards a corpse, De la Rey and Kemp closed in upon this force in the wild region of the Zwartruggens. Once again the British were completely unaware of their presence as Kekewich made his camp on the eastern bank of the Selous River. Good sites safe from Boer attack were hard to find in this broken and bushy country and Kekewich's camp had one serious defect. He had to choose between placing his pickets on the far bank of the river, where they would be too far away to be of much use, or on the near side where they would give him little warning of an attack. Kekewich opted for the latter course and sent the Derbyshires to guard his southern perimeter, while the yeomanry and the Scottish Horse manned most of the riverbank and his northern and eastern flanks.

De la Rey, who had assembled 1,500 men, planned to catch the British unawares, attacking from the river with his main force while two flanking detachments assaulted from the east. But at 4.45am a patrol of the 27th (Devonshire) Company Imperial Yeomanry stumbled across some of the Boers in the riverbed and opened fire. De la Rey was compelled to launch his attack before some of his force was in place. The Boers charged through the scrub on the east bank of the river and overwhelmed two small yeomanry pickets who resisted desperately. By 5am several hundred Boers were on the crest of the steep river bank pouring fire into the camp as it became dimly visible in the dawn. Kekewich, having got into a mess, proceeded to extricate himself with commendable coolness. The British suffered terrible casualties as the men stumbled out of their blankets into devastating Boer fire but within minutes, despite terrified horses and mules stampeding through the camp, a firing line was established on the slope to the west.

Kekewich then ordered a squadron of the Scottish Horse to saddle up and try to outflank the Boers, but this proved too ambitious. One of the Scottish Horse later recalled: "I had the saddle almost on one of my ponies when he was hit in two places. Two men trying to saddle alongside of me were both shot dead and Lieutenant Wortley was shot through the knee. I ran back to where I had been firing from and found the Colonel slightly hit, the Adjutant wounded, and dying and wounded all around." Kekewich was wounded twice, but although the British casualties were rising the main Boer attack gained no further ground and when Commandant Boshoff got into the camp with a few men he was bayoneted by Farrier-Sergeant Kirkpatrick of the Scottish Horse. The two flank assaults came to nothing, but a rumour that the Boers were about to attack from the north or east produced the decisive moment of the action. Major Watts of the Derbyshires collected up some men to beat off this feared attack, but, when it failed to materialize, he instead advanced north-west towards the left of the main Boer assault. As he did so he was joined by men of the Scottish Horse and the yeomanry who with bayonets fixed outflanked the Boers and at 6am charged down the riverbank. The Boers began to retreat and within a quarter of an hour the last of them were galloping away over the horizon. The British had saved themselves but were unable to pursue De la Rey because almost every horse in the camp had been killed or wounded.

Kekewich had lost 214 officers and men, almost a quarter of his strength, killed and wounded in an action which had lasted only an hour and a half. Of these seventy-one came from the Scottish Horse which had thirteen officers wounded, two of whom subsequently died. The yeomanry had thirty-six casualties of whom twelve were killed or fatally wounded. The Boer losses are thought to have been about sixty in the engagement which left both sides with some cause for satisfaction. De la Rey had succeeded in giving the British yet another bloody nose and had temporarily crippled the only column operating in the area at that time. The British, although caught napping once more, had shown courage and determination in beating off their attackers. In particular the yeomanry and the Scottish Horse had fought as well as the veteran infantry and the 7th Battalion had atoned for the shame of Vlakfontein.[17]

The following month De la Rey and Kemp struck again in the western Transvaal. This time their target was a column commanded by Lieutenant-Colonel Stanley von Donop which was marching to Zeerust. The 1,000-strong column, which included 680 men of the 5th Battalion Imperial Yeomanry, was surprised by the Boers at Kleinfontein at 7am on 24 October. The British were stunned to see 500 horsemen charge out of the woods around the road in three groups, each two or three lines deep. Riding like a regiment of European cavalry, the Boers went straight for the centre of the convoy shooting native drivers and seizing wagons. Some of the attackers fell on the rearguard which included a company of yeomanry which lost a quarter of its number and half its horses. The column had now been cut in two and it was two hours before von Donop was able to relieve the rearguard. The Boers were finally beaten off after they had driven away twelve wagons and inflicted eight-four casualties on the British of which half came from the yeomanry.[18]

Kitchener was becoming depressed by his inability to crush the commandos and was under increasing pressure from the British Government and press because of his failure to deliver victory. Rumours were circulating that he was about to be sacked and the catastrophe which befell Colonel George Benson's column at Bakenlaagte on 30 October did nothing to improve the Commander-in-Chief's morale. Benson, a Royal Artillery officer, was one of that rare breed of enterprising commanders who had adapted superbly to the demands of guerrilla warfare. In recent months his column had roamed the eastern Transvaal and with the help of good intelligence had had a series of successes against the Boers. The latter now decided that it was time to strike a blow against this thorn in their side. They chose their moment well for Benson's column was alone in the district, north-west of Ermelo, and he had recently had to exchange many of his seasoned troops for less experienced men. With about 2,000 men under his command, including 434 from the 2nd Scottish Horse, he set off north-west from Syferfontein on 30 October. Throughout the day the Boers gathered around him in increasing strength, threatening his rearguard, as he struggled towards a farm where he planned to camp for the night. At midday 500 Boer reinforcements under Louis Botha arrived, having ridden the last thirty miles without drawing rein and the commandos prepared to attack.

The British rearguard, which had been joined by Benson himself with two weak squadrons of Scottish Horse, was in a particularly vulnerable situation as it withdrew to a ridge south of the camp called Gun Hill. Botha seized the moment and ordered a charge. The Scottish Horse and some mounted infantry raced for the hill pursued by 900 Boers firing from the saddle or waving their rifles and shouting. As the British horsemen reached the hill, where two guns had been sited, Major Frederick Murray, commanding the Scottish Horse, shouted: "Stop and hold the ridge or else they'll lose the guns." With a few exceptions the men obeyed him, spreading out in a line along the hill. The Boers swept over some unfortunate British infantry in their path and flung themselves from their horses in dead ground at the foot of Gun Hill. The battle which ensued was the stuff of which Victorian and Edwardian military legend was made, full of individual gallantry and heroic, sometimes pointless, sacrifice. Captain Thomas Lloyd of the Coldstream Guards, Benson's Assistant Staff Officer, galloped up to the rear of the guns, dismounted and threw his reins to a trooper. At that moment both the trooper and the horse were shot dead but Lloyd sauntered, upright, unarmed and apparently oblivious to the slaughter around him, towards Benson before himself falling riddled with bullets. Some men risked their lives for more reason. Squadron

Quartermaster Sergeant Warnock of the Scottish Horse, who had previously served for twenty-one years in the King's Own Scottish Borderers, took charge of two ammunition carts at the rear of the hill and with two other men crawled up with boxes of cartridges. He then seized a dead man's rifle and picked off Boers before collapsing after being wounded three times.

No reinforcements reached them, the men in the rest of the scattered British force not realizing the extent of the crisis around the guns, and after a quarter of an hour Benson was mortally wounded and the Boers captured the hill. The defenders had been almost wiped out, all but six of the seventy-nine Scottish Horse on the hill being killed or wounded, Murray being among the dead. Altogether the column lost more than 350 men, including 120 prisoners. The Boers, who had suffered nearly 100 casualties, were unable to press home their advantage against the rest of the column but took away the captured guns. Benson died later that night, his death providing a boost to Boer morale. The tragedy was that he should have been back in camp directing his entire force not playing the hero on Gun Hill. His instincts, so sure when he was the aggressor, let him down when he was the one being attacked.[19] Kitchener wrote gloomily to Brodrick: "What makes me most anxious is, if they can act in this way with Benson's column, how far easier it would be for them to catch some of my less efficient columns."[20]

In Britain moves were already under way to raise more yeomanry. Despite renewed appeals to the War Office to organize a system of drafts to keep the second contingent up to strength, nothing was done and the force's numbers dropped just as the first contingent's had. Instead it was decided to raise fresh units and in September an appeal was launched for former members of the Imperial Yeomanry to re-enlist for further service. Lord Scarborough was optimistic that large numbers would come forward but Lucas was more sceptical and, not for the first time when it came to yeomanry recruiting, was proved right. Most of the old yeomen had had enough of trekking. In just over a month only 330 men came forward and even when the appeal was widened to include former colonial troops and mounted infantrymen, the final tally amounted to forty-six officers and 891 men.[21] These formed two battalions, the 25th, from the Sharp-shooters, and the 26th, which was named Younghusband's Horse after its commander who had led the 3rd Battalion Imperial Yeomanry in South Africa in 1900. The 25th sailed in October and November while Younghusband's Horse did not embark until February the following year. The Veteran Yeomanry, as it has been dubbed, was formed from good raw material but was too few in numbers and too late in the war to be of more than limited use.[22]

Appeals to the Volunteer Force for recruits produced similarly dismal results. Roberts had discussions with the Lord Mayor of London and the Lord Provost of Glasgow about launching similar recruiting campaigns to those which had proved so successful in 1900. The talks were not encouraging and he admitted to Kitchener in November: "They both seemed to think that the time had passed for volunteers to leave their civil occupations and, as it would not do to have anything like a failure, I have advised Brodrick to let the matter drop."[23] A plan to recruit a brigade of cyclists and infantry on the CIV model in London and Liverpool also fell through. Eventually in January an appeal for a third wave of Volunteer Service Companies was made but only eight whole companies and forty drafts totalling 2,410 officers and men were raised.

Few men wanted to volunteer to serve on infantry pay, but the prospect of five shillings a day and free passage to South Africa in the twilight of the war still drew new recruits to the yeomanry. After the Veteran Yeomanry failed to attract men, the Government decided to recruit a third contingent through the yeomanry regiments, avoiding many of the mistakes which had been made during the raising of the first two. The system of sending out men in drafts, which had proved so disastrous for the second contingent, was scrapped in favour of ready-formed battalions, medical standards were to be rigorously observed, Scottish recruits were to be sent to Edinburgh instead of to Aldershot and every yeoman was to be given a pay book before he embarked.[24] Most crucially they were to get at least two months training. Roberts promised Kitchener: "I will take care that each regiment is as efficiently officered as is possible under the circumstances and that every man goes through the riding school and a course of musketry." Finding the right officers quickly proved a problem for almost every candidate of even the most modest military ability was already serving in South Africa. A few yeomanry officers from the first contingent rejoined, but Roberts admitted: "The officers are the weak point, a few are good but many struck me as being indifferent. I am seeing what can be done to remedy this but there are very few officers left!"[23]

But there was no problem in finding recruits and within three weeks of the appeal going out in December 349 officers and 6,429 men had joined and another 10,000 could easily have been found. They were formed into thirteen battalions training at Aldershot, Edinburgh and the Curragh. These included the 29th, raised by Lord Longford, designated the Irish Horse, and the 31st, recruited by Viscount Fincastle VC, inevitably known as Fincastle's Horse. Most of of the men had no previous military experience and Capt R.S. Britten, a first contingent man who had taken a commission in the 38th Battalion, told his father: "At present my battalion is in a hopeless muddle." But a daily routine at Aldershot which included more than three hours' stable duty and nearly five hours of mounted drill began to work wonders. At the beginning of March Britten wrote: "My men begin to ride fairly well and tomorrow I shall drill them with rifles on horseback for the first time."[25] The contrast with the training of the second contingent was total but this thorough instruction had some ironic consequences. Some of the recruits complained that they had been kept at Aldershot too long and so lengthy was their training that by the time most left for South Africa the war was virtually over.

Kitchener's gloom after Benson's death at Bakenlaagte did not last long. He began to implement the policy of 'protected areas', proposed by Milner, clearing districts of the guerrillas and re-establishing civilian life where possible. The Commander-in-Chief had doubts about the plan but set to work with his usual energy using the blockhouse system which he had established in early 1901 originally to protect the railways. The system had gradually expanded during the year but now construction went into overdrive. By the end of the war the blockhouses had become a vast grid across South Africa, more than 8,000 of them connected by 3,700 miles of barbed wire fencing.

But it was several months before the system was fully established and in the meantime British fortunes varied wildly. On 13 November Hickie sent two companies of Imperial Yeomanry from the 2nd and 6th Battalions to reconnoitre northwards from Brakspruit in the western Transvaal. They were caught and destroyed losing nine dead, fifteen wounded and sixty-six prisoners. But little more than two weeks later Methuen's scouts and men of the 19th (Lothian and Berwick) Company Imperial Yeomanry captured the rear of a Boer convoy at Kleinplaats in the same region. At Tigers Kloof, near Bethlehem in the Orange Free State, an attempted ambush by De Wet on a column of Imperial Light Horse and 400 men of the 11th Battalion Imperial Yeomanry was a dismal failure. To De Wet's fury only one third of his men charged and their intended victims proved too steady for those who did attack.

The Boers did everything they could to harass the men building the blockhouses, who were by now working at a furious pace. A 300-strong commando near Frankfort in the Orange Free State was causing particular problems for the construction gangs just before Christmas, 1901, and Kitchener ordered two of his column commanders to deal with it. Unfortunately the two forces separated, leaving that commanded by Lieutenant-Colonel Frederick Damant in a vulnerable position. Damant had only three weak squadrons of Damant's Horse, the famous 'Tigers' once commanded by Rimington, and the 30th (Pembrokeshire), 31st (Montgomeryshire) and 91st (Sharpshooters) Companies Imperial Yeomanry with two guns and a pom-pom. He then further weakened his position by extending this 550-strong force over too wide an area, placing himself and his staff on a hill called Tafel Kop overlooking the Wilge River. Only the guns escorted by forty-five men of Damant's Horse and forty from the 91st Company were now with him and the Boers seized the opportunity. This time there was no headlong charge. The burghers, many of whom were dressed in British uniforms, moved slowly towards Tafel Kop in a formation habitually used by the yeomanry. This and the fact that the advancing men occasionally fired volleys towards some Boers further away convinced Damant's men that they must be British.

It was not until the Boers were virtually on top of them that the British realized their mistake. The commandos then galloped flat out towards the highest point of Tafel Kop which, in yet another blunder, Damant had failed to occupy. Realizing the danger he was in, Damant collected some yeomanry and raced to forestall them. The Boers got there first and opened fire on the guns and their escort left without shelter below them but despite this hopeless situation the small British force fought with astonishing courage. Damant himself was wounded four times and the men of the regiment which bore his name were decimated. Twelve of the Sharpshooters were killed, including their commander Captain Charles Gaussen, and eighteen wounded of whom two later died. After nearly an hour's fighting the Boers moved down the hill, smashing the Maxim gun, rolling the pom-pom over the crest and pillaging the dead and wounded. They were eventually driven off by the other two yeomanry companies and the rest of the Tigers. Damant lived to fight again but he had taken too many risks against a devious foe.[26]

A greater disaster soon befell the British in the Orange Free State on the morning of Christmas Day, 1901. The defeat inflicted on the 11th Battalion Imperial Yeomanry at Tweefontein was the work of De Wet, not a man to rest from his sworn task of harrying the British even during the supposed season of goodwill. The disaster was typical of many suffered by Kitchener's forces, poor intelligence compounded by bad defensive dispositions and sheer stupidity. The weakest point of any blockhouse line was always its head and by 24 December the eastern portion of the great line being built from Harrismith to Kroonstad had reached Tradouw, east of Bethlehem. Rundle, commanding the British forces in the area, split up and fatally weakened the troops guarding the head of the line after receiving intelligence reports which said that there were few Boers in the area. About 400 men of the Imperial

Yeomanry with one gun and a pom-pom, all commanded by Major George Williams of the South Staffordshire Regiment, were on a hill called Groenkop, near Tweefontein, south of the line. Rundle was three miles north with a 350-strong force, while 150 infantrymen guarded the blockhouse gangs at Tradouw, three miles to the east and the Imperial Light Horse was 13 miles away at Eland's River Bridge. De Wet watched the British movements with grim satisfaction and marked down the Tweefontein force for destruction while his hungry men thought of the rations which could provide them with a Christmas feast.

Rundle's foolhardiness risked his men but it was Williams's negligence which sealed the fate of the 11th Battalion. Groenkop is a 270 ft high hill which provided a fine observation point and commanded the convoy road from the south. The ascent from the east is gentle but the approach from all other sides is steep and rocky, the western frontage being the most difficult of all. Disregarding the lessons which should have been learned in two years of war, Williams assumed that an attack up the steep slopes was highly unlikely, whereas to De Wet it was the obvious route. Williams placed no pickets at the bottom of the cliff and only a handful of sentries at the top where they were unable to see most of the slope. He compounded this error by his choice of sentries. The yeomanry force consisted of four companies, the 34th and 35th from Middlesex and the 36th and 53rd from West and East Kent respectively. Three of these were good units but the 35th was down to forty men and was as demoralized and inefficient as it was weak in numbers. On the night of the 24th it was this company of dubious value which provided two-thirds of the sixty men on picket duty around the British camp and all the sentries along the western rim of the kopje. Perhaps their vigilance was also lessened by the feeling that because it was Christmas the Boers would not attack that night.

De Wet watched the British from an observation point south of Tweefontein Farm for three days. Meanwhile reinforcements had brought his strength up to 1,000 men and on the night of the 24th all but 100 of these moved quietly off across the plain, riding in single file. The night was moonlit but the commandos were protected by the shadows of passing clouds, a light veil of mist and above all by the fact that most of the British sentries were looking the wrong way. By 2am, with the sleeping yeomanry unaware of their presence and those few awake doubtless thinking of happier Christmases at home, the Boers were massed in the dead ground at the foot of the kopje. They dismounted silently and two storming parties scaled the cliff in stockinged feet while a few were left to guard the horses and some went round to the east to await developments.

It was not until both parties were almost on the crest that the first challenge was given and a warning shot fired. All the sentries except one were immediately shot down by the attackers, the survivor later admitting that he saw the Boers but that they were "too many to fire at", which probably meant that he ran away. De Wet's men charged onto the plateau which commanded the British tents pitched to the east of the summit. Some of the yeomanry took the same view of the situation as the sentry and in the first twenty minutes of fighting about a quarter of them fled half-dressed and often unarmed from the camp. The rest mounted a very creditable defence considering that they were surprised and frightened and fighting in pitch darkness. "The sentry's challenge and the first shot woke me," one of those who stayed, Private Archie Bowers of the 36th Company, recalled. "I yelled out, bullets were ripping our tent and I seized the nearest rifle I could feel in the dark." Outside the tent Bowers sought cover as soon as possible. "I saw one sack full of oats on the ground and crawled to it for shelter," he said. "One yeoman was hiding behind it and I joined him. Bullets were ripping the sack to bits. A bullet went through my pal's belly and he yelled and clawed me in agony and soon died. On my right a few yards away was a bigger pile of oatsacks with three men behind them and I crawled and joined them."

The 35th Company had effectively ceased to exist, but about fifty men of the 34th tried to regain the western part of the plateau. They were enfiladed by Boer fire from the north and decimated. The 53rd under Captain Henry Crawley managed to make its way along the south of the plateau to some sangars, but the 36th never managed to regroup coherently. The Boers then charged shoulder to shoulder and, despite being briefly checked by fire from the 53rd, had soon taken the whole plateau. The guns were lost, Williams was killed, his adjutant, Lieutenant George Grice, fell mortally wounded and the remnants of the 34th were destroyed. Below the eastern edge of the plateau the tiny band from the 36th lying behind the oatsacks rallied, led by twenty-year-old Lieutenant Jack Watney. "I saw swarms of Boers rise up shouting and shooting and rush down the hill," said Bowers. "Young brave Watney, revolver in hand, shouted 'Come on boys, charge'. Watney and the two others were at once riddled, I was bowled over and lost my rifle." Somehow Bowers survived unhurt but the memory of the gallant young officer stayed with him for the rest of his life. "Always so smart, I can see and hear him now," he wrote almost eighty years later.

The Boers now advanced through the camp killing, looting and taking prisoners and the fighting moved to the southern edge of the plateau where the 53rd Company was holding on. When it became clear that the camp had fallen, the yeomen tried to retreat down the cliff but De Wet was having none of it. He sent one force of Boers to their flank from which they opened a destructive fire while another worked round to their rear and cut off their retreat. About twenty of the 53rd managed to escape, the rest being killed or captured. The last shot was fired at about 3.15am, only an hour and a quarter after the Boers had started to climb up to the plateau. The yeomanry lost six officers and fifty-two men killed or mortally wounded, five officers and sixty-five men less grievously hurt and three officers and 158 men captured unwounded. The total of 289 yeomen killed, wounded or taken prisoner was almost all of those who had stayed to fight and the 11th Battalion had been virtually destroyed, while the Boers had only fourteen killed and thirty wounded.

Back in the camp Bowers was pushed into a tent and told by a Boer, "If you move I'll shoot you." He was astonished to discover that the man who had issued this threat was none other than De Wet himself, a legend to the yeomen suddenly all too real on a bloody Christmas morning. The Boers helped themselves to a huge breakfast before towing away the British guns and transport wagons and, unusually, taking their prisoners with them. They were eventually released, some as far away as Basutoland, and had to walk back almost naked under the burning sun. The British pursuit of De Wet was completely ineffective and he vanished westwards into the foothills of the Langberg.[27]

The blame for the disaster was fixed firmly on Williams for his carelessness. Kitchener thought it was also due to "Christmas slackness". He told Brodrick: "We shall always be liable to something of the sort from the unchecked rush of desperate men at night." It was a depressing end to 1901 for the Commander-in-Chief who feared that Tweefontein would give the Boers new heart in the New Year, but the defeat made him even more determined to complete the blockhouse lines and start the great drives which he hoped would finally destroy the commandos.

By 5 February Kitchener was ready to go and four columns totalling 9,000 men, approximately one soldier for every ten yards, swept from east to west across a great slice of the north-eastern Orange Free State. More troops reinforced the blockhouse lines and seven armoured trains fitted out with guns and searchlights steamed up and down the railway lines alongside the blockhouses. Duncalf and his fellow yeomen found themselves part of this awe-inspiring human steamroller. "We have been having it very hard recently," he wrote to his family on 18 February. "We have been lying on the veldt about five yards apart for three or four nights to stop the Boers from breaking through."[9] The results of the drives were mixed, the first accounting for only 285 out of an estimated 2,000 Boers in the area, but another at the end of the month leading to the capture of an entire 650-strong commando only a few miles from Tweefontein. The positive side for the British was that the Boers could not sustain these continuous losses. But the drives were not decisive and in early March the two men Kitchener most wanted to capture, Steyn and De Wet, broke through three blockhouse lines and fled into the Transvaal where they linked up with De la Rey.

The latter's hunting ground in the south-western Transvaal was the scene of two defeats for the British, one a major humiliation, in late February and early March. At Yzerspruit on 25 February De la Rey attacked a convoy which was being escorted to nearby Klerksdorp by 230 men of the 5th Battalion Imperial Yeomanry, 225 Northumberland Fusiliers and a few other troops. At 4.30am Lieutenant-Colonel William Anderson, commanding both the yeomanry and the column, ordered his men to set out for Klerksdorp which was now tantalizingly close. De la Rey, who had come to the area with more than 1,500 men in search of adventure, supplies and revenge for some setbacks, planned to start with a frontal assault which he hoped would draw off as many of the escort as possible. He would then launch a second attack on the rear of the column, followed by a third on the flank to complete the rout. At first all did not go well for the Boers. Anderson's artillery poured such a heavy fire on the riflemen who began the attack from a wood that they ran for shelter. Fearing for the safety of his flank, the British commander hastily sent 150 men to guard it just in time to prevent a spectacular charge by 900 mounted Boers from rolling up the entire column. Four times the Boers, led by Kemp, charged and four times they were driven back by steady fire from the flankguard, while Anderson seized this opportunity to send an officer galloping to Klerksdorp to get help.

But time was now running out for the convoy. Celliers, who was supposed to have attacked the rearguard before Kemp assaulted the flank, finally arrived with 500 men. The men of the rearguard held him off until their ammunition ran out, despite the fact that just a short distance behind them in the convoy were three ammunition carts As they retreated the Boers rode through them into the convoy, while Kemp's men poured in a heavy fire and Anderson was forced to surrender. There could be no criticism of the courage shown by his men, 187 out of 490 having been killed or wounded, the yeomanry's casualties being twenty-eight dead and thirty-four wounded. The British immediately organized rescue parties, but De la Rey, who had had fifty-one casualties, escaped with his booty. Most of the wagons had been empty, but he seized 170 horses, several hundred rifles and half a million rounds of ammunition.[28]

As soon as Methuen heard of the capture of the convoy he prepared to march from his base at Vryburg, south of Mafeking, to try to prevent De la Rey escaping once more. This led to one of the most embarrassing British disasters of the war, one which came close to breaking Kitchener's nerves completely. By this stage of the conflict most British columns were a heterogeneous mixture of regiments, but even by these standards the force which left Vryburg on 2 March was an extraordinary hotch-potch. Its 1,300 men, 900 of them mounted, were drawn from fourteen different units, some of them of very questionable fighting quality. Most of the mounted troops were South African colonials, including some surrendered Boers. More than 300 were Imperial Yeomanry, made up of 184 men from various companies of the 5th Battalion, 110 from the 86th (Rough Riders) Company and some from the 43rd (Suffolk) Company. The Rough Riders were mostly a raw draft recently sent out by their organizing committee from England and were unfit to take on the experienced Boer fighters.

Methuen believed that De la Rey would try to escape north-westwards to the Marico district by slipping through the gap between Mafeking and Lichtenburg where the blockhouse line had not yet been completed. He proposed to prevent this by linking up with a 1,500-strong column sent from Klerksdorp at a rendezvous 17 miles south of Lichtenburg. Methuen's column was a natural target for De la Rey as it marched north-eastwards. Not only were many of the men likely to flee in the face of a determined assault but Methuen was also burdened with thirty-nine ox wagons and forty-six mule wagons and his progress with unfit animals through an arid region where water was hard to find was painfully slow. On 6 March there was an ominous development when a small Boer force under Van Zyl harassed the column as it approached Tweebosch. "I found the men forming the rear screen, which consisted of the 86th Company Imperial Yeomanry, very much out of hand and lacking both fire discipline and knowledge of how to act," Methuen told Kitchener. "There seemed to be a want of instructed officers and non-commissioned officers." Methuen sent for some artillery whose accurate shellfire drove off Van Zyl's commando and the column camped for the night at Tweebosch. Van Zyl did not go far, linking up with De la Rey and bringing up his strength to nearly 2,000 men who had with them the British artillery captured at Yzerspruit.

At 3am on the 7th the ox wagons lumbered out of Tweebosch, their escort including the 86th Company, which had been removed from the column's vulnerable rear. The main convoy with the mule wagons followed an hour later. De la Rey waited until daybreak before launching his attack at 5am as the head of the column reached De Klip Drift on the Great Hart's River. His skirmishers first assaulted the rearguard on the open, undulating plain and then a more serious attack on the right flank of the main convoy began. The Imperial Yeomanry from the 43rd Company and the 5th Battalion formed an inner screen around the mule convoy and alongside the ox convoy, the latter having halted as the terrified native drivers sought safety under their wagons. Three lines of Boer horsemen galloped across the plain, leapt from their horses and opened fire on the defenders and at 6.30am the 43rd Company was ordered to reinforce the right rear where the attack was at its fiercest. The yeomen never got as far as the outer firing line because De la Rey unleashed a fourth line of attackers.These did not dismount, galloping in firing from the saddle and slicing through the outer defences. Panic broke out among the colonial troops and they fled on horseback, meeting the reinforcing yeomanry coming up the slope. Some of the yeomen turned and galloped away with them but others held firm and formed a defensive line in front of the mule convoy. The mass of fugitives swept along the left flank of both the mule and ox wagons sucking more troops into the rout, including the 86th Company which fled without having fired a shot. They did not draw rein until they reached the top of a rise three miles away and some did not stop even there. Those yeomen who had remained on the right flank of the mule convoy were quickly overwhelmed, the Boers charging through them and capturing the wagons. Then the whole Boer force descended on the ox convoy guarded by regular gunners and infantrymen led by Methuen, who himself became a casualty when his leg was broken by a bullet. His men fought well but no amount of personal bravery could retrieve the force from disaster and they eventually had to surrender. Major Archibald Paris tried to rally some of the fleeing mounted troops, but only forty yeomanry and Cape Police gathered with him in a cattle kraal a mile further up the road. They defended it for two hours before shellfire from the guns captured at Yzerspruit made further resistance impossible.

Methuen's defeat was total and he became the first and only British general to be captured during the war. De la Rey, showing great compassion at a time when the Boers felt understandably bitter about the harsh measures taken by Kitchener, overruled protests from his subordinates and sent him off to a British hospital. Even more remarkably, he telegraphed Lady Methuen expressing concern about her husband's injuries. It was a sign of the mutual respect which the two generals had developed during the conflict. Methuen's column had ceased to exist, losing sixty-eight killed, 121 wounded and about 600 prisoners with the rest scattered for miles around. The yeomanry lost fifteen dead and twenty-seven wounded in a battle in which many of them had disgraced themselves.[29]

The defeat left both Kitchener and the British Government in despair. The Commander-in-Chief shut himself in his bedroom and refused to see anyone or eat anything for two days. He admitted "my nerves have gone all to pieces."[30] A letter from Brodrick can have done little to improve his state of mind. "The loss of prestige by Methuen's capture and the misconduct of the mounted troops seems to us to make it the worst business in the war since Colenso," wrote the Secretary of State for War.[5]

Yet for all the humiliation and despair that it caused among the British, Tweebosch made little difference to the overall fortunes of the two sides. The Boers were now so outnumbered that it was impossible for them to turn a tactical victory into a strategic advantage and the British drives ground on relentlessly. Most of the Boers had now had enough of the war and two weeks after Tweebosch a delegation led by Schalk Burgher, the acting President of the Transvaal, took a train to Pretoria to talk peace terms.

211

The momentum towards peace was now unstoppable but for the moment Kitchener's business was still war. Among the 16,000 troops who now assembled in Klerksdorp to launch a huge drive to flush out the commandos in the western Transvaal were more than 1,600 Imperial Yeomanry and 500 Scottish Horse. The drive was a failure, the 'bag' not what Kitchener had hoped for. Soon afterwards, on 31 March, the 30th, 31st and 91st Companies of Imperial Yeomanry, which had been with Damant at Tafel Kop, were involved in a sharp action at Boschbult to the south of Tweebosch. As part of a mixed force with South African colonials, Canadians and British mounted infantry, they fought off an attack by 2,500 Boers. The yeomen, who lost one man killed and twenty wounded, stood their ground like veterans.

Rooiwal, the last major battle of the war, had an air of unreality about it, an echo of Omdurman, even a whiff of Balaclava. By now De la Rey was away at the peace negotiations and Kemp, never his equal in the art of guerrilla warfare, led the burghers in the western Transvaal. On 10 April another British drive began, aiming to squeeze the Boers up against the Klerksdorp blockhouse line and Kemp thought he sniffed a chance for glory. A reconnaissance early on the 10th showed that the western part of the British line was the weakest and Kemp decided that this should be his target. Unknown to him there had been a mixup in the organization of the British columns and in order to remedy this Kekewich was ordered to move westwards on the evening of the 10th. Rooiwal, where Kekewich concentrated his force and where Kemp planned to attack, had by chance now become the strongest part of the British line.

At 7.15 on a cool sunny morning forty mounted infantry forming the British advance screen saw a remarkable sight. Towards them came 1,500 slouch-hatted horsemen riding knee to knee like regular cavalry. This massive charge swept over the small advance party and continued towards the main British force. Time and again Boer charges had destroyed British columns but on this occasion both terrain and numbers were against them. There was no cover for Kemp's burghers while the stony hillside of Rooiwal hid the size of the opposing force from them. When they charged into view Kekewich's men at first thought they must be British. Then a single horseman galloped in from the plain and shouted the truth and Kekewich and his subordinate Lieutenant-Colonel Harold Grenfell acted quickly. Two field guns and two pom poms came into action on the right, protected by 290 of the South African Constabulary, while 460 men of the Scottish Horse dismounted and lined some mealie fields in the centre. A mixed bag of 420 Imperial Yeomanry, scraped together from several different battalions, were sent to the left of the line. Other troops further away took up their positions, bringing the total of rifles pointed at the Boers to 3,000.

By now 800 Boers, all those who had decided to stay with the charge, were just 600 yards away, led by Commandant F.J. Potgieter, conspicuous in a blue shirt. One of the Scottish Horse called it "the transmigration of the soul of the Dervish into the heart of the Dutchman". The sight was too much for a few of the yeomanry who fled. "I tried to get hold of these faint-hearted ones to line them up on the flank but nothing would stop them," complained Lieutenant Carlos Hickie, Grenfell's signalling officer. But the majority of the yeomanry stayed in line and the British opened fire. Had the fusillade been delivered by regular infantry the Boers would have been destroyed, but the shooting of these irregular troops proved woefully inaccurate. Many of the Boers got within 100 yards of the British line, Potgieter fell shot through the head only 70 yards away. Then, leaving behind fifty dead and another thirty badly wounded, the Boers turned and rode away. Even then they might not have fled had not the Imperial Light Horse been threatening their flank. It was an hour and a half before the British organized a pursuit and so Kemp's force escaped destruction. But the last major Boer fighting force in the field had suffered a significant defeat and the message was not lost on the delegates at the peace talks. The need to end the war was now apparent to all but the most intransigent.[31]

The fighting was not quite finished yet and on 20 April a party of 200 Imperial Yeomanry and mounted infantry which had escorted a convoy to Brindisi in the Orange Free State rashly undertook an expedition against a laager reported to be at

Moolman's Spruit. They were ambushed and among the dead were Captain Sir Thomas Fowler and four of his men from the 1st (Wiltshire) Company Imperial Yeomanry. Fowler, an Old Harrovian baronet, had served with the yeomanry since the raising of the first contingent, had volunteered to stay on with the second and died just six weeks before peace was declared.

The Treaty of Vereeniging was signed on 31 May, 1902, ending a war which had begun, in the eyes of some, as a jingoistic crusade and turned into a weary guerrilla campaign, a very 20th century conflict. Kitchener, sick of the war, pressed for a conciliatory attitude, and the terms accepted by the Boers were not harsh. All their fighting men had to surrender and 21,000, almost twice as many as British intelligence estimated, emerged from hiding. Those who surrendered were not to be deprived of liberty or property, the Afrikaans language was to be allowed in schools and courts, Cape rebels would be disenfranchised but not imprisoned or executed and Britain provided £3 million compensation for war damage. Most importantly of all from the Boers' point of view, military administration was to be replaced by civilian rule as soon as possible and this would be followed by self-government. This meant that the Boers would have a majority among the white voting population despite Milner's dream of flooding South Africa with loyalist settlers. The British had won a military victory but the Boer prize was to be political control of all South Africa for much of the 20th century.

The British Army greeted peace with jubilation and the yeomen and volunteers in South Africa were no exception. "The good news was soon shouted over the camp and the men ran out of their tents shouting and cheering," wrote Hay. "We got a ration of rum and a bottle of whisky among seven men and rockets were set off after dark from the headquarters and the surrounding blockhouses. Of course we were all uproariously happy."[32] The reaction among those men of the Imperial Yeomanry's third contingent who were still on their way to South Africa was more mixed. Britten and the rest of the 38th Battalion did not get the news of peace on board ship for more than a week. He wrote to his father: "Personally I am not sorry but there are several who

214

were anxious to see some fighting and, I suppose, sport a medal. If a man has seen any real fighting and is still anxious for more, I put him down as a damned fool or a liar."[25]

The shooting continued for a short time after the treaty was signed until news of it had reached all the commandos. The Imperial Yeomanry suffered its last casualties on 2 June near Mortimer in Cape Colony when twenty men of the 23rd (Lancashire) Company ran into Boers who did not know that the war had ended two days previously. Two yeomen were killed, another slightly wounded, and Lieutenant H.D. Spratt so badly hurt that he died of his wounds the next day. The third contingent of yeomanry remained in South Africa for most of 1902, policing the peace agreement and dealing with a few remaining rebel bands. Many of the second contingent stayed on as settlers, including Hay who found work in a printing works in Johannesburg. Compared to 1901 there was a more muted reception for those yeomen and volunteers who did return to Britain. Most of the yeomen had gone out for five shillings a day rather than for Queen and country and the job was now done.

Although a minority of yeomen proved unreliable as late in the war as the actions at Tweebosch and Rooiwal, most had earned some respect. This had been won not in the major actions but in the unremitting day-to-day routine of escorting convoys, rounding up Boers and minor skirmishes. But such work did not result in newspaper headlines or win hearts and minds in the House of Commons. "I took out the 60th a few nights ago and made a night march of 15 miles, and two hours after daylight bagged a patrol of seven armed Boers with two horses and a telescope," wrote Lieutenant-Colonel Banon, commanding the 17th Battalion Imperial Yeomanry. "Yesterday with a troop of the 60th we chased four Boers four or five miles and bagged them." Jarvis described a night expedition with men of the Sharpshooters from his 21st Battalion: "Left at 7pm and went 28 miles rounding up some farms. Caught six Boers and collared 160 head of cattle and 300 sheep, two Cape carts, some rifles, ammunition etc and got them all safely in here by 9am yesterday morning. It was a long ride in the time. We covered at least 60 miles and both horses and men did well."[33] In the major actions of the guerrilla war the yeomanry often had to fight in the most difficult circumstances, trying to retrieve desperate situations. Some of these had been brought about by the ineptitude of their own commanders, some by poor intelligence and others by the skill of the guerrilla leaders opposing them. Time and again the yeomen found themselves under attack in the early hours of the day, struggling to resist an enemy whose ability to appear out of nowhere seemed almost magical. Methuen, who saw more of the yeomanry in action than most, said that the second contingent "had their hearts in the right place and did their work intelligently and I have not one single word to say against them".[34] The Royal Commission concluded that "the men of the second contingent, after they had received some training, did well."[35] In the end, against all the odds, the second contingent of the Imperial Yeomanry shook off the title of 'De Wet's Own'.

CHAPTER TEN

AFTERMATH

"It was the worst-run war ever fought by the British," grumbled Archie Bowers almost eighty years later.[1] Yet at the time most of those who had volunteered for the South African conflict took a positive view of their experiences. Some such as Childers cited the self-improvement to be wrung from even the most mind-numbing routines required by military discipline. "Physically and mentally, I, like many others, have found this short excursion into strict military life of enormous value," he wrote of his time with the CIV gunners. "It is something, bred up as we have been in a complex civilisation, to have reduced living to its simplest terms and to have realized how little one really wants. It is much to have learnt the discipline, self-restraint and patience which soldiering demands."[2] Ross took a similar view of his service with the Imperial Yeomanry, ending his memoirs with a line from a poem "God be thanked, whate'er comes after, I have lived and toiled with men."[3]

For others some excitement followed by a new life in South Africa was ample compensation for the hardships of service. Hay decided to settle in Johannesburg after his discharge from the Imperial Yeomanry and concluded: "It has been the stormiest and roughest but after all the most interesting time I have yet had. In this case, as in most others, distance lends enchantment and, as I think over it all, it seems that I have come out of it very well." He was, he added contentedly, "well clad, have a full stomach and have gold in my pocket."[4] The gamble he took when he left Edinburgh to serve in the second contingent had paid off handsomely and there were many like him who bettered themselves in South Africa. Some upper class officers took a loftily patriotic view of their contribution. "We have had to give up much personal comfort, have had to subordinate private aims and ambitions to the common cause – the protection and strengthening of our Empire," wrote Colonel Sir John Gilmour of the Imperial Yeomanry. "We feel we have a bigger stake in it, we feel an increased pride in it."[5]

As the decades passed some veterans took a more sceptical stance. There was time for nagging concerns about farm burning and concentration camps to grow and the relentless criticism of the conduct of the war doubtless played its part. Bowers was still proud enough of his period with the Imperial Yeomanry to complain about not having been awarded one of the two campaign medals for the war but he also talked about the sickness that was endemic. "The cooks when we stopped for the night had to part the rushes and dip their dixies into the grimy water to boil water and make some so-called tea," he said. "It is well known that more soldiers died from enteric fever than from the bullets of the Boers. Can one wonder?" George Ives, the last survivor of the Boer War, who died aged 111 in 1993, was unsentimental about his time in South Africa. "You went to war to kill someone and they tried to kill you back," said Ives, who served in the Gloucestershire Imperial Yeomanry. But he spoke of taking women and children away to the camps and of retaliation against Boers who had stripped British prisoners naked under the sun, not of self-improvement or saving the Empire.[6] It had, the veterans agreed, been a brutal, messy business, a bit of an adventure perhaps, but hardly a crusade.

The quality of the volunteers may have been variable, but their substantial contribution to the war effort in terms of numbers could not be denied. The Imperial Yeomanry, Scottish Horse, CIV, Volunteer Service Companies, medical volunteers and overseas colonial volunteers totalled more than 90,000, approximately one-fifth of the total imperial forces of nearly 450,000. The auxiliary forces in Britain could have been forgiven for thinking that politicians and professional soldiers might now take a more positive view of their role, but it was not to be.

The Royal Commission into the War was scathingly critical of almost every aspect of the Army's performance, including its inability to expand quickly in times of crisis. "The true lesson of the war in our opinion is that no military system will be satisfactory which does not contain powers of expansion outside the limit of the regular forces of the Crown, whatever that limit may be," concluded the Commission. "We regret to say that we are not satisfied that enough is being done to place matters on a better footing in the event of another emergency."[7] Vincent complained that there did not "appear to be the slightest realisation by the Adjutant-General's Department of the great lesson of the war, that it is essential to attract the largest possible number of men to some military training."[8]

A national debate about the reform of the Army began in the wake of this criticism. As far as the auxiliary forces were concerned, it was widely accepted that they were insufficiently well organized or trained to be of much use for home defence, let alone for overseas service. Brodrick produced a set of proposals which were killed off by a Cabinet reshuffle in which he was replaced by Hugh Arnold-Forster. Before Brodrick left the War Office he suggested the formation of a Royal Commission on the Militia and Volunteers, which began work in 1903 under the chairmanship of the Duke of Norfolk. It was not a success, receiving no help from the authorities and proving dilatory partly because the Duke, an amiable man, was unable to control and direct proceedings. Arnold-Forster complained that the Norfolk Commission was "a tiresome thing which never ought to have been created".[9] The Commission eventually concluded that the Volunteer Force was "not qualified to take the field against a regular army", which most politicians and soldiers knew already. It came up with some proposals for reform which were completely overshadowed by its suggestion that the only way of defeating an invasion would be by raising a conscripted army. This outraged Arnold-Forster, who said that the Commission had gone beyond its terms of reference, and he dismissed the report as unimportant. As it gathered dust on a shelf, the tactless and self-opinionated Secretary of State for War set about introducing his own reforms.

Arnold-Forster's scheme, submitted hastily and with almost no consultation, succeeded in outraging almost everybody. For the Regular Army he suggested abandoning the system of linked infantry battalions introduced by Cardwell more than thirty years previously and replacing it with long and short terms of service. The long-service men would garrison foreign stations and provide a striking force, while those enlisting for short service would be stationed in Britain for home defence and to feed the reserve. Half the militia was to be disbanded and the Volunteer Force cut from 346,000 to 200,000, the latter divided into about one-third willing to acquire a high degree of efficiency and the remainder who were not. Arnold-Forster calculated that the reduction in the number of volunteers would save £380,000 which could be used to develop the Volunteer Force's rifle clubs and to provide it with necessities such as transport. Opposed by several Cabinet ministers, three of the four members of the Army Council, supporters of the militia in the House of Lords and the powerful group of MPs, led by Vincent, who lobbied for the Volunteer Force in the Commons, the scheme was in trouble from the start. Arnold-Forster eventually won Cabinet support for some proposals but this became academic when the Conservatives were swept from office by the Liberal landslide in the General Election of 1906.

The Liberals' choice for the War Office, Richard Burdon Haldane, was a philosopher by training, a lawyer by profession and a reformer by instinct, who had not previously taken a great interest in military matters. Unlike his predecessors, he did not have any preconceived ideas on Army reform and he took care to consult as he developed his plans, thus avoiding some of the problems which Arnold-Forster had encountered. He and his military secretary, Colonel Gerald Ellison, drew up a scheme for a two-line Army, an Expeditionary Force of three corps supported by some elements from the militia and yeomanry and a Territorial Force formed from the Volunteer Force and the remainder of the militia and yeomanry. The Territorial Force would be administered by county associations and its role would be to support and expand the Expeditionary Force in the later stages of a protracted war. It would consist of forty-two brigades making up fourteen divisions with the yeomanry, organized into fourteen cavalry brigades, forming its mounted arm and with a full complement of artillery and supporting services.

His aim was to produce a British version of the 'nation at arms' concept based on voluntary service. But Haldane had not taken into account the political squabbling which accompanied any attempt to reorganize the auxiliary forces. In the two years between Haldane arriving at the War Office and the Territorial Force finally coming into existence, he was forced to make a series of concessions to get the measure through Parliament. The militia was taken out of the scheme altogether and converted into the Special Reserve and the role of the county associations was weakened with a proposed elective element being abandoned. The latter concession was the result of pressure from the yeomanry and volunteer commanding officers with whom Haldane held a series of dinners around the country and who were appalled at such a threat to their influence. The associations came into being, but were appointed, their membership being drawn from the county elites who had raised the Imperial Yeomanry and who had long run the auxiliary forces. By November, 1909, no less than 115 members of the House of Lords were serving in the associations and the status quo had been preserved.[10]

But the greatest blow to Haldane's scheme, one that struck at the very heart of it, was the steady retreat from the concept of using the Territorial Force as a reserve for the Regular Army in time of war. In a memorandum written in November, 1906, Haldane stated that the purpose of the proposed force was "to provide for home defence and for the support and expansion of the Expeditionary Force after six months of war . . . These forces will be recognized as the main means of home defence on the outbreak of war, both for coast defence and for repelling possible raids and as the sole means of support and expansion of the professional army in any war engaging the whole of that army and lasting more than six months."[11] This was a bold scheme indeed, a proposal to make the Territorial Force the only vehicle for the expansion of the Regular Army in the event of a major conflict.

The problems soon multiplied, partly because of Haldane's admission that the Territorial Force would need six months' training before it could go to war. This supposed that an enemy would be merciful enough and Regular Army casualties low enough to allow the Territorials so much time. It was also an admission that the part-timers were not fit to take the field against the enemy abroad and, if this was the case, then they might struggle to repel an invasion at home. The National Service League, with Roberts, now removed from the War Office, as its president, was scathing and insisted that conscription was the only answer. This was never a serious political option in peacetime, but the League continued to be a thorn in the side of the Territorial Force right up to the First World War. The Labour Party and the more radical Liberals in the House of Commons wanted the purpose of the force switched from an overseas role to home defence. Haldane also had to accept that the Territorial Force could not include compulsion to serve overseas in its terms of enlistment. He hoped that between one-sixth and a quarter might accept such an obligation in peacetime, but this proved wildly optimistic and by 1913 fewer than 19,000 Territorials, less than ten per cent of the total, had done so.

The force that emerged from the Haldane reforms was an improvement on its predecessor but was not the great new army which he proclaimed it to be. It was organized to go to war with all the necessary gunners, engineers, medical and supply services. Its men had greater obligations than the old volunteers, principally the requirement to be called up for at least six months on the outbreak of war. Short-sightedly Vincent, who had struggled to promote the involvement of the auxiliary forces during the Boer War, opposed the six months requirement in the House of Commons on the grounds that it would cause difficulty with employers. The greatest champions of part-time soldiering too often damaged their own cause by concentrating on narrow self-interest rather than the wider picture. But when Haldane rose to introduce his Territorial and Reserve Forces Bill in the House of

Commons in March, 1907, he declared that the main task of the new force was "to defend our shores" and mentioned no other purpose. Any hope that the new force might be something more than an improved version of the old had gone and with it any possibility that the efforts of the volunteers during the Boer War might be formally recognized by a new role for the Territorials.

From its formation on 1 April, 1908, to the outbreak of war in August, 1914, the Territorial Force was surrounded by enemies and dogged by controversy. The National Service League sniped at it, few senior Regular Army officers with the exception of Haig had any time for it and the press and even some of its own members were critical of it. The effectiveness of the Territorial artillery batteries was ridiculed in the House of Commons. Its recruitment figures attracted the sort of attention and debate that were to surround unemployment statistics later in the century. Helped by an invasion scare the Force reached a strength of 268,776 by June 1909 but it never attained Haldane's target of 312,300 and by September, 1913, had dropped to 236,389.

The Force was mobilized on the outbreak of the First World War, but was quickly pushed into the shadows by a new phenomenon. The Liberal Government recruited an unlikely bedfellow to become Secretary of State for War in the form of Kitchener. As he swept energetically through the War Office, the faults he had displayed during the South African conflict, arrogance, secretiveness and an inability to delegate, were still there for all to see. But Kitchener, almost alone among British leaders, saw that the war would be a long one which would require a mass citizens' army to fight it.

Kitchener decided that the Territorial Force was not the right organization to recruit this army. This was partly the result of his own obsessive nature for he was a man who took soldiering so seriously that he simply could not understand part-timers. For him the Territorials were playing at being soldiers, treating what should be a profession as a hobby. But his experiences during the Boer War played an important part in his decision to create the New Armies. Conveniently forgetting that the greatest problems with volunteer soldiers in South Africa had been with the second contingent of the Imperial Yeomanry, hastily recruited and despatched at his insistence and which had little to do with the auxiliary forces, he damned all part-time soldiers. The Territorial Force was, he sneered, "a Town Clerk's army", an ironic description in view of the fact that local government officers played a key role in raising his new force. The Territorials were allowed to recruit and made a substantial contribution to the war effort, sending 318 battalions overseas, and in public Kitchener praised the force. But in private his dislike of it was both powerful and instinctive and his staff warned senior officers that it was better not to raise the subject.

It was the New Armies, soon dubbed Kitchener's Army, that stole the headlines. New battalions, known as Service Battalions, were recruited for existing infantry regiments as 761,000 men joined the Army in the first eight weeks of the war. The scenes were a repeat of what had happened at the turn of the century after Black Week but on an infinitely larger scale. Many of the units formed were Pals Battalions, raised with War Office approval by the mayors and corporations of large cities, Members of Parliament, leading local citizens or self-appointed committees. These harnessed local pride in Manchester, Sheffield, Leeds, Birmingham and elsewhere and brought together men from the same area to serve together just as the first contingent of the Imperial Yeomanry had done in 1900. In another echo of the Boer War, the committees took responsibility for housing, feeding and clothing their own men until the hard-pressed War Office was ready to take over responsibility for them. This was the last great display of Victorian and Edwardian patriotism, soon to be destroyed by the unrelenting nature of modern industrial-style warfare.

A decade and a half previously the Boer War volunteers, although much fewer in numbers, had been inspired by many of the same feelings as the New Armies. A sense of national crisis combined with patriotism, a spirit of adventure and a widespread blissful ignorance of the realities of war motivated both. For those who had hoped that the Boer War volunteers would lead to professional acceptance of the auxiliary forces, the First World

War was to prove a disappointment. But curiously Kitchener's distrust of amateur soldiers, partly rooted in his experiences in South Africa, led him to create a force which had many similarities to that raised during the Boer War. The men who volunteered between 1899 and 1902 were the forerunners of the British citizen armies which were to wage the two great world conflicts of the 20th century.

APPENDIX I: NUMBER OF VOLUNTEERS DURING THE BOER WAR:

Imperial Yeomanry:

1st contingent 1900	10,921
2nd contingent 1901	16,937
Veteran Yeomanry 1901	937
3rd Contingent 1902	6,778
Total	35,573

Volunteers:

CIV	1,803
Volunteer Service Companies	19,856
(inc gunners and engineers)	
Total	21,659

Colonials (non-South African):

Australia	16,148
New Zealand	6,479
Canada	6,059
India and Ceylon	526
Total	29,212

Scottish Horse:

3,409 officers and men served with the regiment but 1,458 were recruited in South Africa and so I deleted these from the total. I have deleted those recruited via the Imperial Yeomanry or in Australia from the totals for those contingents.

Total: 1,951

Medical Volunteers:

St John Ambulance Brigade	1,900
Volunteer Force	600
Total	2,500

This figure is approximate and does not include the non-SJAB staff of private hospitals, civilian doctors and pharmacists and other non-military personnel.

Overall total   90,895

Every set of figures for Boer War volunteers varies slightly, except for the first contingent of the Imperial Yeomanry. I have tried to produce the most accurate figures possible. Some volunteers served for two periods during the war and will therefore have been counted twice. However it should be remembered that many British and other overseas volunteers made their own way to South Africa where they served in locally raised units. The figures also do not include the full number of medical volunteers. They therefore understate the volunteers' contribution to the war. The full total was probably in excess of 100,000.

APPENDIX II: IMPERIAL YEOMANRY AND CIV CASUALTIES:

Imperial Yeomanry:

	Officers	Other Ranks	Total
Killed	73	632	705
Died of disease	25	909	934
Wounded	121	1,323	1,444
Total	219	2,864	3,083

CIV:

	Officers	Other Ranks	Total
Killed and died of wounds	1	10	11
Died of disease	–	47	47
Wounded	1	57	58
Total	2	114	116

Sources: Colonel Lucas's second report into the Imperial Yeomanry, The South African War Casualty Roll.

APPENDIX III: IMPERIAL YEOMANRY COMPANIES

The first contingent consisted of the 1st to 79th Companies, with the exception of the 64th which was not raised. Most of these companies continued with replacements from the second contingent after the men of the first went home. Companies numbered from eighty upwards were purely second or third contingent units. Those listed as arriving in Beira were part of the Rhodesian Field Force. Where two battalion numbers are given this means that the company switched battalions.

Company	Battalion	County/Name	Arrival In South Africa (1st contingent only, 1900)
1st	1st	Wiltshire	20th March.
2nd	1st	Wiltshire	20th March.
3rd	1st	Gloucestershire	20th March.
4th	1st	Glamorgan	20th March.
5th	2nd	Warwickshire	25th February.
6th	4th	Staffordshire	21st February.
7th	4th	Leicestershire	5th March.
8th	4th	Derbyshire	21st February.
9th	3rd	Yorkshire Hussars	20th February.
10th	3rd	Sherwood Rangers	20th February.
11th	3rd	Yorkshire Dragoons	20th February.
12th	3rd	South Notts Hussars	20th February.
13th	5th	Shropshire	27th February.
14th	5th	Northumberland	27th February.

15th	5th	Northumberland	27th February.
16th	5th	Worcestershire	2nd March.
17th	6th	Ayrshire	19th March.
18th	6th	Queen's Own Royal Glasgow	19th March.
19th	6th	Lothian and Berwick	19th March.
20th	6th	Fife and Forfar Light Horse	20th March.
21st	2nd	Cheshire	25th February.
22nd	2nd	Cheshire	25th February.
23rd	8th	Lancashire	5th March.
24th	8th	Westmorland and Cumberland	5th March.
25th	7th	West Somerset	29th March.
26th	7th	Dorset	23rd March.
27th	7th	Devon	23rd March.
28th	4th	Bedfordshire	5th March.
29th	9th	Denbighshire	5th March.
30th	9th	Pembrokeshire	6th April.
31st	9th	Montgomeryshire	6th April.
32nd	2nd	Lancashire Hussars	25th February
33rd	11th	East Kent	20th March.
34th	11th	Middlesex	20th March.
35th	11th	Middlesex	20th March.
36th	11th	West Kent	20th March.
37th	10th	Buckinghamshire	28th February.
38th	10th	Buckinghamshire	28th February.
39th	10th	Berkshire	28th February.
40th	10th	Oxfordshire	27th February.
41st	12th/4th	Hampshire	23rd February.
42nd	12th	Hertfordshire	28th March.
43rd	12th	Suffolk	23rd February.
44th	12th	Suffolk	28th March.
45th	13th	Dublin Hunt	6th April.
46th	13th/12th	Belfast	28th March.
47th	13th	Duke of Cambridge's Own	8th March.
48th	7th	North Somerset	23rd March.
49th	9th	Montgomeryshire	6th April.

50th	17th	Hampshire	4th May (Beira).
51st	19th/12th	Paget's Horse	4th April.
52nd	19th	Paget's Horse	4th April.
53rd	14th	East Kent	29th March.
54th	13th	Belfast	28th March.
55th	14th/5th	Northumberland	6th April.
56th	15th	Buckinghamshire	10th April.
57th	15th	Buckinghamshire	4th April.
58th	15th	Berkshire	4th April.
59th	15th	Oxfordshire	29th March.
60th	17th	North Irish Horse (Belfast)	4th May (Beira).
61st	17th	South Irish Horse (Dublin)	4th May (Beira).
62nd	14th/11th	Middlesex	3rd May.
63rd	16th/1st	Wiltshire	28th March.
64th	Not raised.		
65th	17th	Leicestershire	4th May (Beira).
66th	16th/3rd	Yorkshire	10th April.
67th	18th	Sharpshooters	4th May (Beira).
68th	19th	Paget's Horse	4th April.
69th	7th	Sussex	24th April.
70th	18th	Sharpshooters	4th May (Beira).
71st	18th	Sharpshooters	4th May (Beira).
72nd	20th	Rough Riders	3rd May.
73rd	19th	Paget's Horse	24th April.
74th	16th/8th	Dublin	3rd May.
75th	18th	Sharpshooters	4th May (Beira).
76th	20th	Rough Riders	3rd May.
77th	8th	Manchester	3rd May.
78th	20th	Rough Riders	3rd May.
79th	20th	Rough Riders	3rd May.
80th	21st	2nd Sharpshooters	
81st	21st	2nd Sharpshooters.	

231

82nd	21st	2nd Sharpshooters.
83rd	21st	2nd Sharpshooters.
84th	22nd	2nd Rough Riders.
85th	22nd	2nd Rough Riders.
86th	22nd	2nd Rough Riders.
87th	22nd	2nd Rough Riders.
88th	9th	Welsh Yeomanry.
89th	9th	Montgomeryshire.
90th	23rd	3rd Sharpshooters.
91st	23rd	3rd Sharpshooters.
92nd	23rd	3rd Sharpshooters.
93rd	23rd	3rd Sharpshooters.
94th	24th	Metropolitan Mounted Rifles.
95th	24th	Metropolitan Mounted Rifles.
96th	24th	Metropolitan Mounted Rifles.
97th	24th	Metropolitan Mounted Rifles.
98th	3rd	North Riding of Yorkshire Volunteer Artillery.
99th	8th	Irish.
100th	5th	Northumberland.
101st	5th	Northumberland.
102nd	5th	Worcestershire.
103rd	2nd	Warwickshire.
104th	4th	Derbyshire.
105th	8th	Manchester.
106th	4th	Staffordshire.
107th	6th	Lanarkshire.
108th	6th	Royal Glasgow.
109th	3rd	Yorkshire Hussars.
110th	2nd	Northumberland.
111th	3rd	Yorkshire Dragoons.
112th	11th	Middlesex.
113th	none	Lovat's Scouts.
114th	none	Lovat's Scouts.
115th	25th	Sharpshooters.
116th	25th	Sharpshooters.
117th	25th	Sharpshooters.
118th	25th	Sharpshooters.
119th	26th	Younghusband's Horse.
120th	26th	Younghusband's Horse.

121st	26th	Younghusband's Horse.
122nd	26th	Younghusband's Horse.
123rd	27th	unknown.
124th	27th	unknown.
125th	27th	unknown.
126th	27th	unknown.
127th	28th	Westminster Dragoons.
128th	28th	Westminster Dragoons.
129th	28th	Westminster Dragoons.
130th	28th	Westminster Dragoons.
131st	29th	Irish Horse.
132nd	29th	Irish Horse.
133rd	29th	Irish Horse.
134th	29th	Irish Horse.
135th	30th	unknown.
136th	not listed, 30th if raised.	
137th	30th	unknown.
138th	30th	unknown.
139th	31st	Fincastle's Horse.
140th	31st	Fincastle's Horse.
141st	31st	Fincastle's Horse.
142nd	31st	Fincastle's Horse.
143rd	32nd	unknown.
144th	not listed, 32nd if raised.	
145th	32nd	unknown.
146th	32nd	unknown.
147th	33rd	unknown.
148th	33rd	unknown.
149th	33rd	unknown.
150th	33rd	unknown.
151st	34th	unknown.
152nd	34th	unknown.
153rd	34th	unknown.
154th	34th	unknown.

155th to 174th not listed but battalions numbered 35th to 39th were raised for the third contingent. At four companies per battalion this corresponds exactly with these company numbers.

175th	29th	Irish Horse.
176th	29th	Irish Horse.

177th	31st	Fincastle's Horse.
178th	none	Lovat's Scouts.

Sources: *British Battles and Medals* published by Spink & Son; Roberts Papers WO105/40; *Imperial Yeomanry Companies of the Boer War* by Paul Till, *Orders and Medals Research Society Journal* Autumn 1992; *Imperial Yeomanry Missing Designations* by Dave Buxton, *Coin and Medal News* August 1987; South African War Casualty Roll.

BIBLIOGRAPHY

Official reports and papers:

Central British Red Cross Committee, Report on Voluntary Organisations in the Aid of the Sick and the Wounded during the South African War.

Dixon, Brig-Gen Henry, Report on the action at Vlakfontein. Command Paper 693.

Elgin, Lord, Report of His Majesty's Commissioners appointed to Inquire into the Military Preparations and Other Matters connected with the War in South Africa.

Gipps, General Sir Reginald, Inquiry into second contingent of the Imperial Yeomanry.

Imperial Yeomanry papers, Public Record Office.

Lucas, Colonel Alfred, First Report of the Deputy Adjutant General of the Force regarding the Home Organisation, Inspection of the Condition of its Base and Advanced Depots and Distribution and Stores in South Africa, 1901.

Lucas, Colonel Alfred, Report of the Deputy Adjutant General of the Force regarding the raising of Drafts and new Battalions for the Imperial Yeomanry in South Africa. Supplementary and Final Report 1903.

Methuen, Lieut-Gen Lord, Report into the action at Tweebosch, Command Paper 967.

Report of the Royal Commission appointed to consider and report on the care and treatment of the sick and wounded during the South African campaign.

War Office papers on use of volunteers and civilians, Public Record Office.

Wilson, Surgeon-General Sir William, Report on medical arrangements during South African War.

Letters, diaries, private papers:

Awdry, Lieut C.S., Wilts Imp. Yeo. Letters. NAM 8307-26.

Bowers, Pte A.D., 36th Coy IY. Memoirs. NAM 7905-17.

Britten, Capt R.S. 37th and 38th Bucks IY. Letters and cuttings. NAM 7812-34.

Colvin, Brig-Gen R.B., Records of time as OC 20th Batt. Imp. Yeo. PRO WO136.

Duncalf, Trooper J., 21st Company Imperial Yeomanry. Letters NAM 8104-56.

Kitchener Papers. PRO 30/57.

Mackenzie, Charles, diary in Green Howards Gazette.

Manisty, Lieut Edward, CIV. Letters to mother. NAM 8005-22.

Power, Lieut W.S., 8th Coy IY. Diary NAM 8303-12.

Rice, Roy, copy of diary in author's collection.

Roberts Papers, PRO WO105/7, 8, 10, 14, 40.

Books:

Amery, L.S., *The Times History of the War in South Africa* 7 vols (1900–1909).

Anglesey, Marquess of, *A History of the British Cavalry* Volume 4 (1986).

Beckett, Ian, *Riflemen Form* (1982).

Beighton, Prof Peter, *Blackpool Division St John Ambulance Brigade, The Early Years* (1998).

Birkin, R.L., *History of the 3rd Regt IY*.

Chandler, David and Beckett, Ian, *Oxford Illustrated History of the British Army.* (1994).

Childers, Erskine, *In the Ranks of the CIV* (1900).

Churchill, W.S., *Ian Hamilton's March* (1900).

Conan Doyle, A., *The Great Boer War* (1903).

Cooke, J.H., *5,000 Miles with the Chesire Yeomanry in South Africa* (1914).

Dooner, Mildred, *The Last Post* (1903).

Fitzgibbon, Maurice, *Arts Under Arms* (1901).

Graham, H., *The Annals of the Yeomanry Cavalry of Wiltshire* Vol II (1908).

Hay, R.D., *Diary of an Edinburgh Trooper* (1903).

Hibbard, M.G., *Boer War Tribute Medals* (1982).

Howe, Countess, *The Imperial Yeomanry Hospital in South Africa 1900–1902.*

Inder, W.S., *On Active Service with the St John Ambulance Brigade in the South African War* (1905).

Josling, Harold, *The Autobiography of a Military Great Coat* (1907).

Lloyd, J. Barclay, *1,000 Miles with the CIV.* (1901).

Mackail J.W. and Wyndham G., *Life and Letters of George Wyndham* (1962).

Mackinnon, Maj-Gen W.H., *Journal of the CIV in South Africa* (1901).

Maurice, Maj-Gen Sir Frederick and Grant, M.H., *Official History of the War in South Africa.* 4 vols (1906–1910).

Pakenham, Thomas, *The Boer War* (1979).

Peel, Hon S., *Trooper 8008* (1902).

Perham, F., *The Kimberley Flying Column.*

Portland Hospital, being an account of the work . . . by the professional staff (1900).

Private Memoir of Sir Thomas Fowler.

Reckitt, B.N., *The Lindley Affair* (1972).

Reid, Brian A., *Our Little Army in the Field* (1996).

Rose-Innes, C., *With Paget's Horse to the Front* (1901).

Ross, P.T.A., *A Yeoman's Letters* (1901).

Smith, Godfrey H., *With the Scottish Rifle Volunteers at the Front* (1901).

Smith-Dorrien, H., *Memoirs of 48 Years' Service* (1925).

South African War Casualty Roll.

Spencer, W., *Records of the Militia and Volunteer Forces 1757–1945.*

Spiers, Edward M., *Haldane, An Army Reformer* (1980).
Wallace, R.L., *The Australians and the Boer War* (1976).
Wetton, T.C., *With Rundle's Eighth Division in South Africa* (1907).
Younghusband, Sir G.J., *Forty Years a Soldier* (1923).

Newspapers, magazine articles etc:

H & B Medals catalogue.
Journal of the Orders and Medals Research Society.
London Scottish Regimental Gazette.
Medal News.
North Wilts Herald.
St John Ambulance Brigade in the Boer War by Lieut-Col R.E. Cole-Mackintosh, article in SJAB Museum.
Soldiers of the Queen.
Swindon Advertiser.
The Times.
The Veteran, Journal of the SA War Veterans Association.
Warminster and Westbury Journal.

SOURCE NOTES

Abbreviations for sources commonly listed below:

Amery: *The Times History of the War in South Africa* edited by L.S. Amery.

Anglesey: *A History of the British Cavalry* Vol IV by the Marquess of Anglesey.

Conan Doyle: *The Great Boer War* by A. Conan Doyle.

Lucas 1: Imperial Yeomanry, Report of the Deputy Adjutant General of the Force 15th May 1901 by Colonel Alfred Lucas.

Lucas 2: Imperial Yeomanry, Report of the Deputy Adjutant General of the Force regarding the Raising of Drafts and New Battalions for the Imperial Yeomanry in South Africa. 1903. By Colonel Alfred Lucas.

NAM: National Army Museum.

Pakenham: *The Boer War* by Thomas Pakenham.

PRO: Public Record Office

RC : Royal Commission on the War in South Africa.

Chapter One: The Crisis (p 1–13)

1 *Times* 15th Jan 1900.
2 RC conclusions p34.
3 Amery Vol III page 5.
4 RC evidence 8033–9.
5 RC appendix 5.

[6] St John Ambulance Brigade in the Boer War by Lieut-Col R.E. Cole-Mackintosh. Article in SJAB museum.

[7] PRO WO32/7887.

[8] PRO WO 32/7887.

[9] Salisbury Papers.

[10] Beckett, *Riflemen Form*.

[11] Confidential Telegrams 1899–1902 no 56.

[12] RC conclusions p70.

[13] J.W. Mackail and G Wyndham, *Life and Letters of George Wyndham*, Vol I p382.

[14] Ibid, p382.

[15] PRO WO32/7866.

Chapter Two: Gentlemen in Khaki (pp 14–40)

[1] Lucas 2 p146.

[2] Graham, *The Yeomanry Cavalry of Wiltshire*, Vol II p63.

[3] Pakenham p253.

[4] *Times* 19th Feb 1900.

[5] *Times* 15th and 22nd Jan 1900.

[6] Rose-Innes, *With Paget's Horse to the Front*.

[7] RC evidence 7281.

[8] WO32/7866.

[9] R. Price, *An Imperial War and the British Working Class*.

[10] RC evidence 6844.

[11] Diary of Roy Rice.

[12] WO108/195.

[13] RC evidence 6477.

[14] RC evidence 7009 and 7197.

[15] Lucas 1 appendix 3 p143.

[16] WO32/7866.

[17] Lucas 1 appendix 36 p171.

[18] Peel, *Trooper 8008 IY*.

[19] Ross, *A Yeoman's Letters*.

[20] WO108/194.

[21] RC evidence 6501.

[22] Lucas 1 chap 8.

[23] Lucas 1 chap 5.

[24] RC evidence 6730.

[25] RC evidence 7368.

[26] RC evidence 7379.

[27] RC evidence 7376.

[28] Mackinnon, *Journal of the CIV in South Africa*.

[29] RC evidence 5453.

[30] and [31] Mackinnon, *Journal of the CIV in South Africa*.

[32] RC evidence 7382–7389.

[33] RC evidence 5453.

[34] Amery.

[35] RC evidence 5560.

[36] Cooke. *5,000 Miles with the Cheshire Yeomanry in South Africa*.

[37] Smith, *With the Scottish Rifle Volunteers at the Front*.

[38] Amery.

[39] Harold Josling Bryant, *The Autobiography of a Military Great Coat*.

[40] Erskine Childers, *In the Ranks of the CIV*.

[41] Rose-Innes, *With Paget's Horse to the Front*.

[42] Mackinnon, *Journal of the CIV in South Africa*.

[43] *The Times* 17th,19th,26th Jan 1900.

[44] RC evidence 7500–7502.

[45] WO32/7866.

[46] *Times* 20th Jan 1900.

[47] *Green Howards Gazette*.

[48] WO108/200.

[49] Lucas 1 chap 2.

[50] *Times* 19th Feb 1900.

[51] Ross, *A Yeoman's Letters*.

Chapter Three: Harsh Reality (pp 41–75)

1   Lucas 1 chap 1.
2   WO108/209.
3   Letters of Lieut C.S. Awdry. NAM 8307-26.
4   Peel, *Trooper 8008 IY*.
5   WO105/14.
6   RC evidence 6731.
7   Letters of Lieut Edward Manisty. NAM 8005-22.
8   RC evidence 7542.
9   WO105/7.
10 Mackinnon, *Journal of the CIV in South Africa*.
11 RC evidence 10312.
12 RC evidence 7404.
13 Lloyd, *1,000 Miles with the CIV*.
14 Mackenzie's diary, *Green Howards Gazette*.
15 Harold Josling Bryant. *The Autobiography of a Military Great Coat*.
16 Smith, *With the Scottish Rifle Volunteers at the Front*.
17 Churchill, *Ian Hamilton's March*.
18 RC evidence 5468.
19 *London Scottish Regimental Gazette* July 1901.
20 Ross, *A Yeoman's Letters*.
21 Rose-Innes, *With Paget's Horse to the Front*.
22 Official History Vol III p34.
23 WO105/7.
24 Cooke, *5,000 Miles with the Cheshire Yeomanry in South Africa*.
25 Research published in H & B Medals catalogue Nov 1997.
26 Amery Vol IV pp227–8 and Official History Vol III pp22–25.
27 Rose-Innes, *With Paget's Horse to the Front*.
28 Amery Vol IV pp231–6, Official History Vol III pp19–22.
29 Amery Vol IV pp243–4, *Times* 11th June 1900.
30 WO105/8.
31 Wetton, *With Rundle's Eighth Division in South Africa*.
32 Childers, *In the Ranks of the CIV*.
33 Author's conversation with Rogers' son.

[34] Official History Vol III pp287–290.
[35] Pakenham pp441–2.
[36] Letters of Lieut Edward Manisty. NAM 8005-22.
[37] Roberts Papers WO105/10.
[38] Letter published *Warminster and Westbury Journal* 13th Oct 1900.

Chapter Four: Disillusion and Departure (pp 76–100)

[1] Mackinnon, *Journal of the CIV in South Africa*.
[2] Childers, *In the Ranks of the CIV*.
[3] Letters of Lieut Edward Manisty. NAM 8005-22.
[4] Ross, *A Yeoman's Letters*.
[5] Wetton, *With Rundle's Eighth Division in South Africa*.
[6] Peel, *Trooper 8008 IY*.
[7] Anglesey.
[8] Cooke, *5,000 Miles with the Cheshire Yeomanry in South Africa*.
[9] Rose-Innes, *With Paget's Horse to the Front*.
[10] *A Private Memoir of Sir Thomas Fowler*.
[11] Lucas 1, appendix 3.
[12] RC conclusions p71.
[13] Lloyd, *1,000 Miles with the CIV*.
[14] Lucas 2, page 13.
[15] White's report WO105/10.
[16] Letter *Swindon Advertiser* 12th Oct 1900.
[17] Report into Capt Graves. WO105/10.
[18] Younghusband, *A Soldier's Memories*.
[19] Anglesey p246.
[20] Research published in H & B Medals catalogue Nov 1997.
[21] Power's letters. NAM 8303–12.
[22] *London Scottish Gazette* April 1901 pp71–75.
[23] Official History Vol IV pp132–3.
[24] Kitchener Papers PRO 30/57/20.
[25] Kitchener Papers PRO 30/57/22.

[26] Cooke, *5,000 Miles with the Cheshire Yeomanry in South Africa*.
[27] Letters of Lieut C.S. Awdry. NAM 8307-26.
[28] RC evidence 7224 and 7227.
[29] Mackenzie's diary, *Green Howards Gazette*.
[30] Harold Josling Bryant. *The Autobiography of a Military Great Coat*.
[31] *North Wilts Herald* 12th July 1901.
[32] *Boer War Tribute Medals* by M.G. Hibbard.
[33] RC evidence 7556 and 7580.
[34] RC evidence 13905.
[35] RC conclusions p66.
[36] RC evidence 15492.
[37] RC evidence 14237.
[38] RC evidence 10366.
[39] RC evidence 6909.
[40] Anglesey p363.
[41] RC evidence 14219.
[42] RC evidence 7278–9.
[43] RC evidence 14242.
[44] RC evidence 13146.

Chapter Five: Triumphs and Disasters (pp 101–126)

[1] Peel. *Trooper 8008 IY*.
[2] WO105/7.
[3] *Times* 9th May 1900.
[4] Smith-Dorrien's despatch WO105/8.
[5] Mackinnon, *Journal of the CIV in South Africa*.
[6] Lloyd, *1,000 Miles with the CIV*.
[7] Churchill, *Ian Hamilton's March*.
[8] WO105/8.
[9] Roberts Papers WO105/40.
[10] B.N. Reckitt, *The Lindley Affair*.
[11] Fitzgibbon, *Arts under Arms*.

[12] WO105/40.
[13] WO105/8.
[14] *Cape Times*.
[15] RC appendices p417.
[16] Holland's evidence to inquiry WO105/40.
[17] Younghusband. *A Soldier's Memories*.
[18] PRO WO128/44 and WO100/126.
[19] RC evidence 13149.
[20] Hansard 1901 4th series, 89, 1090.
[21] Kitchener Papers PRO 30/57/20.
[22] Kitchener Papers PRO 30/57/22.

Chapter Six: The Medical Volunteers (pp 127–145)

[1] RC. Statement of the Army Medical Department.
[2] Report by the Central Red Cross Committee PRO WO108/387.
[3] Lord Wantage, letter to *The Times* 19th March 1900.
[4] St John Ambulance Brigade in the Boer War by Lieut-Col R.E. Cole-Mackintosh, St John Museum, London.
[5] W.S. Inder, *On Active Service with the SJAB in the South African War*.
[6] Prof Peter Beighton, *Blackpool Division SJAB, The Early Years*.
[7] Wetton. *With Rundle's Eighth Division in South Africa*.
[8] Official History Vol IV appendix 7.
[9] *Times*, 15th October 1899.
[10] W.H. Fevyer, *Orders and Medals Research Society Journal*, Winter 1978.
[11] RC, letter from Sir William Wilson appendix 40.
[12] *A Civilian War Hospital*, being an account of the work of the Portland Hospital by the professional staff.
[13] Meurig Jones, *The Welsh Hospital at War South Africa 1900, Soldiers of the Queen no 64*.

[14] Countess Howe, *The Imperial Yeomanry Hospital in South Africa 1900–1902.*

[15] Report on the Medical Arrangements in the South African War by Surgeon-General William Wilson. PRO WO108/390.

[16] The South African War Casualty Roll.

[17] Amery Vol VI page 530.

[18] Ross., *A Yeoman's Letters.*

[19] Harold Josling Bryant. *The Autobiography of a Military Great Coat.*

Chapter Seven: Colonial Volunteers (pp 146–166)

[1] Amery Vol III page 27.

[2] RC conclusions pp77–8.

[3] RC conclusions p69.

[4] RC appendix no 5.

[5] R.L. Wallace, *The Australians at the Boer War.*

[6] Brian A. Reid, *Our Little Army in the Field.*

[7] B.W. Ellis, 'The Fighting Twenty-Nine', *Orders and Medals Research Society Journal* Autumn 1987.

[8] Perham, *The Kimberley Flying Column.*

[9] Colvin Papers, WO136/2.

[10] Amery Vol V pages 520–5, Anglesey p271.Reid pp166–9.

[11] *London Scottish Gazette*, Aug 1901 p143.

[12] Harold Josling Bryant. *The Autobiography of a Military Great Coat.*

[13] Diary of Roy Rice.

Chapter Eight: The Second Contingent (pp 167–189)

[1] Lucas 2, Annexure C, Fanshawe's report.

[2] Hay, *Diary of an Edinburgh Trooper.*

[3] RC evidence 7423.

4 Kitchener Papers PRO30/57/22.
5 Kitchener Papers PRO30/57/20.
6 Lucas 2, Chapter 1.
7 Lucas 2, Appendix 20.
8 RC evidence 5669.
9 Gipps Report WO108/107.
10 RC evidence 7119.
11 Lucas 2, Chapter 5.
12 RC evidence 7258.
13 Lucas 2, Appendix 24.
14 RC evidence 6591.
15 RC evidence 6731.
16 Lucas 2, Appendix 49.
17 RC evidence 7170.
18 Lucas 2, Chapter 2.
19 RC evidence 7163, 7164, 7170.
20 RC evidence 7163.
21 RC 7179–80.
22 Deane's report, Lucas 2, Appendix 49.
23 RC conclusions p69.
24 RC evidence p447.
25 RC evidence p455.
26 RC evidence 5473 and appendix p517.
27 RC appendices p66.
28 J.V. Webb, *Medal News* April 1991.
29 The Veteran, *Journal of the SA War Veterans Assoc* 1951.

Chapter Nine: De Wet's Own (pp 186–216)

1 Cooke. *5,000 Miles with the Cheshire Yeomanry in South Africa.*
2 Diary of Roy Rice.
3 RC evidence 6731.
4 Anglesey p101.
5 Kitchener Papers PRO 30/57/22.

[6] Lucas 2, Appendix 49.

[7] RC evidence 7187.

[8] Amery Vol V pp237–8, 240–1, 432.

[9] Duncalf's letters. NAM 8104-56.

[10] *The Veteran, Journal of the SA War Veterans Assoc* 1951.

[11] *London Scottish Gazette* Dec 1901.

[12] Official History Vol IV pp184–8, RC appendices p519, Amery Vol V pp280–285, Dixons's report Command Paper 693, Kitchener Papers PRO 30/57/22.

[13] Kitchener Papers PRO 30/57/20 and 22.

[14] RC appendices pp518–520.

[15] Official History Vol IV p345; Conan Doyle pp652–3.

[16] Amery Vol V p327, Conan Doyle p631.

[17] Official History Vol IV pp293–298,Conan Doyle pp680–4, Amery Vol V pp376–384.

[18] Official History Vol IV pp299–301, Amery Vol V pp384–5.

[19] Official History Vol IV pp304–315, Amery Vol V pp364–376.

[20] Pakenham p536.

[21] Lucas 2, p56.

[22] E.J. Peacock, *The Veteran Yeomanry in South Africa, Soldiers of the Queen* Sept 1997; Kitchener Papers PRO 30/57/20; Lucas 2 pp42–3.

[23] Kitchener Papers PRO 30/57/20.

[24] Lucas 2 pp42–46.

[25] Britten letters NAM 7812-34.

[26] Official History Vol IV pp389–91, Conan Doyle pp690–3, Amery Vol V pp423–7.

[27] Official History Vol IV pp392–6, Amery Vol V pp431–444, Conan Doyle pp693–6, Bowers's account of Tweefontein NAM 7904–17.

[28] Official History Vol IV pp411–15, Conan Doyle pp719–22, Amery Vol V pp497–500.

[29] Official History Vol IV pp416–22, Conan Doyle pp722–726, Amery Vol V pp501–8, Kitcheners Papers PRO 30/57/22, Methuen's report into Tweebosch Command Paper 967.

30 Packenham pp549–50.
31 Official History Vol IV pp499–505, Amery Vol V pp527–537, Packenham pp557–60, Anglesey pp272–5, Conan Doyle pp733–5.
32 Hay, *Diary of an Edinburgh Trooper*.
33 Lucas 2, pp74–5.
34 RC evidence 14206.
35 RC conclusions p74.

Chapter Ten: Aftermath (pp 217–225)

1 Interview *Radio Times* July/August 1979.
2 Childers, *In The Ranks Of The CIV*.
3 Ross, *A Yeoman's Letters*.
4 Hay, *Diary of an Edinburgh Trooper*.
5 Anglesey p277.
6 *Sunday Express* 8th Nov 1992, *Daily Telegraph* 15th April 1993, *Daily Mail* 16th April 1993.
7 RC conclusions p83.
8 RC appendices p517.
9 Beckett, *Riflemen Form*.
10 *Oxford Illustrated History of the British Army*.
11 Esher Papers 16/8.

INDEX

251

253